The
South Carolina
Encyclopedia Guide to
SOUTH CAROLINA WRITERS

I0634441

South Carolina Encyclopedia Editorial Advisory Board

The
South Carolina
Encyclopedia Guide *to*
SOUTH CAROLINA WRITERS

Edited by Tom Mack

Foreword by George Singleton

A Project of the Humanities Council[SC]

The University of South Carolina Press

Published by the University of South Carolina Press
Columbia, South Carolina 29208

www.sc.edu/uscpress

Manufactured in the United States of America

23 22 21 20 19 18 17 16 15 14   10 9 8 7 6 5 4 3 2 1

Library of Congress Cataloging-in-Publication Data

South Carolina encyclopedia guide to South Carolina writers / edited by Tom Mack ;
foreword by George Singleton.
    pages cm. — (The South Carolina encyclopedia guides series)
    Includes bibliographical references.
    ISBN 978-1-61117-346-8 (hardback) — ISBN 978-1-61117-347-5 (paperback) —
ISBN 978-1-61117-348-2 (ebook) 1. Authors, American—South Carolina—
Biography—Dictionaries. 2. South Carolina—Intellectual life—Dictionaries. 3. South
Carolina x In literature—Dictionaries. 4. Authors, American—Biography—Dictionaries.
5. South Carolina—Biography—Dictionaries. I. Mack, Tom, editor.
    PS266.S6S67 2014
    810.9'975703—dc23

                                                                    2013036696

Editorial Staff

Contents

Dates following authors' names indicate the year of induction in the
South Carolina Academy of Authors.

Series Editor's Preface

The South Carolina Encyclopedia was published in 2006 to be a "people's encyclopedia," a comprehensive single-volume print reference for anything that anyone wanted to know about the Palmetto State's rich cultures and storied heritage, from prehistory to the present. Including nearly two thousand entries and five hundred illustrations, the encyclopedia was the result of a six-year collaboration between the Humanities Council[SC], the Institute for Southern Studies at the University of South Carolina, and the University of South Carolina Press. Nearly six hundred contributors came together to write more than one million words depicting our state's representative people, places, and things. The encyclopedia is an authoritative and entertaining compilation of essays covering an array of topics ranging from war and politics to arts and recreation, from agriculture and industry to popular culture and ethnicity. As diverse as the populations that live within the thirty-one thousand square miles that make up the Palmetto State, the entries included in *The South Carolina Encyclopedia* were chosen to best represent the many facets of our shared experiences that remind us of who we are, where we come from, what we have in common, and why we are distinctive.

Thanks to the generosity and vision of the Humanities Council[SC] and the collaboration and cooperation of the University of South Carolina Press, selected portions of the multiyear project that became the widely praised and bestselling print encyclopedia are now available in a new way through this South Carolina Encyclopedia Guides Series. The guides highlight, in an easy-to-access digital format, specific topic areas from the original print version. Where appropriate, entries have been updated or added. For example, the guide to the counties has been updated to include more recent population data, and the guide to the governors has been expanded to include all individuals who have been governor—whether elected or constitutionally succeeding to the office. Where possible, illustrations have been included and, in some cases, new illustrations not part of the print edition have been added.

In March 2012 the venerable *Encyclopedia Britannica* announced that after 244 years, it would cease publishing its print edition and focus solely on the digital version of its content. This transition is indicative of an unquestionable trend toward the digitization of reference materials to serve better the needs of the diverse range of users who have embraced the technology that brings this content to you via a whole host of devices—a technology that continues to revolutionize the ways that sound scholarship is made available and useful for an interested public.

The South Carolina Encyclopedia Guides Series—because of its digital format and its focus on thematic segments—expands the accessibility and functionality of the content created in the print encyclopedia and invites new readers to understand better the hundreds of people, places, and things that have defined the South Carolina experience.

WALTER EDGAR

Foreword

Aristotle could not have written the *Nichomachean Ethics* in the state of South Carolina because that tome is all about moderation and South Carolina is a big old state of excess only. There is little notion of moderation. We have the beautiful Grand Strand plus the bottom end of the Blue Ridge Mountains. But then we have that Savannah River Nuclear Site in Aiken County and the nearly-disastrous atomic bomb hole near Florence in Mars Bluff. We have the classic row houses of Charleston plus more people living in trailers per capita than anywhere else in the United States. We have produced Strom Thurmond of the Dixiecrat era and the forward-thinking Reverend Jesse Jackson. We have BMW, Michelin, and Sunoco—and we have cotton mills that have either burned down mysteriously or faded into skeletal remains to be renovated into outlandishly priced condominiums. There is that "peachoid" water tower thing outside of Gaffney on I-85 and then the Abbeville Opera House. Just in case anyone thinks the opera house might be too beautiful for a small town, there is a place called Roughhouse Billiards a few doors down to even everything back out.

We have refurbished and renovated Greenville, but then there is Pedro's South of the Border down near Dillon. We pride ourselves on good, level-headed, brilliant, ex-governor Richard Riley—who later became the best U.S. secretary of education ever—and then we have Preston Smith Brooks who beat the hell out of Senator Charles Sumner with a cane because Sumner compared Brooks to Don Quixote. Who wants to be compared to Don Quixote?

There is the incomparable Eartha Kitt, who sang at least one song in French, and then later starred as Cat Woman on *Batman*—then there is a man named Barney Odom who had a canine named Flat Nose the Tree-climbing Dog who probably showed up on *The Tonight Show* more often than Eartha Kitt.

We can brag about the public South Carolina Governors' School for the Arts and Humanities and then shrink back embarrassed at the line of schools making up the Corridor of Shame.

There is the bizarre fire-eater and secessionist Laurence Keitt, who once attempted to choke a Pennsylvania congressman, and then David Drake, known as Dave the Slave, who was not supposed to know how to read and write but who put out clay pots and jugs that now sell for thousands upon thousands of dollars.

There is fire-hot Blenheim's Ginger Ale and the Salley Chitlin Strut. We have the Trappist monastery Mepkin Abbey and we have the Darlington International Speedway that is "Too Tough to Tame."

There is nothing inbetween in these parts.

It is this notion of excess that gives all of our writers the daily conflicts that may arise when two or more excessive people, places, or ideas clash. You do not have to be the smartest person in the world as long as you are blessed to be plopped down between North Carolina and Georgia. You do not even have to sit down and invent stories of your own when you are living in a place where strangers possessed with all kinds of odd notions are willing to tell their most personal secrets, quirks, habits, and scams.

So it should be no surprise that South Carolina has produced, encouraged, sponsored, and/or nurtured so many writers over the past few hundred years. Could James Dickey have written *Deliverance* without understanding the inherent excesses of a primordial forest-turned-water-skiing Mecca? Could Dorothy Allison have written *Bastard out of Carolina* without her upbringing? I doubt that Max Steele would have even considered his classic short story "Ah Love! Ah Me!" without intuiting the unspoken-but-omnipresent class system of mid-twentieth century Greenville.

Would Pat Conroy have written his many great novels if his father had been stationed in Jacksonville or Camp Pendleton? Could Josephine Humphreys have penned *Rich in Love* while living in, say, Delaware? Ron Rash's mill poems would never emanate from the state of Oregon, and his novels and short stories would never have germinated in Vermont. Padgett Powell's *Edisto* would not be the same if titled *Monhegan*, or *Staten*, or *Maui*. Likewise, William Price Fox's *Southern Fried* would never be a classic had he been living elsewhere and chosen *Nor'eastern Boiled*.

I daresay that all of the writers within this volume owe their connections to the Palmetto State for the prose, poetry, and plays they have offered the world.

At times, I know, South Carolina—especially in the realm of politics—has been the brunt of jokes. The political landscape changes, evolves, diminishes, disappears. Fortunately, though, we can pride ourselves on past writers and look forward to the ones our state will forge out yearly.

GEORGE SINGLETON

Introduction

When it was first published in 2006, *The South Carolina Encyclopedia* was heralded as "a treasury of enlightened facts"; "a spectacular compendium of people, places and history"; and a "tremendous contribution to our shared understanding of the heritage and culture" of our state. In the intervening years, countless readers have verified the truth of these assertions as this one-volume reference work, a groundbreaking collaboration between the Humanities Council[SC] and the Institute for Southern Studies at the University of South Carolina, has become the go-to resource for anyone trying to learn more about the Palmetto State.

In part because of the success of this landmark volume, the University of South Carolina Press, under the leadership of its new director Jonathan Haupt, decided in 2012 to expand the encyclopedia's range and potential impact by publishing a series of guides focused on specific topics addressed in the initial publication. Among the first such encyclopedia guides were separate volumes devoted to South Carolina governors, hall of fame inductees, and the role of our state in the American Revolution.

The present volume is the latest addition to this series of informative guides. As such, it builds upon the information contained in the original 2006 encyclopedia by updating the entries on South Carolina writers contained therein and augmenting that list with new essays on additional authors, past and present, who have contributed to our state's distinctive literary heritage.

Although the origins of South Carolina as a separate political and geographical entity can be traced to the early part of the eighteenth century—the boundary between North and South Carolina was fundamentally set in 1735—it would not be until the next century, the nineteenth, that anything resembling a literary tradition might be said to arise. A contributing factor was the initial absence of a general readership; illiteracy was a common condition during the colonial period, and even after statehood, the lack of any widespread support for public education meant that a substantial percentage of the population would remain functionally illiterate well into the twentieth century.

Still, with the establishment of a wealthy, privately educated planter class came some interest in letters. One of the most important antebellum periodicals, the

Southern Quarterly Review, was published in Charleston from 1842 to 1855 and revived in Columbia from 1856 to 1857. Among its editors was William Gilmore Simms, who might appropriately be called the father of South Carolina literature. A member of the planter class by marriage, he devoted much of his life to telling the story of the Palmetto State in novels, poetry, essays, and reviews.

It is safe to say that most of the state's earliest authors were affiliated with the planter aristocracy and defenders of its conservative ideals and that it was not until after the War Between the States, when the political and economic power shifted from the lowcountry to the midlands and upstate, that other literary voices of any significance emerge. That trend would continue into the twentieth century; and as one can readily see in the pages of this book, to the ranks of white male authors would eventually be added a host of native-born female authors and writers of color as well as literary practitioners from other parts of the country lured to our state for its natural beauty and recreational resources.

Thus, the literary history of South Carolina mirrors the history of the state—an inexorable evolution from a singular, largely elitist vision to a more diverse, multi-cultural imaginative response to shifting social reality.

This progressive, more communal trajectory is reflected in the current guide, which contains 128 entries on authors from the late-eighteenth century to the present written by over seventy scholars, mostly resident in South Carolina but sometimes hailing from other parts of our country and abroad. Furthermore quite a few of the articles in this volume are the happy product of one creative writer responding to the life and work of another. For example, in the pages of this guide, Jon Tuttle, our state's most important contemporary playwright, reflects on the achievements of William Ioor, the father of South Carolina drama; accomplished poet Phebe Davidson writes about her fellow bards: Dorothy Perry Thompson, Cathy Smith Bowers, and Carrie McCray Nickens; Harlan Greene, novelist and modern authority on all things Charleston, sums up the career of John Bennett, the individual arguably most responsible for fueling the early-twentieth-century artistic renaissance in "the Holy City."

Nearly every entry contains not only essential biographical facts about its subject but also some interpretive and evaluative judgments, in an attempt to place each writer in the context of South Carolina's literary tradition. The contributors to this guide have also paid particular attention to those writers whose work has been recognized by induction into the South Carolina Academy of Authors, which serves as our state's literary hall of fame. In the table of contents, the names of current members of the Academy are followed by their year of induction.

Several years ago, when my name was first placed in nomination for the board chairmanship, I reacted with a combination of shock and consternation. After all, taking the helm of an important statewide organization is not a venture to be taken lightly, and in my case, as a relatively new member of the board of governors, I had much to learn about the South Carolina Academy of Authors, which was then poised to enlarge its presence in the cultural life of our state.

The primary mission of the South Carolina Academy of Authors is to identify and recognize the state's distinguished writers, living and deceased, and promote the reading of their works. Founded in 1986, the organization, which was established on the campus of Anderson College by a small group of engaged individuals, has grown in the last quarter century to boast a revolving, twenty-five-member board of governors from all parts of the state. It is the duty of this board to select the writers to be inducted into the academy.

To recognize these inductees, who number nearly seventy to date, the board sponsors an annual ceremony. These gala events are held in a different part of South Carolina each year, generally alternating among municipalities in the low-country, the midlands, and the upstate. The typical induction ceremony features scholars who summarize the achievements of each inductee with special reference to that individual's relationship to the cultural life of our state; each inductee, in turn, delivers a short acceptance speech. George Singleton's entertaining and insightful address at his induction at USC-Upstate in 2010 forms the nucleus of his fine foreword to this volume.

In recent years, the ceremony has become the centerpiece in a series of public programs held in the host city over a three-day weekend. In 2013, for example, the induction ceremony and reception took place on April 27 at the Ernest F. Hollings Library on the campus of the University of South Carolina in Columbia, but there were other events scheduled for that celebratory weekend. On April 26, for example, National Book Award-winning poet Terrance Hayes, a 2013 inductee, gave a free public reading at Harper College on the USC horseshoe; and the morning of April 27, Alao Folasado gave a lecture entitled "Seeds Planted with Pens: Harvesting the Bounty of Black SC Writers" at a special brunch, both sponsored by the academy. Thus, the annual induction programming has expanded over the years beyond the ceremony itself to encompass additional opportunities to showcase the work of the distinguished academicians in a given year.

Efforts have also been made to enlarge the scope of the annual celebration beyond the borders of the host city. To that end, the board of governors decided in 2010 to partner with public and academic libraries across the state. Each year, during the month of the spring induction, our library partners host displays on the works of each year's inductees, often augmenting their permanent collection of each writer's work with new acquisitions.

A second major goal of the academy is to encourage and support emerging writers in South Carolina. Accordingly, the board initiated in 2009 an annual poetry fellowship in memory of academy inductee Carrie McCray Nickens, who began writing poetry relatively late in life but nevertheless carved out a significant career within a very short time. In 2011 the board also revived an annual fiction fellowship. Each fellowship is awarded through an open competition with a statewide call for submissions announced each fall; recipients of both fellowships are honored at a special brunch scheduled for the same spring weekend as the induction ceremony. Both awards currently carry a thousand-dollar stipend.

Over the years, these fellowships have made a difference in the careers of some of our state's most notable authors. In 2011, for example, at the induction ceremony held that year on the campus of the University of South Carolina Aiken, Sue Monk Kidd, who was being honored for her contribution to South Carolina letters, made mention during her acceptance speech of the receipt of fiction fellowships from the academy in 1994 and 1996. This early validation of her work, she asserted, gave her the encouragement to continue to pursue her goal of writing a novel. As every reader knows, her early efforts at fiction writing would eventually culminate in her first novel, the bestselling *The Secret Life of Bees.*

Returning to my own personal narrative, I would like to report that I finally accepted the nomination to be board chair five years ago, and I am happy that I did. Thanks to the fine work of my fellow board members, especially such veterans as Thomas Johnson, Oliver Bowman, Charles Israel, Ellen Hyatt, Libby Bernardin, and Sally Hare, a solid foundation had already been set; it was left to me to build upon their groundbreaking work. Thus, as I have mentioned above, the board has expanded our public programming, revivified our fellowships, developed a statewide network of library partners, and launched a new website: www.scacademyofauthors.org.

I have come to look forward to each year's induction and its attendant activities, and I happily anticipate welcoming many more of South Carolina's notable writers as members of the academy of authors. Each year's crop of inductees brings surprises, not just from the living authors. Sometimes even the dead offer revelations. Shortly after we announced the names of the writers to be honored at the 2011 induction at USC Aiken, for example, came the report of the discovery of a long lost manuscript by one of our inductees, the late Gamel Woolsey. A small press in the United Kingdom had heard of our plan to induct Woolsey that year into the academy and contacted me about their imminent publication of her novel *Patterns on the Sand,* whose manuscript had been gathering dust in a Texas library for decades. Resident in the South Carolina lowcountry, the characters in Woolsey's novel share the potentially stultifying fate of their socialite author had she not escaped upper-class Charleston in the early twentieth century and made her way to bohemian Greenwich Village in New York City. In short, because of this happy coincidence, the board of governors was able to forge a transatlantic alliance with the British publisher to herald the posthumous publication of a "new" book—it was actually written in 1947 in England—by a long-neglected Carolina native whose reputation may now be on the point of resurrection.

Although not every writer's life is marked by tales of buried treasure, there is so very much more to learn about the literary figures associated with our state. Shedding light on their evolving legacy is the principal goal of this volume.

~

Adams, Edward Clarkson Leverett (1876–1946). Physician, fiction writer, playwright. Adams was born in Weston, Richland County, South Carolina, on January 5, 1876, the eldest son of James Ironsides Adams and Caroline Pinckney Leverett. He was educated in the public and private grade schools of Gadsden and Columbia, and later at Clemson College, Maryland Medical College in Baltimore, the Charleston Medical College (where he received his M.D.), the University of Pennsylvania, and Rotunda Hospital in Dublin, Ireland. On June 10, 1910, Adams married Amanda M. Smith. They had two children.

Adams served in the United States Army during the Spanish-American War. He volunteered again for active duty during World War I, serving in France as a captain in the Eighty-First ("Wildcat") Division. He returned to Columbia in 1918. After several years of medical practice, Adams retired to devote more of his time to farming on his Bluff Road plantation, to run unsuccessfully for lieutenant governor in 1922, and to write sketches, two books, and a play about the black inhabitants of Richland County.

Adams's books and stories about the African American residents of lower Richland County brought him both regional and national attention as an author who was able to present the black dialect with great precision and also as a white author who unhesitatingly portrayed the hardships of racial prejudice in the 1920s and 1930s. His first volume, *Congaree Sketches,* was published by the University of North Carolina Press in 1927. Here he introduced the poor blacks of the Congaree swamp and their meticulously rendered dialect that would form the imaginative foundation for the many stories that followed. The first collection was immediately successful. After reading a copy of *Congaree Sketches* brought to him by a Scribner's representative, the editor Maxwell Perkins wrote to Adams directly; and Adams's next volume, *Nigger to Nigger,* appeared under the prestigious Scribner's imprint in 1928. The chairperson of the board of the National Association for the Advancement of Colored People (NAACP), Mary White Ovington, who had earlier remarked on the high quality of Adams's insights into the mind of African Americans in *Congaree Sketches,* also admired *Nigger to Nigger* for its poignant descriptions of the tragic lives of its poor black characters.

With the 1929 publication of *Potee's Gal: A Drama of Negro Life Near the Big Congaree Swamps,* Adams was thrust directly into the spotlight of public opinion when the Stage Society of Columbia adopted it for production with an entirely black cast. The great public outcry against this decision overwhelmed the quality of the play and the objections of Adams and his many friends. After a bitter exchange of letters with their detractors in the local newspapers, the Stage Society's board of governors canceled the two productions that had been scheduled for February 5, 1929. *Potee's Gal* was never produced on the stage.

Adams died at his home in Columbia on November 1, 1946. He was buried in the cemetery at St. John's Episcopal Church in Congaree. JACOB RIVERS

Adams, Edward Clarkson Leverett. *Tales of the Congaree.* Edited by Robert G. O'Meally. Chapel Hill: University of North Carolina Press, 1987.

————. Vertical Biographical File and Papers. South Caroliniana Library, University of South Carolina, Columbia.

Allan, Glenn (1899–1955). Journalist, novelist, and short story writer. Born in Charleston, South Carolina, on November 15, 1899, Allan was the son of James Allan and Maria Heriot. He grew up in the nearby town of Summerville. Allan entered the Citadel but joined the military in his sophomore year and was assigned to officers' training camp in Plattsburg, New York, where he was commissioned a second lieutenant in the infantry. He served in various posts, was mustered out in January 1919, and returned to the Citadel, graduating in 1920. Thereafter he went to work for the H. K. Leiding brokerage and import firm in Charleston, leaving in 1922 to work on a dude ranch in Taos, New Mexico. In his spare time, Allan began to write for southwestern newspapers. His first full-time job as a journalist was for the *Greenville* (South Carolina) *Piedmont* as a sports writer, followed by stints on the *Asheville Citizen* and the *Atlanta Journal.* He gave up journalism temporarily to show jumping horses along the eastern seaboard. Concurrent with that enterprise, he and a friend launched *Turf and Tanbark,* a horse magazine that failed.

Allan joined the staff of the *New York Herald Tribune* in 1930 and later was one of the journalists who helped launch the features service of the Associated Press. In 1932 he published his first and only novel, *Old Manoa,* a story of quaint and stereotypical Kentucky characters enmeshed in an improbable plot. He joined the editorial staff of the *New Yorker* in 1936. For years he had been writing freelance articles on sports and selling short stories to pulp magazines, encouraged by the Charleston writer Octavus Roy Cohen. It was the steady purchase of his works by the *Saturday Evening Post* that prompted him to try fiction writing full-time. He returned to Summerville, living with his mother, summering with her at Pawleys Island. Several of his stories of poor white, quaint, colorful, and ignorant "swampers," some of them showing their comic attempts to survive in a changing South, were collected in a volume of linked tales, *Little Sorrowful* (1946). The book carried an opening essay by Allan's mother, and one swamp tale was sold to a film company.

Allan's most popular creation, however, was "Boysi," a comical, stereotypical black servant getting his way with his white employers. He based the character on family servants and wrote the stories, he said, to counter the image of the Negro current in some southern writing. The stories were immensely popular for a time, and a collection of them appeared in 1946 as *Boysi Himself.* Allan's works were light, mildly amusing, and comforting to those who liked to see no change in the status quo. However, they fell quickly out of favor and out of print.

An ardent sportsman and foxhunter, Allan committed suicide on July 23, 1955. He was buried in Summerville's St. Paul's Episcopal Church. HARLAN GREENE

"Glenn Allan, Author, Found Fatally Shot." Charleston *News and Courier,* July 24, 1955, A11.

"Glenn Allan Is Buried at Summerville." Charleston *Evening Post,* July 25, 1955, A2.

Jones, Katherine M., and Mary Verner Schlaefer. *South Carolina in the Short Story.* Columbia: University of South Carolina Press, 1952.

Tobias, Rowena Wilson. "Summerville Writer Finds South's Present Better Copy than Its Past, Would Keep 'Honest.'" Charleston *News and Courier,* April 7, 1940, 3–iii.

Allen, Gilbert Bruce (b. 1951). Poet, fiction writer, editor, educator. Gilbert Allen was born in Rockville Centre, New York, on New Year's Day, 1951, to Joseph Aloysius Allen and Marie Skocik. He grew up in Long Island and married Barbara Jean Szigeti in 1974. Allen attended Cornell University, completing three degrees there—a Bachelor of Arts degree in 1972, a Master of Fine Arts in 1974, and a doctorate in 1977. From 1972 to 1975 he was a Ford Foundation fellow. Allen moved to South Carolina in 1977, becoming a professor of English at Furman University and establishing his residence in Travelers Rest.

Allen's first collection of poetry, *In Everything: Poems, 1972–1979,* appeared in 1982 and was followed by three other volumes: *Second Chances* (1991), *Commandments at Eleven* (1994), and *Driving to Distraction* (2003). In addition to poems, he has published articles and short stories. His work includes more than three hundred contributions to magazines such as *American Scholar, Cortland Review, Emrys Journal, Georgia Review, Shenandoah, Pembroke, Image, Southern Humanities Review,* and *College English.* Allen served as assistant editor of the journal *Epoch* from 1972 to 1977 and has edited *Furman Studies.*

In 1991, along with fellow Furman English professor William E. Rogers, Allen became cofounder and coeditor of Ninety-Six Press. Focusing primarily on the works of South Carolina poets, the press has produced twelve books to date, including *45/96: The Ninety-Six Sampler of South Carolina Poetry.* Allen also continues to compose his own prose pieces.

Allen's poetry combines contemporary philosophical concerns with a format more aligned with earlier poetic styles. As he puts it, most of his published work "tries to document the experience of living in America during the latter half of the twentieth century," combining "both the impulse to believe and the inclination to be skeptical." Along with the theme of family relationships, many common topics in his poetry include parts of nature, particularly cats, trees, and winter. "How anyone gets an idea about anything," Allen says, "is one of the great mysteries."

In 2007, his poem sequence entitled "The Assistant" won the Robert Penn Warren Prize from the *Southern Review;* that same year his chapbook *Body Parts* was published by the SC Poetry Initiative. Allen was inducted into the South Carolina Academy of Authors in 2014. AMY L. WHITE

Allen, Gilbert. "Timber." *Southern Review* 36 (winter 2000): 1–2.
———. "Walking through St. Patrick's, Finding St. Joseph off the Side." *Southern Review* 34 (summer 1998): 405–406.

Allen, William Hervey, Jr. (1889–1949). Poet, novelist. The son of William Hervey Allen, Sr., and Helen Eby Myers, Hervey Allen is known to literary historians as a southern writer although he was born in Pittsburgh, Pennsylvania, on December 8, 1889, and spent the first thirty years of his life in the north. Allen was educated in the public schools of Pittsburgh and received a Bachelor of Science degree in economics from the University of Pittsburgh in 1915 after a sporting accident cut short his promising career at the U.S. Naval Academy. While serving in the U.S. Army during World War I, Allen fought in the Meuse-Argonne offensive in France. By the time of the armistice in November 1918, he had risen to the rank of first lieutenant. After a brief period of graduate study at Harvard, Allen was hired as an English instructor at Porter Military Academy in Charleston in 1919.

Allen's move to Charleston coincided with the beginnings of the Poetry Society of South Carolina. Along with John Bennett and Dubose Heyward, Hervey Allen was a driving force behind this organization. In 1922 he and Heyward coauthored *Carolina Chansons: Legends of the Low Country,* a book of local color verse that was enthusiastically received by northern critics, especially by Harriet Monroe, founding editor of *Poetry* magazine. In fact, when Monroe published a special southern issue of *Poetry* in April 1922, Heyward and Allen were chosen as guest editors. In their introduction to this special issue, the two South Carolinians advocated a poetic regionalism that would keep its distance from the main currents of modernism.

In 1922 Heyward moved from the Porter Academy to the High School of Charleston. In 1925 he left South Carolina permanently for a series of jobs in academia and publishing. On June 30, 1927, he married Annette Hyde Andrews of Syracuse, New York. They had three children.

Although Allen spent only six of his sixty years in South Carolina, his association with the Poetry Society came at a crucial time in his development as a writer. His book *Israfel: The Life and Times of Edgar Allan Poe* (1926) traced Poe's complex relationship with Charleston in a manner that had never been previously attempted.

Moreover, the regionalist aesthetic he was calling for continued to permeate his own verse.

In 1933 Allen published his long historical novel *Anthony Adverse*, which sold 395,000 copies in its first year. By 1968 sales had passed three million, thus making Allen's book one of the best-selling historical novels of all time. Set in early nineteenth-century America and Mexico, this picaresque tale of adventure captivated Depression-era audiences until it was eclipsed by *Gone with the Wind*. Even as he was living far from South Carolina, Allen was using his experience in Charleston in his Civil War novel *Action at Aquila* (1938). Although he could have lived comfortably on his royalties from *Anthony Adverse*, Allen continued writing until shortly before his death of a heart attack on December 28, 1949. He was buried with full military honors at Arlington National Cemetery. MARK WINCHELL

Aiken, David. *Fire in the Cradle: Charleston's Literary Heritage*. Charleston: Charleston Press, 1999.
Slavick, William H. *Dubose Heyward*. Boston, Mass.: Twayne, 1981.

Allison, Dorothy (b. 1949). Novelist, poet. Allison was born on April 11, 1949, in Greenville, South Carolina, a self-proclaimed bastard child of an unwed teenage mother, Ruth Gibson Allison, who dropped out of seventh grade to work as a waitress. Allison was raised in extreme poverty by her mother and an abusive stepfather, who repeatedly beat and raped her from the time she was five to eleven years old. Though Allison's mother contributed to this scarring childhood by tolerating her husband's violence, she invested in Allison's future by keeping a jar of money for her daughter's college education and thus taught her bright daughter that she had a right to excel. Allison was the first in her family to finish high school and went on to Florida Presbyterian College (now Eckerd College) on a National Merit Scholarship. She earned a master's degree in anthropology at the New School for Social Research in New York.

In the early 1970s, Allison joined a lesbian-feminist collective and severed all ties to her family until 1981. She credits the women's movement with making her writing career possible, nourished by women friends and lovers who initially helped her overcome a "terrible drive" to burn her journals, stories, and poems.

The Women Who Hate Me (1983), a collection of poetry, published in an expanded version in 1991, focuses on lesbian sexuality and relationships between women. *Trash* (1988) includes stories and poetry with a lesbian-feminist emphasis that were inspired by Allison's working-class, poverty-stricken childhood. "Ours is a culture that hates and fears the poor, queers, and women," she says. "The people I love most are the people society doesn't like."

Allison received mainstream recognition with her first novel, *Bastard out of Carolina* (1992), which in 1996 was adapted to a film directed by Anjelica Huston.

The semi-autobiographical narrative, which takes place in Allison's hometown, explores themes of poverty and choice through the eyes of Bone Boatwright, who draws strength from family stories and, despite beatings and sexual abuse, finds her own voice and identity. Allison takes up the notion of storytelling as both a survival tool and a weapon in two works of nonfiction, *Skin: Talking about Sex, Class, and Literature* (1994) and *Two or Three Things I Know for Sure* (1995), a lyrical memoir.

Cavedweller (1998), Allison's second novel, follows the character Delia and her attempt to come to terms with her past and its losses. Set in Cayro, Georgia, *Cavedweller* explores the connection between identity and place and continues Allison's desire to record the lives of marginalized southerners. The numerous women who populate the novel meet or live in a world of headstrong Baptists, truck farms, trailers, convenience stores, and beauty parlors. Underneath hides an underworld of caves, mapped or unmapped, in which Delia's daughter Cissy seeks refuge and comfort. Metaphorically representing a journey into the past, the silences of stories, the lesbian body, and more, the caves also suggest the writer's ambition to uncover the "harder truths" and map paths to redemption. The text was adapted for the screen in 2004; the film version starred Kyra Sedgwick and Kevin Bacon.

Although she has accepted visiting appointments at Emory University (2008) and Davidson College (2009), Allison's permanent residence is now in northern California where she lives with her son, Wolf Michael, and her partner, Alix Layman. California is also the setting of her long-anticipated third novel entitled *She Who*, which focuses on the lives of three women coping with the aftermath of personal violence. CLARA JUNCKER

Griffin, Connie. "Going Naked into the World: Recovery and Re/presentation in the Works of Dorothy Allison." *Concerns* 26, no. 3 (1999): 6–20.

Iring, Katrina. "'Writing It Down So That It Would Be Real': Narrative Struggles in Dorothy Allison's *Bastard Out of Carolina*." *College Literature* 25 (spring 1998): 94–107.

Megan, Carolyn E. "Moving toward Truth: An Interview with Dorothy Allison." *Kenyon Review* 16 (fall 1994): 71–83.

Allston, Washington (1779–1843). Poet, painter. Born on a rice plantation on the Waccamaw River close to Georgetown, South Carolina, Allston was the son of Rachel Moore Allston and Captain William Allston, an army officer who fought at the Battle of Cowpens. Washington Allston's ancestors arrived in South Carolina around the year 1685. They founded a wealthy and influential plantation dynasty. Allston, a descendant of two of South Carolina's colonial governors, John Yeamans (1672–1674) and James Moore (1719–1721), was one of the first noted individuals to be named after George Washington.

In 1781 Washington Allston's father returned home from the Battle of Cowpens and died from what was thought to have been poisoning by a servant. Immediately prior to Captain Allston's death, he requested that his son be brought to his bedside and is reported to have spoken the words, "He who lives to see this child grow up will see a great man."

Rachel Moore, Washington Allston's mother, later married Dr. Henry Collins Flagg, master of the property now known as Brookgreen Gardens. Allston's education began at an early age, and at the request of Dr. Flagg, he was sent to study at Mrs. Colcott's School in Charleston. He then departed Charleston for college preparation with Mr. Robert Rogers, of Newport, Rhode Island. Allston entered Harvard University in 1796 at the age of seventeen. According to personal letters, Allston was fond of reading and writing but wanted to concentrate more on painting. At Harvard, he was at first attracted to Della Cruscan poetry, then later abandoned it for "the manliness of [Charles] Churchill." His poems occasionally appeared in a section entitled "Poet's Corner" of the periodical *Centinell*. During his senior year at Harvard, he was appointed to deliver a poem at a fall exhibition. Because of the popular reception of that first effort, he was asked the next winter to deliver another poem on the solemn occasion of the death of George Washington.

Upon graduation from Harvard in 1800, Allston returned to South Carolina and later sailed to England where he studied at the Royal Academy for three years. He visited Paris and then lived in Rome for four years. During his time spent in Europe, he became friends with Samuel Taylor Coleridge and Washington Irving. In 1809 he returned to America and lived in Boston where he married the sister of the Reverend Dr. William E. Channing, a Unitarian clergyman. He returned to London in 1811; and in 1813, the same year his first wife died, he published *The Sylphs of the Seasons, with other Poems.*

This first of Allston's significant published works consists of sixteen poems and tales, six of which were sonnets devoted to famous artists such as Michelangelo, Rafael, and Rembrandt. Allston's last sonnet in the collection is dedicated to his friend, Benjamin West, who was president of the Royal Academy during the time of his studies. Reviews of his work, both visual and verbal, were mixed. In 1842 an anonymous reviewer in *Graham's Magazine* described Allston as one of the American literati. On the subject of his paintings, the reviewer commented, "we have here nothing to say" and "the most noted of them are not to our taste." Of the poems, the reviewer opined that they were "not all of a high order of merit; and, in truth the faults of his pencil and of his pen are identical." That initial appraisal, however, was contradicted in 1856 when publisher Evert Duyckinck avowed, "[Allston's] poems, though few in number, are exquisite in finish, and in the fancies and thoughts which they embody. They are delicate, subtle, and philosophical."

In 1830 Allston married the sister of Richard N. Dana and resided in Cambridgeport, Massachusetts, where his studio was often the focus of considerable interest to some of the leading figures of American Romanticism, including Ralph Waldo Emerson, Margaret Fuller, and Sophia Peabody, who was later to marry Nathaniel Hawthorne.

In 1842 his Italian romance, *Monaldi: a Tale*, was published; however, it was reported to have been written as early as 1821. Duyckinck described *Monaldi* as an Italian story of "jealousy, murder, and madness. [The title character] Monaldi is suspicious of his wife, kills her in revenge, and becomes a maniac. The work is entirely of a subjective character, dealing with thought, emotion, and passion, with a concentration and energy for which we are accustomed to look only to the greatest dramatists."

After Allston's death, his theories on art and writing were published as *Lectures on Art, and Poems* (1850). Allston wrote detailed thoughts not only on his own work but also on art and poetry in general: "Thus the wildest visions of poetry, the unsubstantial forms of painting, and the mysterious harmonies of music, that seem to disembody the spirit, and make us creatures of the air,—even these, unreal as they are, may all have their foundation in immutable truth; and we may moreover know of this truth by its own evidence."

Although he devoted his life to both the visual and literary arts, Allston was more recognized for his painting than his writing. His *Moonlit Landscape*, completed in 1819 and now part of the permanent collection of the Museum of Fine Arts, Boston, and his *Ship in a Squall*, completed before 1837 and now part of the permanent collection of the Fogg Art Museum, Cambridge, Massachusetts, are recognized as two of his finest works. CURTIS R. ROGERS

Duyckinck, E. A. "Washington Allston." *Cyclopedia of American Literature*. Vol. 2. New York: Charles Scribner, 1856.

Flagg, Jared B. *Life and Letters of Washington Allston*. New York: Charles Scribner & Sons, 1892.

Gragg, Rod. *Planters, Pirates & Patriots: Historical Tales from the South Carolina Grand Strand*. Gretna, La.: Pelican Publishing, 2006.

Hubbel, Jay B. *The South in American Literature: 1607–1900*. Durham: Duke University Press, 1954.

Poe, Edgar Allan. "A Chapter on Autography [part III]." *Graham's Magazine* 20 (January 1842):44–49.

Ashmore, Harry Scott (1916–1998). Journalist, editor, Pulitzer Prize winner. Born in Greenville, South Carolina, on July 28, 1916, to William Green Ashmore and Nancy Elizabeth Scott, Harry Ashmore grew up in relative poverty but obtained a general science degree from Clemson College in 1937. Thanks to the exceptional skills he demonstrated as editor on both his high school and college newspapers, Ashmore decided to pursue a journalism career in his hometown, where he married Barbara Edith Laier, a faculty member at Furman University, in 1940.

Ashmore's reputation as a journalist grew during his time at the *Greenville Piedmont* and *Greenville News*, garnering him a Nieman Fellowship at Harvard University in 1941. After a stint in the United States Army during World War II, Ashmore became an editorial writer for the *Charlotte* (North Carolina) *News;* his work for that paper led to a job at the *Arkansas Gazette* in 1947.

One of several southern journalists whose "liberal" views on desegregation and civil rights attracted national attention and local scorn, Ashmore won a Pulitzer Prize for his editorials opposing Arkansas Governor Orval Faubus's attempt to stop the integration of Little Rock's Central High School in 1957. However, Ashmore shunned the "liberal" tag, claiming to be a gradualist—supporting the removal of the "separate but equal" system by degrees.

Ashmore's 1954 book, *The Negro and the Schools,* summarized a massive Ford Foundation research project on the disparate biracial educational system in the South. Chief Justice Earl Warren of the U.S. Supreme Court later told Ashmore that the findings of this study influenced the court's desegregation implementation decision.

After leaving the *Gazette* in 1959, Ashmore served as editor in chief of *Encyclopaedia Britannica* and joined Robert Maynard Hutchins's Center for the Study of Democratic Institutions in Santa Barbara, California, where he lived until his death. During his career Ashmore wrote ten books, many of which discussed the changing attitudes in the New South. He explained, "All of these books of mine, with all the examining, I'm trying to examine my own attitude. How did I get to this point from where I started? What changed my mind?" Ashmore was inducted into the South Carolina Academy of Authors in 1995, three years before his death in Santa Barbara on January 20, 1998. NATHANIA K. SAWYER

Ashmore, Harry S. *Civil Rights and Wrongs: A Memoir of Race and Politics, 1944–1996.* Rev. ed. Columbia: University of South Carolina Press, 1997.
———. *An Epitaph for Dixie.* New York: Norton, 1958.
Sawyer, Nathania K. "Harry S. Ashmore: On the Way to Everywhere." Master's thesis, University of Arkansas at Little Rock, 2001.

Babcock, Havilah (1898–1964). Short story writer, educator. Babcock was born on March 6, 1898, in Appomattox, Virginia, the son of Homer Curtis Babcock and Rosa Blanche Moore. He earned an A.B. from Elon College in 1918, then pursued graduate studies at Columbia University, the University of Virginia (A.M., 1923), and the University of South Carolina (Ph.D., 1927). On June 3, 1919, he married Alice Hudson Cheatham. Babcock briefly taught high school English in Virginia before joining the faculty at the College of William and Mary in 1921. In 1926 he came to the University of South Carolina (USC) on a year's sabbatical leave. During what he initially regarded as a temporary residency in South Carolina, Babcock found the people, school, and state so hospitable that he stayed thirty-eight years, joining the English department and becoming a fixture at the university.

At USC, Babcock became himself an institution about whom truths and legends were freely circulated. He might, some of his former students have reported, begin a class with the offer, "I'll give twenty-five cents to anyone who can spell Houyhnhnm," and reportedly he once greeted students with a broadside of snowballs after a rare southern snowfall. His jovial bond with students made his courses the most sought after at the university, causing students to sign up a year in advance for his English 129 course entitled "I Want a Word." In this vocabulary and semantics course, students learned of the charm and power of words as they listened to Babcock reveal their nuances and connotations.

Babcock was equally at home in the field as at the blackboard. He used the outdoors as a canvas to draw a vast array of colorful characters, becoming a master of the hunting and fishing tale. His stories were replete with references to English and American literature. More than one hundred of his stories found their way into print in a variety of newspapers and magazines, including *Field and Stream.* Anthologies of his works include *My Health Is Better in November* (1947), *Tales of Quails 'n' Such* (1951), *I Don't Want to Shoot an Elephant* (1958), and *Jaybirds Go to Hell on Friday, and Other Stories* (1964). His writing traveled the literary spectrum with ease. In his novel *The Education of Pretty Boy* (1960), Babcock wrote of a young boy's gun-shy bird dog because he thought the dog "was too pretty not to be immortal."

Babcock's writings continued their popularity years after his death. A reviewer from the *New York Times* once compared his writing to "a rare old Bourbon you want to make last as long as possible." A counterpart at *Field and Stream* applied a similar metaphor: "Like a good wine [Babcock's stories] grow better with age." Babcock died in Columbia on December 10, 1964, and was buried in Appomattox, Virginia; he was posthumously inducted into the South Carolina Academy of Authors in 2001. FRANCIS NEUFFER

Babcock, Havilah. *The Best of Babcock.* New York: Holt, Rinehart, and Winston, 1974.
Neuffer, Claude Henry. "Havilah Babcock: Virginia Carolinian." *Georgia Review* 21 (fall 1967): 297–310.

Baldwin, William Plews, III (b. 1944). Novelist, poet, nonfiction writer. Baldwin was born in McClellanville, South Carolina, on October 27, 1944. He is the son of William P. Baldwin, Jr., a wildlife biologist and real-estate broker, and Agnes Leland, a title researcher and historian. He was raised in the lowcountry in Savannah,

Georgia, and in Bluffton and Summerville, South Carolina. He graduated from high school in Summerville in 1962. Baldwin married Lillian Morrison on August 15, 1965, and they have two sons, Aaron and Malcolm. Baldwin is a would-have-been architect with two degrees from Clemson University, a B.A. in history (1966) and an M.A. in English (1968). After university he returned to McClellanville and has remained in the area, where he has made a living by crabbing, oystering, shrimping, serving as a magistrate, writing screenplays for Hollywood, designing and building houses, and writing fiction.

Baldwin has said: "I think of myself as a novelist. Whenever I get ahead in life, I write a novel, which is why I stay broke." His first novel, *The Hard to Catch Mercy* (1993), was universally well received, winning the Lillian Smith Award for Fiction and becoming a Book-of-the-Month Club selection. In the oral tradition of the South, the novel is narrated by the fourteen-year-old Willie T. Allson, who in the year 1916 is sent on a mythic journey to gain his manhood. With humor and passion Baldwin tells the entertaining and anecdote-filled story of the Allson family and their life in the South Carolina lowcountry. The landscape comes to life, and the characters stand out as highly original and yet convincingly real human beings of that place and time. It is a grotesque, violent, and above all compelling story of initiation and recognition. The boy learns about revenge, death, sex, the abiding influence of the past on the present, the "failures" of his family's collective memory, and the possibility of happiness. All in all, Baldwin's first novel was a splendid entry for him into the ranks of accomplished South Carolina novelists.

The fun Baldwin had with his stereotyping of classic southern fiction in his first novel was continued, and perhaps exaggerated, in his second, *The Fennel Family Papers* (1996). In this novel he satirized a young historian's pathetic attempt to get tenure by securing and publishing the historic papers of an ancient, notorious, and decadent family, the Fennels. This Swiftian tale of the eccentric South Carolina family, who supposedly were keepers of the lighthouse of Dog Tooth Shoal since before the Revolutionary War, is darkly comic. From the story of the naively ambitious academic's research among the violent and mad members of the Fennel family, Baldwin created unforgettable and hilarious satire.

Baldwin has also published with the photographer Jane Iseley four nonfiction books about historic Charleston and the plantations of the lowcountry. He has also published two oral history reports featuring Mrs. Emily Whaley (1913–1998), grande dame of Charleston society, and her recollections of her garden, cuisine, recipes, and entertaining. In a similar vein is his oral history report *Heaven Is a Beautiful Place* (2000), based on his conversations with Genevieve C. "Sister" Peterkin (b. 1928), which is a memoir of life at Murrell's Inlet on the South Carolina coast. The screenplay for that book—*Heaven Is a Beautiful Place*—won Baldwin a Silver Remy at the Houston Film Festival in 2012.

Baldwin's third novel *A Gentleman in Charleston and the Manner of His Death* (2005) is a mixture of fiction and historical fact based on the prominent Charleston newspaper editor Francis W. Warrington's life and his violent death in a duel on March 12, 1889. The novel evokes the language of both polite upper-class society and intimate domestic or hidden lives. The novel is most effective as a study of turbulent gender patterns, the codes of honor in the Old South society, and their dramatic consequences.

With *The Unpainted South* (2011) Baldwin, together with photographer Selden Hill, continued to document the South with an emphasis on the lowcountry. The newest element in his work is poetry, which won him the Benjamin Franklin Award from the Independent Book Publishers Association. Baldwin, who is a member of the South Carolina Poetry Society, has continued his lyrical celebrations of the state's natural resources, lifestyles, cuisine, oral history, and architecture in *These Our Offerings* (2012), a book with photographs by Selden Hill, Sharon Cumbee, and Robert Epps. JAN NORDBY GRETLUND

Abbott, Reginald. "*The Hard to Catch Mercy:* A Review." *Southern Quarterly* 32 (summer 1994): 169–71.

Baldwin, William, Currie McCullough, and Bradford Collins. *William McCullough, Southern Painter in Conversation with William Baldwin, Southern Writer.* Charleston: The History Press, 2006.

Barrett, James Lee (1929–1989). Screenwriter. Once described as "perhaps the most prolific hyphenate (writer-producer) in Hollywood," James Lee Barrett was born on November 19, 1929, in Charlotte, North Carolina, the son of James Hamlin Barrett and Anne Blake. He grew up in Anderson, South Carolina. Following the early death of his mother, he was reared by four schoolteacher aunts and was remembered as an independent and mischievous boy who chafed under the hand of authority. He served as a reporter for his high school newspaper and attained the rank of Eagle Scout in a local Boy Scout troop.

Barrett pursued his education at Anderson College, Furman University, Pennsylvania State University, Columbia University, and the Art Students League in New York. After a stint in the U.S. Marine Corps, he moved to New York City, where, failing to place any of the numerous short stories he had written, he began to try his hand at writing material for television. His first breakthrough was the production of his teleplay *Cold Harbor,* and soon thereafter Barrett was writing for the big New York television market: *Kraft Theatre, Playhouse 90,* and *Armstrong Circle Theatre.* One of his Kraft teleplays, *Murder of a Sand Flea,* based on a Marine experience, caught the eye of the actor Jack Webb, who brought Barrett to Hollywood to adapt the text into a movie. It was released in 1957 as *The D.I.,* and Barrett remained in the film capital for the rest of his life.

During the next thirty years Barrett wrote the scripts for some of Hollywood's most successful film and television productions. Among his most popular films were *The Greatest Story Ever Told*, *The Green Berets*, and *Smoky and the Bandit*. His screenplay for the comedy *The Cheyenne Social Club* won a Writers Guild of America award in 1970. One of his most enduring works has been the film *Shenandoah*, whose star, James Stewart, became a good friend. Barrett's musical book for the stage version of *Shenandoah* won him a Tony Award.

Barrett's made-for-television films include *Belle Star*, *Angel City*, *The Day Christ Died*, *Mayflower: The Pilgrim Experience*, *The Law & Charlie Dodge*, *April Morning*, *Stagecoach*, *Poker Alice*, *Vengeance*, and *The Quick and the Dead*. He created pilots for such productions as *The Doctors Brandon*, *Big Bad John*, *The Judge*, *When the Whistle Blows*, *Running Hot*, *The Cowboys*, *You the Jury*, and *Big Man, Little Lady*. He wrote the seven-hour, three-part miniseries *The Awakening Land* and the holiday special *Stubby Pringle's Christmas*. He developed *In the Heat of the Night* for television and was the originator of the popular series *Our House*. "I've told mostly about people," Barrett remarked near the end of his career. "And that, really, is what makes a good motion picture—the people and how real they are. Always the people."

Barrett was a member of the Academy of Motion Picture Arts and Sciences; the Writers' Guild of America, West; the Dramatists' Guild; and the Authors' League of America. In 1998 he was inducted into the South Carolina Academy of Authors. He and his wife, Danish-born Merete Engelstoft Barrett, were the parents of five children. Barrett died of cancer on October 15, 1989, at his home in Templeton, California. THOMAS L. JOHNSON

Barrett, James Lee. Papers. South Caroliniana Library, University of South Carolina, Columbia.

Bass, Jack (b. 1934). Journalist, biographer, educator. Born in Columbia, South Carolina, Jack Bass is the youngest of seven children born to Nathan and Esther (Cohen) Bass. His father Nathan Bass emigrated from Lithuania and moved to the town of North, South Carolina, after marrying Esther Cohen, a Polish immigrant from Brooklyn, New York. Bass became the sixth member of his family to attend the University of South Carolina in Columbia, where he received his Bachelor of Arts in 1956. While at USC he served as chief editor for the school newspaper, the *Gamecock*, and worked as an intern for the sports department of the Charleston *News and Courier*. In 1957 Bass married his first wife Carolyn McClung. After graduation he served for three and a half years as a naval flight officer, stationed primarily in San Diego. In 1960 Bass returned to Charleston, taking a position with the Charleston *News and Courier* where his journalistic focus switched from sports to politics.

In 1961 Bass moved back to Columbia, working for the *Columbia Record* before moving to the *State* as part of their governmental affairs staff. While in that position, Bass became interested in the changing politics of the South in connection with the civil rights movement, a major theme in his writing. In 1965 he received a Nieman Fellowship for journalism from Harvard University. As part of his fellowship, he studied current constitutional issues and American constitutional development at the Harvard School of Government.

In 1966, after completion of his fellowship, Bass accepted a position as Columbia Bureau chief for the *Charlotte Observer,* a position he held for seven years during the height of the civil rights movement. Bass reported on the tragedy of the Orangeburg Massacre as it unfolded on the campus of South Carolina State College on February 8, 1968 with fellow journalist Jack Nelson, Atlanta Bureau chief for the *Los Angeles Times.* Bass's coverage of the massacre earned him the award for South Carolina Newspaperman of the Year in 1972. Collaboration between Bass and Nelson later produced *The Orangeburg Massacre* (1970), an account of the event unveiling governmental cover-ups and highlighting journalistic misinformation. Although both authors received positive reviews from critics and historians, the book met with considerable public backlash that limited its distribution. Despite its controversial release, however, Bass and Nelson's work became the definitive account of the massacre and its aftermath.

From 1967–71 Bass entered the academic field as a part-time lecturer in journalism at the University of South Carolina and began work on his second book, *Porgy Comes Home: South Carolina after Three Hundred Years.* The book, published by the R. L. Bryan Company of Columbia (1972), details the history of South Carolina from settlement through the civil rights era.

In 1973 Bass accepted a position as a visiting research scholar in the Institute of Policy Science and Public Affairs at Duke University to work on his third book, a follow-up to V. O. Key's foundational 1941 volume *Southern Politics: State and Nation.* Bass received Ford and Rockefeller Foundation grants to complete his research on *Transformation of Southern Politics: Social Change and Political Consequence since 1945* (1976) co-authored with Walter DeVries. This state-by-state analysis of eleven southern states focuses on political and societal changes and features extensive data and interviews.

In 1974 Bass gained an insider's view of the U.S. political system working with Congressman Brian Dorne during the latter's failed bid for the office of South Carolina governor. From 1975 to 1978 Jack Bass served as writer-in-residence and research scholar at South Carolina State College in Orangeburg, South Carolina, while concurrently completing his Masters of Arts in journalism at the University of South Carolina (awarded in 1976). During this time Bass became a frequent non-staff correspondent for several prestigious newspapers and journals including the *New York Times,* the *Washington Post, Newsweek, The Nation, The New Republic,* the *Philadelphia Inquirer,* and *Life.*

In 1978 Jack Bass returned to Columbia and unsuccessfully ran for U.S. Congress as a Democrat for the Second Congressional District against Congressman Floyd Spence. Following the election, he became the director of American South Special Projects at the University of South Carolina where he worked for five years producing the fourteen-part television course *The American South Comes of Age.* Soon after, Bass produced his fourth book *Unlikely Heroes: The Dramatic Story of the Southern Judges of the Fifth Circuit who Translated the Supreme Court Brown Decision into a Revolution for Equality* (1981), which focuses on four judges: Chief Judge Elbert Tuttle, John Minor Wisdom, John Robert Brown, and Richard Rives. *Unlikely Heroes* examines the Federal Fifth Circuit Court's ruling on landmark cases like Brown v. The Board of Education and the impact those decisions had in shaping southern politics and race relations.

In 1984 Bass married his second wife Alice R. Calsaniss and, three years later, accepted a position as professor of journalism for the University of Mississippi, where he worked for twelve years. In 1993 Bass published *Taming the Storm: The Life and Times of Judge Frank M. Johnson, Jr. and the South's Fight over Civil Rights,* devoted to Johnson's precedent-setting decisions as federal judge for Alabama. In this volume, Bass documents Judge Johnson's rulings as integral to the civil rights movement, citing landmark cases beginning with Browder v. Gayle (1956), which integrated public transit in Montgomery by declaring segregation unconstitutional. The book received the prestigious Robert F. Kennedy Book Award.

In 1994 Bass married South Carolina author and television personality Nathalie Dupree. Bass completed his doctorate in American studies from Emory University in 1998. His dissertation, *A Biography of Strom Thurmond,* served as the basis for his work with Marilyn W. Thompson entitled *Ol' Strom: An Unauthorized Biography of Strom Thurmond,* published in 1998 by Longstreet Press and nominated for a Pulitzer Prize. The biography quickly became the definitive text on the controversial southern senator.

In 2000, Bass accepted a position at the College of Charleston, where he currently serves as a professor of humanities and social science. After Strom Thurmond's death in 2003, he and Thompson paired up again for a second book on Thurmond entitled *Strom: The Complicated Personal and Political Life of Strom Thurmond,* published in 2005.

In 2009 Bass's eighth book, *The Palmetto State: The Making of Modern South Carolina* was published by the University of South Carolina Press. The book, co-authored by W. Scott Poole, outlines the unique political and cultural history of South Carolina and the effects that the state's past has had on its modern identity and culture. In 2011 Bass received the Governor's Award in the Humanities from the Humanities Council^{SC} for outstanding achievement in humanities research, teaching, and scholarship.

His ninth book, *Justice Abandoned* (Pantheon, 2012), returns to a discussion of constitutional law, focusing on the Supreme Court's interpretation of the fourteenth amendment. In 2013 the South Carolina Academy of Authors inducted Bass in recognition of his distinguished contributions to South Carolina's literary legacy. AMANDA RACHELLE WARREN

Epps, Edwin C. *Literary South Carolina.* Spartanburg, S.C.: Hub City Writers Project, 2004.
Jack Bass, interview by Ferrel Guillory, 15 April 2011, Southern Oral History Program Collection at the Southern Historical Collection, Louis Round Wilson Special Collections Library, UNC-Chapel Hill.

Bennett, John (1865–1956). Fiction writer, artist. The son of John Bennett and Eliza Jane McClintick, Bennett was born in Chillicothe, Ohio, on May 17, 1865. Wanting to become an artist, he had to work to support his family instead. In the 1880s he published prose and silhouettes for children in *St. Nicholas Magazine.* The publication serialized his most famous work, *Master Skylark,* which appeared in book form in 1897. A tale of Shakespeare's time, it was considered one of the best American historical novels for children. Its success convinced Bennett to drop out of the New York Art Students League and write another book. In 1898 ill health drove him to Charleston, where he renewed his acquaintance with the Smythe family, whom he had met a few years before at Salt Sulphur Springs, West Virginia. Bennett's second book, *Barnaby Lee,* was published in 1902. Its proceeds enabled him to marry Susan Smythe the same year. Turning his attention to the riches of the area, he wrote *The Treasure of Peyre Gaillard* (1906).

During these years Bennett tried to interest publishers in African American spirituals, and he made a close study of Gullah, the language of lowcountry blacks. He also studied black folklore, amassing tales of the disappearing oral tradition. He presented a lecture on this subject in 1908, but the local press castigated him for using blacks as a subject. Dejected, he nearly gave up writing. During World War I, he came into contact with the younger DuBose Heyward, as they raised money for Liberty Loans. After the war, when the Pittsburgh native and war veteran Hervey Allen came to town, Heyward and Allen became friends, and both turned to Bennett, who mentored them in weekly "fanging" sessions. Stirred by the new spirit of modern poetry, Allen, Heyward, and Bennett joined with a group of fledgling women poets under Laura Bragg, including Elizabeth von Kolnitz (later Hyer) and Josephine Pinckney. Together they launched the Poetry Society of South Carolina in 1921. Bennett agreed to participate only after being assured that he would be a figurehead. But as the careers of the younger artists took off, Bennett was left to run the organization.

Bennett published one folktale, *Madame Margot,* in 1921 but was not able to complete the collection as *The Doctor to the Dead* until 1946. In the interim he published a collection of his earlier silhouette tales, *The Pigtail of Ah Lee Ben Loo* (1928). Although his published work is notable, perhaps his greatest personal contribution to arts and letters was to the individuals he mentored and the fields of study that he fostered. He was a pioneer in the study of many African American and other historical topics and was instrumental in the creation and publication of Heyward's landmark novel *Porgy* (1925). As founder and sustainer of the Poetry Society of South Carolina, Bennett was a key player in the revival of literary and cultural life in the city and the state. The father of three, Bennett died on December 28, 1956, and was buried in Magnolia Cemetery; he was posthumously inducted into the South Carolina Academy of Authors in 1998. HARLAN GREENE

Greene, Harlan. *Mr. Skylark: John Bennett and the Charleston Renaissance.* Athens: University of Georgia Press, 2001.

Billings, John Shaw (1898–1975). Journalist, editor. Billings was born on May 11, 1898, at Redcliffe Plantation in Beech Island, South Carolina, the eldest son of John Sedgewick Billings and Katherine Hammond. He was the great-grandson of James Henry Hammond, the eminent South Carolina politician of the antebellum era. Although a South Carolina native, Billings resided during much of his life in New York City. During his childhood, however, the family made many extended visits to Redcliffe.

After graduating in May, 1916 from St. Paul's School in Concord, New Hampshire, Billings enrolled at Harvard University. He left college in January 1917 to fight in World War I. Initially Billings drove both trucks and ambulances for the French military; however, following America's entry into the fighting in April 1917, he transferred to the U.S. Army Air Corps. At his discharge in January 1919, he held the rank of second lieutenant.

On returning to the United States, Billings went back to Harvard. Although a good student, Billings grew bored with his academic routine. In January, 1920 he became involved with a gubernatorial campaign in Connecticut. That autumn he dropped out of Harvard one term short of graduation. In 1921 he became a political reporter for the Brooklyn *Daily Eagle.* Ten months later he was assigned to the paper's Washington bureau. In September 1922, during a visit to Redcliffe, Billings met Frederica W. Wade, a Beech Island neighbor. They were married on April 19, 1924, at Beech Island Presbyterian Church.

In 1928 Billings succeeded Henry Cabot Lodge II as the Washington, D.C. correspondent for *Time,* a weekly newsmagazine. Billings relocated to New York City in January 1929 when he became national affairs editor of *Time.* During the next quarter-century, he rose steadily within the Time Inc. editorial hierarchy. In

November, 1933 he was promoted to managing editor of *Time*. Three years later he assumed the managing editorship of *Life*, a new weekly pictorial magazine. The eight years in that position were considered the most noteworthy of his journalistic career. When he retired in May 1954, Billings was the editorial director of all Time Inc. publications. Only Henry R. Luce, the editor in chief, possessed more editorial authority.

In March 1935 Billings's aunt Julia Hammond Richards died, leaving Redcliffe Plantation without an occupant. As the most affluent Hammond descendant, Billings agreed to purchase the property; and during the next several decades, he spent a considerable personal fortune renovating the entire estate, especially the big house. On retiring, Billings returned permanently to Redcliffe, spending his last years there.

Following a long illness, Frederica Wade Billings died in 1963. Billings subsequently married Elise Lake Chase of Augusta, Georgia, on September 10, 1963. Because his only child, Frederica Wade Billings, had died in childhood, he bequeathed Redcliffe Plantation in 1973 to the state of South Carolina. The property was to become a state park after his death. Throughout much of his life Billings had maintained an extensive daily diary; increasingly frail heath finally forced him to curtail that activity in June 1974. Fourteen months later, on August 25, 1975, Billings died in Augusta, survived by his second wife. He was interred in the Hammond family cemetery at Redcliffe. MILES S. RICHARDS

Billings, John Shaw. Papers. South Caroliniana Library, University of South Carolina, Columbia.

Bleser, Carol, ed. *The Hammonds of Redcliffe.* New York: Oxford University Press, 1981.

Morris, Sylvia Jukes. *Rage for Fame: The Ascent of Clare Boothe Luce.* New York: Random House, 1997.

Swanberg, W. A. *Luce and His Empire.* New York: Scribner's, 1972.

Williams, William Bates. "John Shaw Billings: The Man behind the Editor." Master's thesis, University of South Carolina, 1978.

Blackwell, Elise (b. 1964). Novelist, nonfiction writer, educator. Born July 18, 1964 in Austin, Texas, Elise Blackwell grew up in and around Baton Rouge, Louisiana. She started writing at age five, when her maternal grandfather offered her a dollar for every story she wrote. After attending Sherwood Middle School and University High School, Blackwell enrolled at Louisiana State University where she worked as a DJ at the KLSU radio station. She earned a B.A. in English in 1986 and lived briefly in Albuquerque, New Mexico, and Boston, Massachusetts, before moving to California to attend the M.F.A. Creative Writing Program at UC-Irvine, where she finished her degree in 1990. In 1989 she married novelist David Bajo and moved to San Diego, where she spent eight years working as a freelance writer, editor, and translator; traveling extensively in Mexico; and raising rare fruits and vegetables. During this period, she participated in the Seed Saver's Exchange, an organization dedicated to preserving and sharing heirloom fruits and vegetables.

In 1997 Blackwell gave birth to a daughter, Esme Claire Bajo, and moved to Northern California for a year and a half and then to Princeton, New Jersey, where she worked as a senior copywriter for Princeton University Press. From 2003–2005 Blackwell taught at Boise State University, before accepting a position in the English department at the University of South Carolina.

Currently associate professor of English and director of the M.F.A. Program in Creative Writing at the University of South Carolina, Blackwell teaches courses in prose writing. In acknowledgment of her work in the classroom, she won the Department of English Excellence in Teaching Award in 2008 and the Michael J. Mungo Undergraduate Teaching Award in 2009. A member of the PEN American Center, Blackwell has served on the AWP Board of Directors since 2012 and continues to appear as a reader and presenter at literary events around the country.

In 2003 Blackwell's first book *Hunger* appeared in print, garnering substantial critical and popular attention. Enriched by her experience with Seed Saver's Exchange, *Hunger* is narrated by a fictional scientist working at the N.I. Vavilov Research Institute of Plant Industry during Hitler's siege of Leningrad when hundreds of thousands of civilians died of starvation. Charged with protecting and maintaining the institute's collection of rare seeds, tubers, and fruit, the narrator staves off starvation by secretly eating the carefully preserved samples. Against a backdrop of heroism and deprivation, the narrator slowly emerges as an amoral survivor, driven to betrayal by his sensual appetites. *Hunger* was named one of the "Best Books of 2003" by the *Los Angeles Times;* and the *Sydney Morning Herald* named it one of the "Best Reads of the Year." Since its appearance, it has been translated into Spanish, French, Hebrew, and Portuguese and adapted for the stage by Chicago's Lifeline Theater.

In 2007 Blackwell's second novel *Grub* was published by the Toby Press. A modern reworking of George Gissing's *New Grub Street,* a classic satire of the Victorian literary marketplace, *Grub* follows the intertwining struggles of group of writers as they establish and maintain literary careers in contemporary New York City. *Grub* was named a "Best Book of 2007" by *Kirkus* and the "Finest Book of the Year" by the Morning Advocate (Louisiana). The year 2007 also saw the publication of Blackwell's third novel, *The Unnatural History of Cypress Parish,* which Blackwell rewrote in light of Hurricane Katrina's impact on the Louisiana coast. Like her novel *Hunger, The Unnatural History of Cypress Parish* explores the impact of a historical disaster on ordinary peoples' relationships and values. Set in a fictional parish in Blackwell's native Louisiana, *Unnatural History* is narrated by a ninety-five-year-old hydraulics expert Louis Proby, who, on the eve of Hurricane

Katrina's landing, recalls his boyhood experience with both political corruption and personal betrayals during the 1927 Great Flood. Part coming-of-age story and part meditation on the nature of human history, *The Unnatural History of Cypress Parish* was named "Louisiana Book of the Year" by the *Monroe News Star* and "Best Book of 2007" by the *New Orleans Times—Picayune*.

In 2010 Blackwell's fourth novel, *An Unfinished Score,* was published by Unbridled Books. The novel follows the struggles of a married musician, Suzanne, who has been blackmailed into completing the unfinished score of a violin concerto started by her lover, a famous conductor who died unexpectedly. Developing themes that Blackwell also explores in *Grub* and in her nonfiction writing, *An Unfinished Score* traces the complex and sometimes devastating interactions between an artist's social and interior lives; the novel was named "Best Independent Press Book of the Decade" by the *Huffington Post* and "Best Book of 2010" by the *Athens Banner-Herald.*

In addition to her novels, Blackwell writes regularly for *The Chronicle of Higher Education,* describing professional and academic trends in the field of creative writing and analyzing their effects on writers and their work. Her story "Necrotic" won the 2012 flash fiction contest sponsored by the *Newport Review,* and her short pieces "Carolina Dog" and "Before Texas" appear in the anthologies *Carolina Writers and Their Literary Dogs* and *A Shared Voice: A Conversation in Narrative by Twenty-four of the Finest Fiction Writers in America* respectively. DAVID BRUZINA

Blackwell, Elise. "Blackwell on Writing: The Long and the Very Short of It." *The Chronicle of Higher Education,* January 1, 2012.

Blair, Frank (1915–1995). Broadcaster, author. Born in Yemassee, South Carolina, on May 30, 1915, Blair was the son of telegrapher Frank S. Blair and Hannah Pinckney. He attended the College of Charleston in 1933. On October 20, 1935, he married Lillian Stoddard. They had eight children. During World War II he served in the U.S. Navy as a flight instructor and transport pilot, attaining the rank of lieutenant.

A deep-voiced newscaster, Blair got his start in broadcasting in October 1935, when he convinced officials at WCSC-Radio in Charleston to let him start a news show. From this fifteen-dollar-a-week job he moved on to Columbia and Greenville stations, then to WOL in Washington, D.C., where he worked from 1939 to 1942. After World War II he briefly managed station WSCR-Radio in Scranton, Pennsylvania.

Blair joined NBC-TV in 1950 and moderated *The American Forum of the Air,* a debate program. He was named Washington, D.C., correspondent for the *Today Show,* which was launched on January 14, 1952, as an experimental morning news program. The innovative enterprise eventually won acclaim with Dave Garroway and Jack Lescoulie as hosts and Blair as newscaster. Blair worked with twenty-five different hosts during his twenty-three years on the show. In his autobiography, *Let's Be Frank about It,* Blair described the pressures of the job and his bouts with alcohol abuse. He resigned from the show on March 14, 1975, and retired to Hilton Head Island, South Carolina, but continued recording commercials and syndicated radio programs.

Blair was honored by Georgetown University, where he was a broadcast instructor; Xavier University; the University of Missouri; and the Boy Scouts of America. He received honorary degrees from Nasson College, Le Moyne College, Niagara University, and the Citadel. He died at Hilton Head Island on March 14, 1995. ROBERT A. PIERCE

Blair, Frank. *Let's Be Frank about It.* Garden City, NJ: Doubleday, 1979.

Bowers, Cathy Smith (b. 1949). Poet, educator. Cathy Smith Bowers was born in Lancaster, South Carolina, on November 15, 1949. One of six children born to millworker Edward Sorrel Smith and his wife Mary Helen McManus Smith, she was educated in the public schools, graduating from Lancaster High School in 1968. Subsequent to her graduation, she attended Winthrop University (then Winthrop College) in Rock Hill, South Carolina, receiving her B.A. in English in 1972. Beginning in 1973, she worked as a teacher of high school English in South Carolina for ten years, completing a master's degree in English (also at Winthrop) in 1976. Her years as a high school English teacher ended when she became an English instructor at Queens University in Charlotte, North Carolina, where she would also serve as director of composition from 1989 to 1995 and Poet-in-Residence from 1996–2004. Presently she holds faculty positions with the Queens University M.F.A. and Creative Writing Program; Wofford College in Spartanburg, South Carolina; and the Haden Institute in Hendersonville, North Carolina, and Niagara Falls, Canada. Bowers currently lives in Tryon, North Carolina.

Her work reflects a life marked by considerable achievement, both literary and professional, as well as considerable sorrow. Because her parents had separated when she was in her teens, she was estranged from her father for many years, though they were reunited before his death. A deeply loved younger brother Paul was lost to AIDS, and an older brother Gary died as a result of drug and alcohol complications. Her first marriage, to Dennis Carl Bowers, ended in divorce in 1994. Her second husband, Jerry Scott Stockdale, died by suicide in 2005. All of this, along with an acute consciousness of the value and beauty of everyday life, are present in Bowers's books of poems, which range from compellingly lyrical free verse to adroit formal experimentation.

Bowers's work has garnered considerable acclaim; in 1990 she won the General Electric Award for Younger Writers and a South Carolina Poetry Fellowship from the South Carolina Arts Commission. Her first book of poems, *The Love That Ended Yesterday in Texas*, originally published by Texas Tech in 1992 and reissued by Iris Press in 1998, won first place in that year's inaugural Walt McDonald First Book Series competition. Other awards include the JB Fuqua Distinguished Educator Award from Queens University and the Gilbert-Chappell Distinguished Poet Award from the North Carolina Poetry Society in 2006 and 2007. In February 2010, she was named Poet Laureate of the State of North Carolina.

Bowers's second book of poems, *Traveling in Time of Danger*, published by Iris Press in 1999, marked her continued development as a free-verse poet who handles line and image with remarkable dexterity. With *A Book of Minutes*, published by Iris Press in 2004, the poet broke new ground, writing each poem in the poetic form called "the minute," which consists of sixty syllables broken into three four-line stanzas with a fixed rhyme scheme, a poetic challenge that Bowers rose to with superb use of image, line, and rhyme pattern. Like her earlier books, *The Book of Minutes* is strongly rooted in the poet's life experience as she pursues her work of rendering life—from its grittiest to its most beautiful—as art.

By the time Iris Press published her fourth book of poems in 2009, *The Candle I Hold Up to See You*, Cathy Smith Bowers's reputation in poetry was well established. Her poems appear regularly in publications such as the *Atlantic Monthly*, *Poetry*, the *Kenyon Review*, *Shenandoah*, the *Southern Review*, and the *Georgia Review*. Her most recent collection of selected and previously unpublished poems, *Like Shining from Shook Foil*, was published by Press 53 in February, 2010, as a commemoration of the tenth anniversary of the Queen's MFA program.

Smith Bowers is very clear about the force and value of poetry and acutely conscious of its ability to alter the shape of a life. She once stated, "Poetry saved my life. I could have been the poster child for the one least likely to succeed at anything. And yet my life has been blessed because I dared attempt to say the unsayable, to express, in words I did not know I possessed, the inexpressible mysteries of this life." PHEBE DAVIDSON

Bowers, Cathy Smith. Personal Interview. August 30, 2012.

Boyd, Blanche McCrary (b. 1945). Novelist, educator. Boyd was born in Charleston, South Carolina, on August 31, 1945, the daughter of Charles Fant McCrary and Mildred McDaniel. She attended Duke University, earned her B.A. from Pomona College in 1967, and received a Wallace Stegner Fellowship from Stanford University, where she completed her M.A. in 1971. Boyd joined the faculty at Connecticut College in 1982. In 1988 she was awarded a National Endowment for the Arts Fiction Fellowship. Four years later she received the Lambda Literary Award for her novel *The Revolution of Little Girls*, and in 1993–1994 she received a Guggenheim Fellowship.

Boyd has published four novels: *Nerves* (1973), *Mourning the Death of Magic* (1977), *The Revolution of Little Girls* (1991), and *Terminal Velocity* (1997). The last two are part of a trilogy telling the story of Ellen Burns, a Charleston native who experiences an unsatisfying marriage, experiments with heavy drinking and drugs—Boyd herself struggled with substance abuse until she kicked the habit in 1981—and loses herself through various affairs and lifestyle changes. Part three of the trilogy is tentatively titled *Children of Nod*. While each novel can be read on its own, Boyd explains that they are ultimately meant to be viewed together, "like transparencies that alone show complete images, but reveal a unique perspective when combined."

Boyd's fiction reveals a deep concern with the culture of the South. Much of her work addresses civil rights injustices or gender-identity issues within southern culture. *Mourning* is about three girls raised in the South during the 1950s and 1960s who are disillusioned with racism and class discrimination. Boyd's 1981 collection of essays, *The Redneck Way of Knowledge: Down-Home Tales*, features autobiographical accounts of the South Carolina world she knows well. One critic described Boyd's literary voice as "wild, original, witty, imaginative . . . the direct, buckshot explosion of a lady red-neck turned narrator." Boyd is known for capturing both the tumult of a time period and a region's response to such social change.

Boyd's work has won wide recognition. The *Atlanta Journal-Constitution* praised *The Revolution of Little Girls* as "funny . . . lively and wry, insightful and poignant. [A] psychedelic and unsettling journey into a Southern heart of darkness." A reviewer for *Publishers Weekly* said that Boyd has "established a solid reputation as one of America's most unpredictable literary outlaws." Such attention to the more controversial issues addressed in her writing is balanced with compliments on the craft of her fiction. Her work has also been published in periodicals such as *Esquire, New York Times Magazine, Premiere,* and *Voice Literary Supplement.* Divorced in 1971, Boyd created a life partnership with Leslie Hyman in 1999, and the couple have two children, both twins. AMY L. WHITE

Cole, Clarence Bard. "The Revelations of Blanche McCrary Boyd." *Christopher Street* 14 (October 1991): 11.
Gordon, Emily. "Terminal Velocity." *The Nation* 265 (September 1997): 32.
Schuessler, Jennifer. "Blanche McCrary Boyd: Writing Against Gravity." *Publishers Weekly* 244 (June 1997): 64.

Brawley, Benjamin Griffith (1882–1939). Scholar, editor, educator, clergyman. Brawley was born on April 22, 1882, in Columbia, South Carolina, to prominent Baptist parents. His father, the Reverend Edward McKnight Brawley, is remembered as the founder of Morris College in Sumter. "My mother [Margaret Saphronia Dickerson] was from Columbia," Brawley wrote in 1925, "and it was in Columbia, almost in the shadow of the State House, that I first sat up and took notice." A gifted and enthusiastic student, he earned degrees from the University of Chicago (A.B., 1906) and Harvard (M.A., 1908). In 1912 Brawley married Hilda Damaris Prowd. The couple had no children. In 1921 he was ordained as a Baptist minister by the Massachusetts Baptist Convention. For two years in the early 1920s he served as pastor of the Messiah Baptist Church of Brockton, Massachusetts.

Between 1902 and 1939 Brawley taught English at various predominantly black colleges in the South. He was twice at Atlanta Baptist College (later Morehouse College): from 1902 to 1910 and again from 1912 to 1920. The fellow South Carolinian, educator, and writer Benjamin Mays singled Brawley out as one of the "few able, dedicated teachers who made the Morehouse man believe he was 'somebody.'" From 1923 to 1931 Brawley was on the English faculty at Shaw University in Raleigh, North Carolina. He served as professor of English at Howard University in Washington, D.C., during two separate periods: from 1910 to 1912 and from 1931 until his death.

Brawley developed into a prolific writer, contributing works to such periodicals as *Bookman, Dial, North American Review, Sewanee Review,* and *Reviewer.* But it was in his writing and editing of books about the African American experience that he pioneered. While he was teaching at Morehouse in 1909, a student pleaded with him to write a textbook that would enable black students to learn something of the experiences and accomplishments of their own people. Four years later, in 1913, Macmillan published his book *A Short History of the American Negro.* In the ensuing years Brawley wrote or edited *History of Morehouse College* (1917), *Africa and the War* (1918), *Your Negro Neighbor* (1918), *New Era Declamations* (1918), *The Negro in American Literature in the United States* (1918), *Women of Achievement* (1919), *A Social History of the American Negro* (1921), *A Short History of the English Drama* (1921), *Freshman Year English* (1929), *Dr. Dillard of the Jeanes Fund* (1930), *History of the English Hymn* (1932), *The Negro Genius* (1937), and *The Best Stories of Paul Lawrence Dunbar* (1938). In 1925 Knopf published his college textbook *New Survey of English Literature.* The University of North Carolina Press published three of his last five books: *Early Negro American Writers* (1935), *Paul Lawrence Dunbar: Poet of His People* (1936), and *Negro Builders and Heroes* (1937).

By the mid-1930s the U.S. Works Progress Administration in South Carolina had identified Brawley as one of the state's half-dozen outstanding African Americans. Perhaps his chief significance as a writer lay in his ability to articulate what he referred to as "the Negro problem"—the presence and plight of blacks in America. In a 1922 article in *The Bookman,* Brawley noted "the strange prominence of the Negro throughout the whole course of American history." Brawley insisted on articulating a positive black self-awareness, which was not typical of literature about African Americans at the time. "Literature should be not only history but prophecy," he wrote, "not only the record of our striving but also the mirror of our hopes and dreams." He later expanded his interest beyond the well-being of African American boys and girls alone. "What we want," he declared, "is that every boy and girl shall receive the full promise of American life. No one is so high that he does not need our interest, nor is anyone so low that he should not have his chance."

Brawley died on February 1, 1939, at his home in Washington, D.C. In 1991 he was posthumously inducted into the South Carolina Academy of Authors.
THOMAS L. JOHNSON

Brawley, Benjamin G. "The Negro in American Literature." *The Bookman* 56 (October 1922): 137–41.
———. Papers. Moorland-Spingarn Research Center, Howard University, Washington, D.C.
Parker, John W. "Benjamin Brawley—Teacher and Scholar." *Phylon* 10 (first quarter, 1949): 15–24.
———. "Benjamin Brawley and the American Cultural Tradition." *Phylon* 16 (second quarter, 1955): 183–94.
———. "A Bibliography of the Published Writings of Benjamin Griffith Brawley." *North Carolina Historical Review* 34 (April 1957): 165–78.

Bristow, Gwen (1903–1980). Novelist. Gwen Bristow, who would come to be referred to as "Carolina's Best Seller," was born in Marion, South Carolina, on September 16, 1903, the daughter of the Baptist minister and hospital superintendent Louis Judson Bristow and Caroline Cornelia Winkler. She made her writing debut in 1916 in Columbia's *State* newspaper as a seventh-grade Taylor School reporter. Although she attended Columbia High School, she graduated at Abbeville, where her father had returned as pastor. After attending Anderson College for a year, she transferred to Judson College in Marion, Alabama, where in 1924 she received her A.B. degree. In 1925, following a year's study at Columbia University's Pulitzer School of Journalism in New York, she became a reporter for the *Times-Picayune* in New Orleans. There she met and married Bruce Manning, a newspaper reporter who eventually became a Hollywood screenwriter and film producer. Together they collaborated on the writing of four mystery novels between 1930 and 1932: *The Invisible Host* (1930), *The Gutenburg Murders* (1931), *Two and Two Make Twenty-Two* (1932), and *The Mardi Gras Murders* (1932).

By the summer of 1934 they had moved to California, where Bristow began to experiment with historical fiction. The result of this was the publication of *Deep Summer* (1937), her first bestseller and the first installment in her Louisiana Plantation Trilogy. The next two in the series soon followed: *The Handsome Road* (1938) and *This Side of Glory* (1940). Her World War II romance novel, *Tomorrow Is Forever,* appeared in 1943 and in 1946 was made into a film starring Orson Welles and Claudette Colbert. The next two novels, *Jubilee Trail* (1950) and *Celia*

Garth (1959), became Literary Guild selections. By the time of the publication of the latter book, which is a story of Charleston in the Revolutionary War, sales of Bristow's books had reached nearly three million copies, exclusive of book clubs. *Calico Palace,* her last novel, was published in 1970. Bristow's final book, *Golden Dreams,* came out in 1980 and was a nonfiction account of the gold rush and the founding of California.

Natural storytelling ability, neatly devised and detailed plots, sharply drawn characters, a telling eye for landscape and its detail, the use of common sense, a gift for dramatic effect, and emotional sincerity were the characteristics of Bristow's work that critics and reviewers singled out for praise. Margaret Wallace spoke of her "solid and versatile talent as a novelist." The critic Susan Quinn Berneis claimed that Bristow's greatest skill was reserved for "the unfolding of American history as displayed around the lives of the people who created it." And Eugene Armfield remarked that she belonged "among those Southern novelists who [were] trying to interpret the South and its past in critical terms." Furthermore, her books had universal appeal: various ones were translated into German, French, Italian, Norwegian, Danish, Swedish, Finnish, Czechoslovakian, Dutch, Spanish, and Portuguese.

Bristow died in New Orleans on August 16, 1980. On April 15, 2000, she was posthumously inducted into the South Carolina Academy of Authors. THOMAS L. JOHNSON

Bristow, Gwen. Papers. South Caroliniana Library, University of South Carolina, Columbia.

Lowry, Julia B. "Carolina's Gwen Bristow Finds She's Obliged to Write!" Columbia *State Magazine,* November 5, 1950, 6–7.

MacNebb, Betty L. "Gwen Bristow: Carolina's Best Seller." *South Carolina Magazine* 12 (July 1949): 8, 10.

Theriot, Billie J. "Gwen Bristow: A Biography with Criticism of Her Plantation Trilogy." Ph.D. diss., Louisiana State University, 1994.

Bruccoli, Matthew J. (1931–2008). Scholar, editor, publisher. Born in the Bronx, New York, in 1931, Matthew Bruccoli was a student at the Bronx High School of Science. Earning a bachelor's degree at Yale University in 1953, he went on to Cornell University but transferred to the University of Virginia for his master's degree (1956) and doctorate (1960). Bruccoli taught at the Ohio State University before joining the faculty at the University of South Carolina. There he remained from 1969–2005, retiring as the Emily Brown Jefferies Distinguished Professor of English. William Grimes of the *New York Times* states that even after his retirement, Bruccoli "continued to cut a dash on campus" and was readily known for "his vintage red Mercedes convertible, Brooks Brothers suits, Groucho mustache and bristling crew cut." Unique also during his years at USC was Bruccoli's New York accent.

While at Cornell, Bruccoli attended literature courses taught by Vladimir Nabokov and eventually edited Nabokov's letters (1940–1977) with the writer's son Dimitri Nabokov; the collection was published in 1989. It is, however, as a scholar of the works of F. Scott Fitzgerald that Bruccoli is known around the world. According to Charles Scribner in his foreword to *The Short Stories of F. Scott Fitzgerald*, Bruccoli's devoted interest in Fitzgerald's writing began in 1949 when he listened to Fitzgerald's story "The Diamond as Big as the Ritz" on the radio. Eventually, he was to write a dozen books on Fitzgerald and his work. Bruccoli's long-term commitment to Fitzgerald's legacy culminated in 1994 when, with the encouragement of his wife Arlyn and help from Fitzgerald's daughter Scottie, he established the Fitzgerald collection housed at the Thomas Cooper Library of the University of South Carolina in Columbia. Today that collection includes books, proofs, letters, inscriptions, photos, memorabilia, screenplays, and paintings about and by both Fitzgerald and his wife Zelda.

Though renowned as a Fitzgerald scholar, Bruccoli also dauntlessly wrote and edited dozens of other books. For instance, while general editor of the *Pittsburgh Series in Bibliography*, Bruccoli collaborated with Richard Layman to produce *Ring W. Lardner: A Descriptive Bibliography*, which was published in 1976. Bruccoli and Layman's collaboration eventually became a partnership (known as Bruccoli Clark Layman) that produced limited first editions. Those limited editions, in turn, resulted in the eventual establishment of the *Dictionary of Literary Biography* and helped precipitate Bruccoli's becoming director for the Center of Literary Biography at the Thomas Cooper Library (University of South Carolina). To date, the *Dictionary of Literary Biography* comprises 400 volumes of reference, including short biographies of over 12,000 writers.

Among other scholarly offerings and projects, Bruccoli worked steadfastly at editing various series: *Lost American Fiction, Understanding Contemporary American Literature, Understanding Contemporary British Literature,* and *Gale Study Guides*. For a time, Bruccoli was also editorial advisor to the *Paris Review* and literary personal representative for the estate of James Dickey. In addition to works aforementioned, Bruccoli is also the author of books about or the editor of works by Raymond Chandler, Ernest Hemingway, John O'Hara, and Thomas Wolfe, to name a few.

In all volumes edited by Bruccoli, readers can expect to find interesting, critical details in the preface and notes; sometimes the editor offers his own insight into the art of writing and the abiding value of literary effort. For instance, in *The Short Stories of F. Scott Fitzgerald: A New Collection* (1995), Bruccoli reminds readers: "Literature is what lasts." In the introduction to John O'Hara's *Gibbsville, PA* (2004), Bruccoli argues: "All great fiction writers are great social historians." In that work, he also cautions: "A writer who can't be trusted for details can't be trusted for anything else."

It is no wonder that Matthew J. Bruccoli came to be so trusted and honored. Among his many achievements were receipt of the Thomas Cooper Medal of the University of South Carolina (1999); invited lectureships in Italy (1996), Norway (1999), and at Illinois State University (1997 and 1998); and induction into the South Carolina Academy of Authors (2001). Matthew J. Bruccoli referred to himself as a "bookman who likes to write." In his many published works, he became the writer to whom other writers, "bookmen," researchers, scholars—new and established—turn. ELLEN E. HYATT

Bruccoli, Matthew J., ed. *Gibbsville, PA: The Classic Stories by John O'Hara.* New York: Carroll and Graf Publications, 1992.

———, ed. *The Short Stories of F. Scott Fitzgerald: A New Collection.* New York: Scribner, 1995.

Epps. Edwin, ed. *Literary South Carolina.* Spartanburg, S.C.: Hub City Writers Project, 2004.

Grimes, William. "Matthew J. Bruccoli, 76, Scholar Dies." *New York Times,* June 6, 2008.

Smith, Kathryn. "Bruccoli Speaks at Banquet." *Anderson Independent-Mail,* April 29, 2001, 4C.

Burroughs, Franklin Gorham, Jr. (b. 1942). Essayist, environmentalist, educator. Burroughs was born on March 7, 1942, in Conway, South Carolina, to Franklin Gorham Burroughs, Sr. and Geraldine Bryan. In 1964 he earned his B.A. from the University of the South, and then at Harvard University he completed his A.M. in 1965 and his Ph.D. in 1970. In 1968 he began teaching at Bowdoin College in Maine, where he continued until his retirement in the fall of 2000. He was inducted into the South Carolina Academy of Authors in 2012.

Burroughs's work, often compared to that of New England essayist and poet Henry David Thoreau, was collected in *Best American Essays* in 1987 and 1989. In 1989 he was awarded the Pushcart Prize for nature essays. His collection *Billy Watson's Croker Sack* appeared in 1991, followed by a paperback edition in 1992. That same year his book *Horry and the Waccamaw* was published, and it was later reprinted in 1998 with the title *The River Home: A Return to the Carolina Low Country.*

The River Home tells the story of Burroughs's canoe trip down the Waccamaw River, focusing on the South Carolina counties of Horry and Georgetown, the same country landscapes that he remembered from childhood. His journey was inspired by his discovery of Nathaniel Holmes Bishop's *The Voyage of the Paper Canoe* (1878), recounting that author's East Coast river voyage. Donald Dederick wrote that Burroughs's story "is not simply a recapitulation of a famous canoe trip, but a well-written tribute to an area and its people, economy, and history." *The River*

Home is about the intimate relationship between human beings and the land—about how people's customs and language reflect their environment in complex ways.

In 1999 Burroughs's "Compression Wood" was collected in *Best American Essays*. Part literary analysis and part personal narrative of a trip to South Carolina, the piece once again takes up his familiar theme of the relationship between people and place. Driving north through Pennsylvania after visiting his native Conway, Burroughs thinks about the questions "What do you do?" and "Where do you come from?" Along with philosophical speculation and poetry analysis, the essay accomplishes a sketch of a man called McIver, whom Burroughs has grown up with and who embodies his environmental values. Working with lumber salvaged from Hurricane Hugo wreckage, McIver says, "People who don't work with primary resources don't understand reality. And not understanding reality is a functional definition of insanity."

"Compression Wood" contains astute cultural observation as well: "When you stop for gas in the Virginia tidewater, you hear that something has happened to the language. Tongues seem to have lost their agility. Vowels and consonants thicken and soften; cadences and sentences ooze and eddy and ebb, and you can stand there, half listening to the attendant and half thinking of the silt-laden, leisurely rivers and streams and swamps that wind through this flat country and in fact created it." The essay's insights reflect much of Burroughs's philosophy: "Where you're from is never simply a matter of geography. It involves intersections of history, economics, family, and so forth, as well as the coordinates of latitude and longitude. Self-location, with or without maps, is ultimately as complicated and incomplete a process as self-knowledge."

In 2009, Burroughs won the prestigious John Burroughs Award for natural history writing for his nonfiction volume entitled *Confluence: Merrymeeting Bay*. With photographs by Hellen Perry, the book focuses on the residents of Maine who live at the junction of two major rivers with two separate watersheds. AMY L. WHITE

Burroughs, Franklin. "Compression Wood." *American Scholar* 67 (spring 1998): 123–37.

Crum, Robert. "Book Reviews—'Billy Watson's Croker Sack' by Franklin Burroughs." *Georgia Review* 45 (winter 1991): 808.

Dederick, Donald H. "Sports & Recreation—'Horry and the Waccamaw' by Franklin Burroughs." *Library Journal* 117 (January 1992): 140.

Ives, Nancy R. "Literature—'Billy Watson's Croker Sack' by Franklin Burroughs." *Library Journal* 116 (January 1991): 104.

Burton, Orville Vernon (b. 1949). Historian, educator, institute director. Orville Vernon Burton returned to his hometown of Ninety-Six, South Carolina, after sojourning in the north for over thirty years. In his 2004 autobiographical sketch and again in his presidential address at the Southern Historical Association's 2012 meeting, he focused on the peculiarities and peccadilloes of a southerner displaced in the north. He characterizes his adult life as one of "crossing boundaries, boundaries of race, geography, class and status." In fact, he admits, "I have crossed so many boundaries that sometimes I no longer know where I belong. . . . But, I do know where I am from."

Burton grew up in the rural, cotton mill town of Ninety-Six and attended a small high school where everyone knew each other. Burton himself was on the football team. Commenting on the fact that his coach, who was also the history teacher, would let his players skip class in order to get more practice on the field, Burton confessed: "We did have a very good football team and won the state championship, but I learned very little about history in high school. I did read a lot, including all the history and biographies in the bookmobile that visited every other week. Also, as I rolled newspapers for my paper route each morning, I read three different papers with totally contrasting political views, which was intriguing to me." Burton's self-education and close reading of the "abuses of the past" took him to Furman University where he graduated with a B.A. in history in 1969. His quest for knowledge and deep curiosity eventually led him to the north where he would continue his education by earning an M.A. and Ph.D. at Princeton University. Moving from New Jersey to Illinois for his first academic post, Burton began his long exile from his beloved but blighted South.

At the University of Illinois, where he is now emeritus University Distinguished Teacher/Scholar and professor of history, African American studies, and sociology, Burton was recognized for his outstanding mentorship and teaching. In 1999 he was named the National Research and Doctoral University Professor of the Year by the Carnegie Foundation. He is a leader of the movement to bridge the cyber world and academe, as both the founding director of the Institute for Computing in Humanities, Arts, and Social Sciences at UIUC and as Distinguished Professor of humanities and computer science and director of the CyberInstitute at Clemson University. When Burton first returned to the South, he was the Mark W. Clark Visiting Distinguished Chair at the Citadel. Later, he spent two years as the Burroughs Distinguished Professor of history and culture at Coastal Carolina University, where he followed in the footsteps of his colleague and friend, Charles Joyner.

In his hundreds of scholarly articles and sixteen books, Burton has focused on the American South and its painful history of race relations. *In My Father's House are Many Mansions* (1985) casts light on the violence of black and white relations in Edgefield, South Carolina. Noting how few scholars until that time had studied southern family life, he wrote: "This history of family and community in nineteenth-century Edgefield, South Carolina, is intended to convey the enormous richness and complexity of family and community life, a life complicated by the violent strains of slavery, Civil War, freedom, Reconstruction, and Redemption." Researching the family papers, letters, slave narratives, and church records of the residents of Edgefield—an area called a "district of devils" by Parson Weems— unveiled the "ties that bound black and white together."

Burton followed the influential, Edgefield-based Pickens family into another book that he co-edited with his wife, Georganne. *The Free Flag of Cuba* by Lucy Holcombe Pickens, Governor Francis W. Pickens's third wife, is a work of romantic fiction inspired by the 1851 filibustering campaign in Cuba, an unauthorized military incursion focused on fomenting revolution. The Burtons uncovered Lucy's lost novel, written under the pseudonym, H.R. Hardimann, and annotated the historical details in the book.

Burton is perhaps best-known for his monograph on President Abraham Lincoln. In *The Age of Lincoln*, Burton identifies Lincoln's "southernness" as key to his affirmation of freedom and liberty for all. The companion website that Burton manages for the book allows readers to engage in their own analysis and interpretation of many primary source documents that undergird the research. Here Burton's twin pillar strengths of computing and humanities research are provided to the general public, free of charge. MAGGI M. MOREHOUSE

Burton, O. Vernon. *The Age of Lincoln.* New York: Hill and Wang, 2007.
———. *In My Father's House Are Many Mansions: Family and Community in Edgefield, South Carolina.* Chapel Hill: University of North Carolina Press, 1985.
———. "The Southerner as Stranger." Presidential Address presented at meeting of the Southern Historical Association, Mobile, Alabama, 2012.
———. "Stranger in a Strange Land: Crossing Boundaries." In *Shapers of Southern History: Autobiographical Sketches by Fifteen Historians.* Edited by John Boles. Athens: University of Georgia Press, 2004.
———. and Georganne B Burton, editors. *The Free Flag of Cuba: The Lost Novel of Lucy Holcombe Pickens.* Baton Rouge: Louisiana State University, 2002.
"Interview with Orville Vernon Burton," conducted by Roy Rosenzweig in *History Matters.* City University of New York, and George Mason University, http://historymatters.gmu .edu/d/6164. August, 2001.

Byars, Betsy Cromer (b. 1928). Novelist. Byars was born in Charlotte, North Carolina, on August 7, 1928, the daughter of George Guy Cromer and Nan Rugheimer. After attending Furman University in Greenville, South Carolina, she graduated in 1950 from Queens College in Charlotte with a Bachelor of Arts in English, although she had begun college as a mathematics major. On June 24, 1950, she married Edward Ford Byars, a professor of engineering and a writer. Byars began her writing career with magazine articles until dedicating herself to children's literature. In

1962 her first book, *Clementine,* was published. It was the first of many books that Byars would create from her personal experiences.

Among her numerous novels, Byars's most popular work is perhaps *The Summer of the Swans* (1970), the story of a young girl named Sara and her experiences with her mentally handicapped brother, Charlie. This book won many honors, including the John Newbery Medal from the American Library Association. In total, Byars has written more than fifty books, including *The Night Swimmers* (1980), which won the American Book Award for children's fiction; *Wanted . . . Mud Blossom* (1991), which won an Edgar Award for the best mystery for young people; and *Keeper of the Doves* (2002). Several have been adapted for television. In her autobiography, *The Moon and I,* published in 1991, Byars used the arrival of a blacksnake she named Moon to reveal her insights on a writer's life along with anecdotes from her childhood.

Byars has three daughters and a son. With her daughters Betsy Duffey and Laurie Myers, she wrote *My Dog, My Hero* (2000). Byars resides in Seneca, South Carolina. R. F. STALVEY

Byars, Betsy. *The Moon and I.* Englewood Cliffs, NJ: J. Messner, 1991.

Cash, Wilbur Joseph (1900–1941). Journalist, social commentator. A writer and an acerbic commentator on southern life, Cash was born in the mill village of Gaffney, South Carolina, on May 2, 1900. The oldest child of John William Cash, who managed the company store for a local cotton mill, and Nannie Lutitia Hamrick, he was named Joseph Wilbur Cash. Disliking his first name, Cash reversed the order and used the initial J. rather than Joseph. Cash graduated from Boiling Springs High School in North Carolina in 1917 and enlisted in the Students' Army Training Corps—a home-front service during World War I. Following the end of his enlistment, Cash entered Wofford College. After one year at Wofford, Cash attended Valparaiso University in Indiana and then in 1920 enrolled at Wake Forest University in North Carolina. At Wake Forest he wrote for student publications and discovered the writings of H. L. Mencken.

After graduating in 1922, Cash attended law school for a year and then tried teaching—first at Georgetown College in Kentucky and later at Hendersonville School for Boys in North Carolina. Returning to writing, Cash had a brief stint with the Chicago *Post* before joining the *Charlotte (N.C.) News* in 1926. In 1928 ill health forced him to return to Boiling Springs. He edited the short-lived *Cleveland (N.C.) Press* and in 1929 wrote "Jehovah of the Tar Heels," which appeared in Mencken's *American Mercury.* "Jehovah of the Tar Heels" was an exposé of the anti-Catholicism of U.S. Senator Furnifold M. Simmons, an anti-Al Smith Democrat. Later that year his second article, "The Mind of the South," caught the attention of the editors at Alfred A. Knopf. In March 1936 the publisher contracted with Cash to write a history of the South. Finding freelancing difficult in the dark days of the Depression, Cash returned to the *Charlotte News* in 1935 and stayed there until 1940. While in Charlotte, he married Mary Ross Northrop on Christmas Day 1940.

Cash's masterpiece and only book, *The Mind of the South*, appeared in February 1941 to wide critical praise. An instant classic that has not been out of print since its initial publication, the work sought to dispel myths about the "Old South" by tracing the pervasive influence of racism on southern history and culture. Antebellum ideals remained dominant in the twentieth-century South, despite the upheavals of the Civil War, Reconstruction, industrialization, urbanization, and Depression. Indeed, Cash's compelling chronicle of the persistence of an Old South mentality, especially its emphasis on race, individualism, and agriculture, led the author to assert that much of southern history has been a march "from the present toward the past." National publications hailed *The Mind of the South*, and even many southern reviewers found much to admire in Cash's penetrating analysis of the region.

Awarded a prestigious Guggenheim fellowship, W. J. Cash traveled with his wife to Mexico, where he planned to write his first novel. In Mexico, Cash's history of psychological instability, alcohol abuse, and ill health caught up with him. Ill with dysentery and in a state of paranoia—he claimed that he was being chased by Nazi spies—and depression, Cash eluded his five-month bride, who summoned the local police to search for her distraught husband. On July 1, 1941, he was found in the Hotel Reforma hanging by his own necktie. Cash's body was cremated and his ashes buried in Sunset Cemetery, Shelby, North Carolina; he was posthumously inducted into the South Carolina Academy of Authors in 1995. ALEXIA JONES HELSLEY

Clayton, Bruce. *W. J. Cash: A Life.* Baton Rouge: Louisiana State University Press, 1991.
Morrison, Joseph L. *W. J. Cash: Southern Prophet.* New York: Knopf, 1967.

Chesnut, Mary Boykin Miller (1823–1886). Diarist. Chesnut was born on her father's plantation near Stateburg in the Sumter District of South Carolina on March 31, 1823. She is recognized as "the preeminent writer of the Confederacy" because of the diary she kept during the Civil War and revised for publication in the early 1880s. No other southern writer of her era possessed the combination of literary cultivation, psychological perception, opportunity to observe closely the upper echelons of the Confederacy, and a willingness to write candidly about people, events, and issues—including slavery. The resulting publication, much revised and more appropriately labeled a memoir, secured her place in southern literary history.

Chesnut was the eldest child of Stephen Decatur Miller and Mary Boykin. Her father, a leader in the states' rights campaign, was elected governor in 1828 and U.S. senator in 1830. Thus, she grew up in a political environment. She received as good an education as could be provided a southern girl of her day, first at home and then at Madame Talvande's French School for Young Ladies in Charleston, where she acquired all of the intellectual and social equipment needed to flourish in her milieu. Her father's death in 1838 ended her carefree childhood, and she soon accepted a marriage proposal from James Chesnut, Jr., whom she had met in Charleston. They were married on April 23, 1840; she was barely seventeen.

Her new home, Mulberry, the baronial Chesnut plantation just south of Camden, was dominated by her parents-in-law, who would live twenty-five more years. Childless, Mary found little satisfaction and suffered bouts of depression and illness in this unfulfilling setting. She regarded her father-in-law, James Chesnut, Sr., as a tyrant and was appalled at the liberties he took with his female slaves. Although the couple moved to their own house in Camden in 1848, it was not until her husband's election to the U.S. Senate in 1858 that she found a society that suited her gifts and her zest for life. In Washington she flourished as a charming literary lady and valuable asset to her husband, attracting the admiration of several prominent men and arousing her husband's jealousy. Among her intimate friends was Varina Davis, wife of the senator and future Confederate president Jefferson Davis. When the secession of South Carolina ended this idyllic life after only two years, Chesnut quickly became an ardent southern patriot.

Chesnut began keeping a diary in February 1861, confessing regret that she had not done so earlier. James's prominent role in the new Confederacy carried her to the centers of action and allowed her to witness and record her impressions of those dramatic times. She was in Montgomery, Alabama, while the provisional Confederate government was being formed, in Charleston for the bombardment of Fort Sumter, and in Richmond when the new government moved to its permanent capitol. All the while she recorded her perceptive observations of people and events, and the frustrations of a spirited woman in a world of men, many of whom she considered too "discrete, cautious, lazy for the roles they were playing." The couple returned to South Carolina in 1862 as James became chairman of the state's executive council. James, urged on by Mary, accepted a post as aide to President Davis in December, and again in Richmond she experienced and wrote about the highs and lows of war. The death of her mother-in-law in 1864 brought them home again to care for his father, now ninety-three and blind.

In early 1865 Union forces ravaged Mulberry, and the Chesnuts took refuge in North Carolina and then in Chester, South Carolina. After the war James inherited his father's property but also large debts. A butter-and-egg business provided the little cash they had for some time, but they grew closer as a couple. Since her father-in-law's will left his property to his son and, on James's death (he died in 1885), to his grandsons, Chesnut found security only in the new Camden home built for her in the early 1870s. There she completed by the mid-1880s the revisions and extensions of her war diary. However, before it was published, Mary Chesnut died of a heart attack on November 22, 1886. She was buried next to her husband in Knight's Hill Cemetery in Camden. Mary Chesnut was posthumously inducted into the South Carolina Academy of Authors in 1987. JAMES O. FARMER, JR.

DeCredico, Mary A. *Mary Boykin Chesnut: A Confederate Woman's Life.* Madison, Wis.: Madison House, 1996.
Muhlenfeld, Elisabeth. *Mary Boykin Chesnut: A Biography.* Baton Rouge: Louisiana State University Press, 1981.
Woodward, C. Vann, ed. *Mary Chesnut's Civil War.* New Haven: Yale University Press, 1981.
Woodward, C. Vann, and Elisabeth Muhlenfeld, eds. *The Private Mary Chesnut: The Unpublished Civil War Diaries.* New York: Oxford University Press, 1984.

Childress, Alice (1920–1994). Actress, theater director, playwright, novelist. Childress was born in Charleston, South Carolina, on October 12, 1920, to Alonzo Herndon and Florence White. Although she was taken to New York City quite early in her life and raised by her grandmother Eliza Campbell, Childress maintained a connection to the lowcountry through a network of Charlestonians living in Harlem. She did not finish high school, opting instead for a life in the theatre, first working professionally as an actress in 1940, when she joined the American Negro Theater. She eventually rose to director, a position she held for nearly twelve years.

Childress acted in plays on and off Broadway and later in films. Her first one-act play, *Florence,* was produced in 1949. *Just a Little Simple,* an adaptation of a Langston Hughes work, followed in 1952. *Gold through the Trees,* the first play by a black woman to be staged professionally in the American theater, was produced in 1952. *Trouble in Mind,* about black actors having to play stereotypical black roles created by whites, won an Obie for best Off-Broadway play in 1956, making her the first woman to win that award. Her work paved the way for later black playwrights such as Lorraine Hansberry.

After her first marriage ended in 1957, she married Nathan Woodward, a future collaborator on many projects. She lectured at colleges and universities in the 1960s. Perhaps her most famous play, *A Wedding Band,* a tale focusing on an interracial love affair in Charleston, circa 1918, premiered at the University of Michigan in 1966. The play was staged by Joseph Papp at the New York Public Shakespeare Theater in 1972 and was televised nationally. *A Wedding Band,* like many of her other works, enthralled some and angered others, prompting periodic banning. Other dramatic works included *The Young Martin Luther King; When the Rattlesnake Sounds; Moms,* about Moms Mabley; *The World on a Hill,* about West Indian life; *Wine in the Wilderness,* about ghetto and middle-class black youths; *Mojo;* and *String,* based on the Guy De Maupassant short story "A Piece of String."

In 1977 Childress published *A Short Walk,* a novel of a woman growing up in Charleston, going into show business, and ending up in New York. Her better-known novels were for young adults and included *A Hero Ain't Nothing But a Sandwich* (1973), a compelling look at a drug-addicted youth with no happy endings inferred; its banning was part of a case taken to the U.S. Supreme Court in 1983. *Rainbow Jordan* (1980), another young adult novel, centered on a daughter perpetually seeking her mother's love. Childress received many national and international awards for individual works and for lifetime achievement.

Considering herself a Charlestonian, she visited the state in 1977 with her husband, with whom she wrote *A Sea Island Song,* a musical and dramatic tribute to the Gullah culture of the Sea Islands. *The Wedding Band* was produced in the state at the time, and "Alice Childress Weeks" were proclaimed in Columbia and Charleston. She brought to all of her audiences, theatergoers and readers alike, intelligence and an unflinching but perceptive look at people and their problems, regardless of race. Childress was inducted into the South Carolina Academy of Authors in 1990; she died in Queens, New York, on August 14, 1994. HARLAN GREENE

Brown-Guillory, Elizabeth. *Their Place on the Stage: Black Women Playwrights in America.* New York: Greenwood, 1988.

Salem, Dorothy, ed. *African American Women: A Biographical Dictionary.* New York: Garland, 1993.

Cleveland, Georgia Alden (1851–1914). Diarist, activist. Georgia Cleveland was born in Laurensville, Georgia, on December 6, 1851, the daughter of Robert M. Cleveland and Fannie Leonard. She spent most of her early years in Bedford County, Tennessee. On November 4, 1871, she married John Bomar Cleveland of Spartanburg, South Carolina. They had seven children. A prominent businessman and industrialist, John Cleveland was related to President Grover Cleveland and served as a delegate to the 1884 Democratic National Convention. Both Georgia and her husband were noted in the Spartanburg community for their generosity, charity, and humanity. They played leading roles in the founding of Converse College in 1889, and their daughters attended school there. They lived within walking distance of both Converse and Wofford, and they were actively involved in each campus's activities, frequently entertaining students in their home.

Georgia Alden Cleveland kept a detailed dairy from 1890 to 1914 in which she chronicled life as an upper-class, married, southern white female. Because of the richness of her entries, she left a legacy of South Carolina upcountry history that is useful on several levels: not only does it document local, state, and regional history but it also serves as a valuable record of Victorian female domesticity and a rare peek into a snippet of southern female life, from the mundane to the grand, over the course of twenty-four years.

Cleveland's diary recorded a myriad of social, political, cultural, educational, and religious activities that filled her active life, including membership in the

Women's Christian Temperance Movement, Daughters of the American Revolution, and United Daughters of the Confederacy. Furthermore, her entries are all-encompassing, acknowledging local, national, and world events as well as the customary domestic activities such as gardening, housekeeping, sewing, and paying social calls, while noting such meticulous details as weather conditions, temperatures, and lists of crops planted. She also wrote of births, deaths, and sicknesses among relatives and friends. She regularly traveled throughout South Carolina and the Southeast, even making a trip to the Chicago World's Fair in 1893, and her descriptions of these destinations provide historically significant details and insights into that period. Nevertheless, her delight in her children, her strong Episcopal faith, and her charity to others are the prominent features throughout her diary that serve to underscore her strong character as an authentic authoress of South Carolina history and southern womanhood.

Cleveland's last diary entry was January 23, 1914. She died in Baltimore on March 1, 1914, following surgery for stomach cancer. She was buried in the Episcopal Church of the Advent Cemetery in Spartanburg. LAURA BARFIELD

Cleveland, Mrs. John B. [Georgia Alden]. "Diary of Mrs. John B. Cleveland." Typescript. South Caroliniana Library, University of South Carolina, Columbia.

"Mrs. Cleveland's Funeral Today." Spartanburg *Herald*, March 3, 1914, 1.

Coker, Elizabeth Boatwright (1909–1993). Novelist. Once referred to by a friend as "South Carolina's First Lady of Letters," Elizabeth Boatwright Coker was born in Darlington, South Carolina, on April 21, 1909, the daughter of Purvis Jenkins Boatwright and Bessie Heard. Her career as a published writer began in 1925 when, as an eleventh-grade student, she won the Poetry Society of South Carolina's Carroll Prize for her poem "Noches." She went on to become editor of the literary magazine at Converse College, where she earned a B.A. in 1929. She later did graduate work at Middlebury College in Vermont. On September 27, 1930, she married James Lide Coker III, who subsequently became president of Sonoco Products Company in Hartsville. The marriage produced two children. Except for summer retreats to Blowing Rock, North Carolina, and periods of schooling and travel, Coker spent the rest of her life in Hartsville.

Between 1950 and 1981 Coker published nine novels in the genre of the historical romance, allowing her to exploit her deep interest in all periods of the southern and South Carolina experience. Her first novel, *Daughter of Strangers* (1950), was a dramatic treatment of racial identity set in New Orleans and the South Carolina lowcountry of the 1830s and 1840s. It remained on the *New York Times* bestseller list for six months and was a selection of the Fiction Book Club. After reading the book, fellow South Carolina writer Chapman Milling claimed that Coker was "a national writer to be reckoned with." Her next novel, *The Day of the Peacock* (1952), was set in a twentieth-century South Carolina mill village and explored the struggle between old wealth and new labor through the lives of those whose existences were tied to "the most modern spinning plant in the new South of today." *India Allan* (1953) shifted in action between South Carolina and Virginia, portraying the lives of South Carolinians caught up in the dramatic events of secession, Civil War, and Reconstruction. Two more novels followed in quick succession, *The Big Drum* (1957) and *La Belle* (1959), the latter a spirited portrait of Marie Boozer, the notorious southern belle who "flirted her way to the top of South Carolina society" before riding away with Sherman's army after the burning of Columbia.

Coker's sixth novel, *Lady Rich* (1963), was distinguished for its Elizabethan English setting. Her 1968 work, *The Bees,* returned to twentieth-century South Carolina for its depiction of a prominent family at odds with itself. *Blood Red Roses* (1977), for which Bantam Books paid at the time a record price for the paperback rights, told the story of Hilton Head Island during the Civil War. *The Grasshopper King* (1981) concerned the doomed Mexican Empire of Maximilian and Carlotta.

In addition to writing novels, Coker reviewed books and published satirical poems in various newspapers, magazines, and anthologies. In 1962 she won the International P.E.N. Short Story Contest of the American Branch of P.E.N. For some four decades she was deeply engaged in other efforts that defined her era's literary and cultural life in South Carolina and the region. She stayed in touch with other writers, encouraged new talent, and appeared as a reader and lecturer in innumerable programs. She taught seminars in colleges and universities and lectured throughout the South. She was inducted into the South Carolina Academy of Authors in 1991, and in 1992 she was selected for membership in the South Carolina Hall of Fame. She died in Hartsville on September 1, 1993, and was buried in Magnolia Cemetery, Hartsville. THOMAS L. JOHNSON

Coker, Elizabeth Boatwright. Papers. South Caroliniana Library, University of South Carolina, Columbia.

Conroy, Pat (b. Donald Patrick Conroy, 1945). Novelist, memoirist. Pat Conroy was born on October 26, 1945, in Atlanta, Georgia, the first of seven children born to Donald Conroy and Frances Peek. Despite numerous moves with his U.S. Marine Corps father, Conroy maintained a southern identity. His father was transferred to Beaufort, South Carolina, in 1961. Conroy enrolled in Beaufort High School, where he starred athletically, academically, and personally. With a difficult home life, Conroy flourished under the encouragement of his English teachers, J. Eugene Norris and R. Millen Ellis, and his principal, William E. Dufford. He enrolled at the Citadel and graduated in 1967. At the Citadel he was captain of the basketball team and selected most valuable player.

After graduation Conroy taught at Beaufort High School, then at the elementary school on Daufuskie Island, a poor, isolated corner of the South Carolina Sea Islands. Fired by school administrators for his unorthodox approach to teaching his nearly illiterate black students, Conroy turned to writing to vent his frustration and earn a living. *The Water Is Wide,* a largely autobiographical novel of his experiences on Daufuskie, was published in 1972 and became a critical and commercial success. Turning to writing full time, Conroy followed with four more novels inspired in large measure by his formative and young-adult years: *The Great Santini* (1976), *Lords of Discipline* (1980), *Prince of Tides* (1986), and *Beach Music* (1995). Each became a national bestseller, and collectively they established Conroy as one of the nation's most popular writers and appealing storytellers. He has also published two works of nonfiction: *The Boo* (1970; a biography of the Citadel's assistant commandant of cadets) and *My Losing Season* (2002; a memoir of his senior year at the Citadel). His first four novels were made into major motion pictures, with the film version of *The Prince of Tides* earning seven Academy Award nominations, including one for Conroy for best screenplay.

After a gap of fourteen years, he published a new novel *South of Broad* in 2009; although the critical reviews were mixed, the book, which is marked by the author's characteristically lush prose, won many readers for its often melodramatic account of a group of friends as they navigate three decades of contemporary history, from the counterculture of the 1960s to the AIDS crisis of the 1980s. The commercial success of *South of Broad* was followed closely by the autobiographical volume entitled *My Reading Life,* culled from the copious notebooks that Conroy has kept for years, detailing his catholic reading habits, including not only the narratives of his fellow southerners but also poetry, philosophy, and history. In 2013 he published *The Death of Santini,* a memoir about his father Donald, the real-life inspiration for the often abusive parent depicted in *The Great Santini.*

At times critics have censured Conroy's novels for their similarity of characters, themes, and setting. Yet these same traits have attracted legions of loyal readers. A consummate storyteller, Conroy relates tales of family conflict, fathers and father figures, racism, and coming of age, all against the consistent backdrop of the South Carolina lowcountry. Humor and pathos are frequent bedfellows. Influenced by Thomas Wolfe, Conroy writes deceptively complex sagas with lyrical descriptions of people and places. Steeped in southern history and mores, his stories connect with readers on a variety of levels.

Conroy's work has been recognized with numerous awards and honors, including the National Endowment for the Arts Award for Achievement in Education (1974), the Georgia Governor's Award for Arts (1978), and the Lillian Smith Award for fiction from the Southern Regional Council (1981). Closer to home, Conroy was elected to the South Carolina Academy of Authors in 1988 and the South Carolina Hall of Fame in 2009, was the first recipient of the Governor's Award in the Humanities for Distinguished Achievement from the South Carolina Humanities Council in 1994, and received the Order of the Palmetto in 2002.

Conroy has been married three times: to Barbara Bolling Jones in 1969, to Lenora Gurevitz in 1981, and to the author Cassandra King in 1995. He has two daughters. Residing on Fripp Island, Conroy continues to pursue his loves—writing, cooking, and living. In 2013 he was named editor-at-large by the University of South Carolina Press and charged with shepherding a new state-based original fiction series. ALEXIA JONES HELSLEY AND J. EUGENE NORRIS

Burns, Landon C. *Pat Conroy: A Critical Companion.* Westport, Conn.: Greenwood, 1996.

Dabbs, James McBride (1896–1970). Writer, educator, theologian, civil rights leader. Born on May 8, 1896, in the Salem community of eastern Sumter County, South Carolina, Dabbs was the son of the farmer Eugene Whitefield Dabbs and Alice Maude McBride. After receiving his private education in the one-room rural Salem School, Dabbs eventually graduated from the University of South Carolina (USC) as one of the top students in the class of 1916. Between 1913 and 1916 he filled pages of the college's literary magazine with his poems, short stories, and prose sketches. In 1917 he earned a master's degree in psychology from Clark University in Worcester, Massachusetts, and then served as a field artillery officer in the U.S. Army (1917–1919). On May 11, 1918, Dabbs married Barnwell native Jessie Clyde Armstrong. The marriage produced two daughters. After teaching in North Carolina from 1919 to 1920, Dabbs returned to USC to teach English. In 1924 he became professor of English at Coker College in Hartsville, where he served as head of the department from 1925 to 1937. He retired in 1942 as a part-time faculty member, commuting from Rip Raps Plantation, his ancestral farm in east Sumter County. Following the death of Jessie Dabbs in 1933, Dabbs married Edith Mitchell on June 11, 1935. They had three children.

Moving to Rip Raps in 1937, Dabbs established a dual pattern of writing and farming that would last the rest of his life. He had begun to establish his reputation as a master of formal and informal essays in the early 1930s, when he began publishing in some of the country's leading journals and rubbing literary shoulders with such writers as Ernest Hemingway, Robert Frost, and Robert Penn Warren. Although he was not one of the twelve contributors to the famous 1930 volume *I'll Take My Stand,* Dabbs did address early on many of the same themes and issues about which the Southern Agrarians wrote: the distinctiveness of the South, the mixed blessings of industrialization, education, the African American presence and identity, and southern religion. However, he "out-Agrarianed" the Agrarians in one respect: he moved back to the farm. The Sumter artist Elizabeth White, his friend, spoke of Dabbs as "a man of letters and of lettuce."

In the 1940s Dabbs began to identify and address the issue of race relations and the inequities experienced by black southerners. At the end of 1946 he wrote a pamphlet entitled *When Justice and Expediency Meet,* in which he stated un-equivocally that "both justice and expediency indicate that the Negro should be permitted to vote in the Democratic primary in South Carolina." By April 1947 he had assumed the chairmanship of the South Carolina Division of the Southern Regional Council, and in 1948 he was a delegate to the Charlottesville Declaratory Conference on Civil Rights, which met to approve "a declaration calling for an end to racial segregation and discrimination."

During the 1950s and 1960s Dabbs attended innumerable conferences as a speaker or resource person on matters of racial equity, human relations, and social justice. He wrote frequent letters to newspaper editors expressing his view that racial segregation was variously unjust, tragic, nonsensical, hypocritical, impractical, discourteous, silly, and un-American. From 1958 to 1964 he served as president of the Southern Regional Council, the Atlanta-based interracial organization that focused on bringing about positive social and political change in the South. Martin Luther King, Jr., in his 1963 "Letter from Birmingham Jail," included Dabbs among the half dozen "white brothers in the South [who] have grasped the meaning of this social revolution and committed themselves to it."

Dabbs was also one of the South's principal twentieth-century Christian churchmen and theologians, although he never claimed this distinction for himself. He certainly was the chief lay theologian of his denomination, the Presbyterian Church of the United States. For more than thirty years he contributed essays and articles to such journals as *Christendom,* the *Christian Century,* and *Presbyterian Outlook.* He served for years on his denomination's advisory committee on Christian Action and permanent committee on Christian Relations. As a member of these two committees he drafted one of the Presbyterian Church's most eloquent theological pronouncements on social justice, "Justice, Law, and Order," which was officially adopted by the General Assembly of his church in 1969. He summed up a lifetime of views on Christian faith, practice, and churchmanship in *Haunted by God.* Published posthumously in 1972, the book focused primarily on the religious significance of southern culture. Despite the presence of evil in southern life and culture, "evils almost beyond compare," he insisted that "somehow we've never ceased being haunted by God."

In addition to *Haunted by God,* Dabbs wrote an autobiography, *The Road Home* (1960), and three other books. *The Southern Heritage* (1958), a history of race relations in the South, won the 1959 National Brotherhood Media Award. In *Who*

Speaks for the South? (1964), Dabbs analyzed southern character, and the book was hailed as "the most perceptive book about the South and the southern mind and southern history since W. J. Cash's *The Mind of the South* (1941)." In *Civil Rights in Recent Southern Fiction* (1969), Dabbs linked his analysis of regional literature "with the relation of blacks and whites. This is the core problem of Southern life."

Dabbs died at Rip Raps on May 30, 1970, and was buried at Salem Black River Presbyterian "Brick" Church. He was posthumously inducted into the South Carolina Academy of Authors in 1990. THOMAS L. JOHNSON

Johnson, Thomas L. *A Day in May.* Hartsville, S.C.: Coker College, 1996.
———. "James McBride Dabbs: A Life Story." Ph.D. diss., University of South Carolina, 1980.

Dawes, Kwame (b. 1962). Poet, editor, novelist, cultural critic. Kwame Senu Neville Dawes was born in Ghana on July 28, 1962 to Sophia and Neville Dawes. His Ghanaian mother worked as a social worker and a sculptor; and his father, a Jamaican-born teacher, poet, and novelist, was an avowed Marxist who moved to Ghana in the 1940s, playing a part in reforming the recently independent nation. In 1971 the Dawes family moved to Kingston, Jamaica, where Neville Dawes was offered a position as deputy director of the Institute of Jamaica. This is where Kwame Dawes fell in love with reggae music. In 1983 his father died in an unfortunate accident.

Kwame Dawes received his B.A. in English from the University of the West Indies at Mona in 1983 and a Ph.D. in comparative literature from the University of New Brunswick in 1992. From 1992 to 2012 he was professor of English and distinguished poet-in-residence at the University of South Carolina. During his tenure, he received numerous awards including the Hugh T. Stoddard Sr. Award for distinguished service as a faculty member in 1994, an Individual Artist Fellowship from the South Carolina Arts Commission in 1996, a Pushcart Prize for his poem "Inheritance" in 2001, and a Guggenheim Fellowship in 2012. In 2009 Dawes was inducted into the South Carolina Academy of Authors. *Poets and Writers* honored him with the 2011 Barnes & Noble Writers for Writers Award, which recognizes writers who give generously to other writers or the broader literary community. In 2012 he joined the faculty of the University of Nebraska as the Glenna Luschel Professor of English and the editor of *Prairie Schooner*.

Dawes first book, *Progeny of Air,* published in 1994, won the Forward Poetry Prize for a first poetry collection, being praised for its sense of craft and its ability to examine aspects of memory with a fresh sense of language. Dawes's second poetry collection, *Resisting the Anomie,* published in 1995, celebrates his multi-nationality. He quickly followed this up with *Prophets* (1995), *Requiem* (1996), *Jacko Jacobus* (1996), and *Shook Foil* (1997). Each poetry collection examines the effects of colonialism on Dawes's fragmented sense of culture and progressively incorporates more and more South Carolina themes. In *Jacko Jacobus,* for example, Dawes reinvents the biblical story of Jacob and Esau, creating Jacko, a trickster who flees his violent brother in Jamaica and finds himself in South Carolina selling crack.

In 1999 Dawes published both *Natural Mysticism: Towards a New Reggae Aesthetic,* a personal narrative that works to restructure the discussion of Caribbean writing, and also *Talk Yuh Talk,* a series of interviews with various West Indian poets.

Dawes's next collection, *Map-Maker,* won the Poetry Business contest in the United Kingdom in 2001 while *Midlands,* also published in 2001, won the Hollis Summers Poetry Prize. Divided into four sections, *Midlands* is organized by Dawes's various cultural influences: Africa, the Caribbean, England, and the American South.

Commissioned by Talawa, England's leading black theatre company, Dawes wrote *One Love,* a play set in the 1970s about a Rastafarian healer in Kingston who takes in a homeless country girl, causing neighborhood unrest. It premiered at Bristol Old Vic Theatre in April 2001 and was published the same year.

In 2002 Dawes published *Bob Marley: Lyrical Genius,* the authoritative critical and cultural examination of Bob Marley's lyrics.

Dawes's collection of short stories, *A Place to Hide and Other Stories* (2003), portrays, through numerous perspectives, a contemporary Jamaican culture struggling with violence and misogyny. In 2003 he also published his *New and Selected Poems, 1994–2002.*

In collaboration with various visual artists, Dawes published in the following year *Bruised Totem,* a series of ekphrastic poems that respond to an exhibit from the Bareiss Family Collection of African Art. Dawes's collaborative projects continued in 2006 when he composed *Brimming,* a poem sequence responding to the paintings of South Carolina artist Brian Rutenberg. The poems themselves explore local racial themes like the lynching of blacks in South Carolina and the Stono slave rebellion of 1738. Also in 2006, Dawes released *Wisteria: Twilight Poems from the Swamp Country,* a series of dramatic monologues based on interviews he conducted in 1995 with seven elderly African American citizens of Sumter County, South Carolina. It was a finalist for the 2007 Patterson Poetry Prize. In 2006 Dawes also collaborated with writer and composer Kevin Simmonds to adapt these poems into the performance *Wisteria: Twilight Songs from the Swamp Country,* which debuted at Royal Festival Hall that same year.

In 2007 two books of Dawes's poetry were published: *Gomer's Song* and *Impossible Flying.* That same year, Dawes released his nonfiction examination of his childhood, *A Far Cry from Plymouth Rock: A Narrative,* in which he examines his lifelong struggle with cultural identity, utilizing his father's notes and papers as well as his own personal recollections.

Dawes's literary romance, *She's Gone,* won the 2008 Hurston/Wright Legacy Award for Best Fiction Debut. His second novel, *Bivouac* (2010), follows Ferron Morgan, a Jamaican who examines the suspicious death of his father in the mid-1980s.

In 2009 Dawes won an Emmy Award for his work on a television project that documented HIV/AIDS in Jamaica and incorporated poetry, photography, and music. Dawes published his poems from this project in *Hope's Hospice* the same year. After the earthquake that devastated Haiti on January 12, 2010, Dawes visited Haiti numerous times to write about the lives of people struggling to survive following that natural disaster. In 2010 Dawes saw the publication of two poetry books: the lyrical narrative, *Back of Mount Peace,* and *Wheels.* Dawes published new and selected poems in 2013 under the title *Duppy Conqueror.*

Aside from being a prolific writer and avid humanitarian, Dawes has edited numerous anthologies such as *Wheel and Come Again: An Anthology of Reggae Poetry* (1998); *Red: Contemporary Black British Poetry* (2009); *So Much Things to Say: 100 Poets from the First Ten Years of the Calabash International Literary Festival* with co-editor Colin Channer (2010); *Hold Me to an Island: Caribbean Place: An Anthology of Writing* with co-editor Jeremy Poynting (2011); and *Seven Strong: Winners of the South Carolina Poetry Book Prize, 2006–2012* (2012).

In 2003 Dawes was appointed director of the South Carolina Poetry Initiative, an organization that promotes poetry in South Carolina. From 2006 to 2012 he was the director of the South Carolina Poetry Initiative's annual book prize competition and editor of the Initiative's chapbook series, publishing dozens of South Carolina poets. In 2012 Dawes wrote the introduction to his father's posthumous collection, *Fugue and Other Writings.* He directs the Calabash International Literary Festival, a yearly event in Jamaica.

Kwame Dawes's writing combines the personal, the mythical, the spiritual, the political, and the cultural aspects of his diverse background. He is part of the New Generation of Caribbean Writers influenced by authors as diverse as T.S. Eliot, Bob Marley, and Derek Wolcott. ROY SEEGER

Collins, Walter P. "Kwame Dawes: An Interview with Walter P. Collins, III." *Obsidian* 8.2 (Fall/Winter 2007): 38–42.

Ross, Sassy. "The Art of Collaboration: An Interview with Kwame Dawes." *Calabash: A Journal of Caribbean Arts and Letters* 5.1 (Summer-Fall 2008): 115–23.

Dickey, James (1923–1997). Poet, novelist, educator. Considered in the 1960s to be the chief rival to Robert Lowell as the major poet of the generation, James Dickey spent almost thirty years as resident poet and Carolina Professor of English at the University of South Carolina in Columbia.

Dickey was born on February 2, 1923, in Atlanta, Georgia, the son of Eugene Dickey and Maibelle Swift. He graduated from North Fulton High School in 1941.

After an unhappy preparatory year at Darlington Academy in Rome, Georgia, he enrolled for the fall semester of 1942 at Clemson College to play football. He performed well only in one game, but his Clemson experience established a basis for a myth of Dickey as sports star. At the end of the football season, he left Clemson to join the U.S. Army Air Corps. He served in the Pacific as a radar observer.

After the war Dickey moved on to Vanderbilt University. He received a bachelor's degree with high honors in 1949 and an M.A. in 1950. He married Maxine Webster Syerson on November 4, 1948. The marriage produced two sons. Dickey taught at Rice University until he was recalled for the war in Korea. After the war he returned to Rice until 1954, when he received a *Sewanee Review* fellowship to spend a year in Europe writing poetry.

On his return, Dickey accepted an instructorship at the University of Florida but resigned in response to verbal flack received from reading a poem in progress, "My Father's Body." After six years as a copywriter and director in advertising firms in New York and Atlanta, he was awarded a Guggenheim Fellowship in 1961. This permitted a return to Europe, where he, like many other southern writers, wrote about the South from a faraway country. He subsequently abandoned his money-making advertising career to go "barnstorming for poetry." Dickey performed well as poet-in-residence at Reed College (1963–1964), San Fernando Valley State (1965), and the University of Wisconsin (1966), climaxed by his appointment as poetry consultant (1966–1968) at the Library of Congress, where he was successful at setting up readings.

In 1968 Dickey was appointed the first Carolina Professor at the University of South Carolina and settled in Columbia, beginning thirty years of distinguished teaching there. Maxine Dickey died on October 27, 1976. Shortly thereafter, on December 30, 1976, Dickey married a student, Deborah Dodson. The couple had one daughter.

Dickey published widely, including books of poetry, fiction, essays, criticism, and children's literature. In two of the three volumes of literary criticism, *The Suspect in Poetry* (1964) and *Babel to Byzantium: Poets and Poetry Today* (1965), Dickey identified the "suspect" in poetry as a failure to involve the reader.

His readings of the Cambridge anthropologists, his discovery of Theodore Roethke, and a friendship with the poet James Wright led to an interest in "country surrealism," a blending of nature and fantasy. Dickey also mastered an empathetic exchange of identity, as with his dog sleeping on his feet or with a dead soldier whose helmet he donned or with a flight attendant falling to her death. "The String," a poem from his first book, *Into the Stone* (1960), introduced the theme of the survivor, beginning with Dickey's view of himself as a replacement child for a dead brother. A plenitude of like poems appeared in *Drowning with Others* (1962), *Helmets* (1964), and *Buckdancer's Choice* (1965), which won the National Book

Award. A climax to the most productive decade of his life came with his novel *Deliverance* (1970), followed by a powerful film version highlighting the naturalism and primitivism of both novel and poetry. His "energized" protagonist or persona "beholds" nature, regains an original relationship, and experiences deliverance from the bonds of civilized life.

Success encouraged Dickey to take greater risks with two big, overly complex novels: one about flying, *Alnilam* (1987), and one about war and killing, *To the White Sea* (1991). Some critics found in Dickey little more than a pretentious "more life school" yearning, while others such as Harold Bloom credited Dickey with a contribution to the American sublime. One thing is clear: the earlier Dickey was largely successful with long lines that advanced both the narrative and the lyric. After the summer of *Deliverance,* the lines "loosened," a split line experiment largely failed, and the dramatic became rhetorical. Most of the "good" poems were written in a decade from the 1960s into the 1970s, with the exception of a few good lyrics in *Puella* (1982) and some good narrative moments in *The Eagle's Mile* (1990). Randall Jarrell said that for a poet to be major, lightning had to strike a dozen poems. It struck enough for Dickey to deserve consideration as South Carolina's best resident poet since Henry Timrod.

The final word on Dickey was "decline"—decline from his reputation as a major poet in the 1960s, decline from his status as a brilliant performer to unseemly public behavior, and decline in health. A South Carolina Academy of Authors inductee in 1990, Dickey died in Columbia on January 19, 1997, and was buried in the All Saints Waccamaw graveyard on Pawleys Island. *The Complete Poems of James Dickey* was published by USC Press in 2013. RICHARD CALHOUN

Calhoun, Richard J., and Robert W. Hill. *James Dickey.* Boston: Twayne, 1983.
Hart, Henry. *James Dickey: The World as a Lie.* New York: Picador, 2000.
Kirschten, Robert, ed. *"Struggling for Wings": The Art of James Dickey.* Columbia: University of South Carolina Press, 1997.

DuBose, Louise Jones (1901–1994). Poet, journalist, editor, educator. Louise Jones DuBose was born near Columbus, Georgia, to the Reverend Frank Dudley Jones of Clinton, South Carolina, and Catherine Wyman of Aiken, South Carolina. Her father served as pastor of the First Presbyterian Church in Clinton and as a member of the faculty of Presbyterian College. Her father's university teaching— he taught history, psychology, and philosophy—inspired DuBose to pursue her own scholarly interests.

DuBose was interested in writing, research, and southern history early on; over time, she added regional music and photography to the list. DuBose preferred to be called "Ms. DuBose," a new form of address, and prided herself on not being a "quiet woman." She attended Agnes Scott College in Decatur, Georgia, and Chicora

College for Women in Columbia, South Carolina, for a short period. In 1918 she began work with the *State* newspaper in Columbia and attended the University of South Carolina where she received her bachelor's degree in 1920.

After graduation, DuBose moved to Columbus, Georgia, where she lived with her aunt Clara Gunby. She worked for the Columbus, Georgia *Inquirer* under her often-used penname Nancy Telfair, writing on everything from national news events to society happenings. She occasionally worked as a sports reporter as well, becoming the first woman in Georgia to report on a professional prize fight.

It was in Columbus that she began writing historical and biographical studies. Her first large-scale work, *Women in Columbus 1828–1928*, remains unpublished, housed in the Simon Schwob Memorial Library at Columbus State University. On the strength of that early effort, however, the Columbus Office Supply Company hired her, as Nancy Telfair, to write the centennial history of Columbus. For this book *A History of Columbus, Georgia, 1828–1928*, she produced a series of biographical "sketches" of over 100 citizens and historical figures.

DuBose returned to South Carolina in 1931, receiving her M.A. in psychology from the University of South Carolina. After graduation, she taught history at USC, and was nearly fired from her position at one point for her then-controversial interest in African American history and culture. Ever the renaissance woman, she also served briefly on the faculty of the Naval Flight Preparatory School as an instructor of mathematics and navigation.

In 1934 she began work as assistant state director of the South Carolina Writers' Project, under Mabel Montgomery. Part of the larger Federal Writers' Project, a program designed in 1935 as part of the U.S. Works Progress Administration, the South Carolina Writers' Project initially had a single goal in mind: to create a detailed guide to the state and its major cities. DuBose worked heavily on the *South Carolina Guidebook* (Oxford University Press, 1941). In a 1981 interview, she recalled time spent on the road conducting interviews, taking photographs, and checking that all directions provided in the guide were correct within a tenth of a mile. The guidebook itself was a collection of nineteen essays on the culture and history of South Carolina, and DuBose's writing, although unaccredited, is thought to comprise the bulk of the collection. An occasional photographer, DuBose also worked on four "picture books" of South Carolina during her time at the SCWP: *Peedee Panorama, Beneath Some Kinds of Sky, Ninety-Six,* and *Sea Islands to Sand Hills.*

Louise DuBose also dabbled in writing for the theater. Although she produced several one-act plays including *Page Boys* and *If I Could Only Tell You,* her only dramatic work to find a publisher was *The Woman from Off: A One Act Play* (1936). Her play *Silver Bullet* won first prize in a competition sponsored by Columbia's Town Theater.

Dubose's exposure to South Carolina's oral history inspired the non-fiction collection *South Carolina Folktales* (University of South Carolina, 1941), featuring animal tales, superstitious practices, and oral narratives passed down through generations in the state's lowcountry. It is an extensive collection akin to Ambrose E. Gonzales's *The Black Border* (The *State,* 1922) in terms of content and linguistic study.

DuBose became an authority on South Carolina folksongs and ballads, especially African American and religious music. She gave several invited lectures on the topic, occasionally joined by her daughter Rowena "Boo" DuBose, who performed many of the pieces.

DuBose's poetry appeared in numerous periodicals including *Bozart, American Mercury, Poetry,* and the *New York Times,* and was reprinted in several anthologies. *Windstar,* her one and only book of poetry, was published in 1943 by Bostick and Thornley. She called the collection of sixty poems her "chiselings of infinity upon the granite rock of doom." Her poetry achieved notable recognition nationwide, receiving awards from the Poetry Society of South Carolina and the Swope Prize for Nature Poetry (1950). Her interest in poetry influenced the formation of the Columbia Chapter of the South Carolina Poetry Society, and she became the director of the group in 1951.

In 1944 DuBose expanded her teaching at the University of South Carolina to include sociology and English. That same year she became associate editor of *South Carolina Magazine.* In October and November of 1945, DuBose took part in a "Goodwill Tour" promoting South Carolina and *South Carolina Magazine,* travelling 5,000 miles from Bangor, Maine, to Key West, Florida, in three weeks and meeting with cultural figures along the way. Her travelogue was published in the magazine.

Around the same time, DuBose began work with the University of South Carolina Press (established 1944), playing an important role in the company's first releases; and in 1950 she became the third chief editor, a position she held for sixteen years.

From 1946 to 1949 DuBose produced over 250 radio scripts for a regular South Carolina series called *Palmetto Landmarks.* The topics ranged from cultural and historical events to local legends and places of regional interest.

In 1962 DuBose published her biography of fellow South Carolinian, artist Blondelle Octavia Edwards Malone. This volume entitled *Enigma: The Career of Blondelle Malone in Art and Society, 1879–1951, As Told in Her Letters and Diaries* (University of South Carolina Press) outlined the sometimes scandalous life of this singular artist and world traveler.

The next year DuBose served as supervising editor of *South Carolina Lives: The Palmetto Who's Who, A Reference Edition Recording the Biographies of Contemporary*

Leaders in South Carolina, with Special Emphasis on Their Achievements in Making it One of America's Greatest States (Historical Record Association). This directory was designed, as she stated in the foreword, to recognize "the men and women responsible for South Carolina's achievements."

Dubose retired from the University of South Carolina Press and academia in 1966, but she remained busy with various clubs and philanthropic organizations. In 1975 she was invited to give a seminar at Columbus College on the role of women in the history of Columbus, Georgia, over forty years after her original study was written.

DuBose, who died in 1994, was posthumously inducted into the South Carolina Academy of Authors in 2001 in recognition of her many literary accomplishments. AMANDA RACHELLE WARREN

Epps, Edwin C. *Literary South Carolina.* Spartanburg, S.C.: Hub City Writers Project, 2004.
Louise Jones DuBose, interview by Thomas L. Johnson, September 21, 1981, South Caroliniana Library Oral History Collection, South Caroliniana Library, University of South Carolina, Columbia.
Louise Jones DuBose Papers, South Caroliniana Library, University of South Carolina.

Dupree, Nathalie (b. 1939). Chef, author, television personality. The author or co-author of thirteen books, Nathalie Dupree initiated what has been called the "new Southern cooking movement" that swept across the United States. In fact, she has been labeled the "doyenne of Southern cooking."

The daughter of Evelyn Cook and Walter G. Meyer, a career army officer, Dupree was born in New Jersey on December 23, 1939. When she was a young child, her father was transferred to Alexandria, Virginia, where she spent the first through twelfth grade. After her parents divorced, Dupree joined her father in Texas for her freshman year of college. At nineteen, she decided she wanted to cook for a living. Her mother suggested that, before she embarked on such a venture, Dupree would be wise to first find a "lady" who made a living as a cook. Dupree soon realized that she had few, if any, female role models in the cooking world.

Undaunted, Dupree moved to London, England, with her first husband, David Dupree, and attended the Cordon Bleu cooking school, the only American in her advanced certificate class. While attending Cordon Bleu, she met Julia Child, who suggested that Dupree consider a career in teaching, advice that would ultimately set a trajectory for Dupree's future. She was chef at a restaurant in Majorca, Spain, before moving to Social Circle, Georgia, in the early 1970s. Dupree opened Nathalie's, a restaurant featuring fresh regional ingredients, inside the couple's antique store just outside of town. She credits Nathalie's as the "beginning of new Southern cooking."

In 1975 Dupree founded a cooking school at Rich's Department Store in Atlanta that attracted a variety of guests and students, including chef Paul Prudhomme, author Pat Conroy, and food writer Shirley Corriher. In the mid-1980s Dupree was a founding member and served as two-term president of what would become the International Association of Culinary Professionals, an organization that sets accrediting standards for cooking schools in the United States.

In 1986 Dupree was contacted by White Lily Flour about hosting a cooking show that focused primarily on the cuisine of the American South. *New Southern Cooking with Nathalie Dupree* led to two more television series, and Dupree soon became the first woman since Julia Child to host more than one hundred televised cooking broadcasts. Ultimately, Dupree would be responsible for more than three hundred half-hour shows for PBS, the Learning Channel, and the Food Network. Dupree's on-air personality combined technical know-how with a charming grace that often resulted in comfortably controlled kitchen chaos.

Dupree is the sole author of ten books and co-author of three more—one with Marion Sullivan and two with her friend and producer, Cynthia Graubart. Not surprisingly, the books consider southern culture, food, and entertaining. Similar to her television shows, Dupree's published works display an unmistakable southern voice, a style that lilts effortlessly from simple breakfast fare through ladies' luncheons and afternoon pick-ups to traditional favorites and formal dinner parties. Dupree's writing seems so at ease, in fact, that one might overlook each work's meticulous research and organization. Two of her books, *Nathalie Dupree's Southern Memories: Recipes and Reminiscences* (1993) and *Nathalie Dupree's Comfortable Entertaining: At Home with Ease and Grace* (1998), earned James Beard Awards, among the highest honors in the field. In 2004 the Southern Foodways Alliance awarded her the Jack Daniels Lifetime Achievement Award.

In the fall of 2012, Dupree and Graubart released *Mastering the Art of Southern Cooking*, whose title is a nod to *Mastering the Art of French Cooking* by her longtime friend Julia Child. The book is both an introduction to southern cooking and an exploration of southern foodways. At 720 pages and with over 200 sources, *Mastering the Art of Southern Cooking* has been called "the most exhaustive and well researched volume on Southern cooking ever published" and "a candidate to replace Mrs. H. R. Dull's classic 1928 cookbook *Southern Cooking*."

Dupree's other books include *New Southern Cooking* (1986), *Nathalie Dupree's Matters of Taste* (1990), *Nathalie Dupree Cooks for Family and Friends* (1991), *Nathalie Dupree Cooks Everyday Meals from a Well-Stocked Pantry* (1995), *Nathalie Dupree Cooks Quick Meals for Busy Days* (1996), *Nathalie Dupree Cooks Great Meals for Busy Days* (2001), *Nathalie Dupree's Shrimp & Grits Cookbook* (2006, with Marion Sullivan), and *Southern Biscuits* (2011, with Cynthia Graubart). She writes a monthly column for the Charleston *Post and Courier* and *Charleston Magazine* and has been featured in *Redbook, Good Housekeeping, Bon Appetit,* the *New York Times,* the *Washington Post,* and other publications.

An excellent storyteller, Dupree relies on narrative to communicate the ideas and culture that lie behind the food. At the heart of her work as both television host and author is a desire to teach people by making food accessible. Dupree avoids any pretense of perfection, preferring instead to help people learn by participating in the process, mistakes and all.

In 2010 Dupree ran a write-in campaign for the United States Senate against incumbent Jim DeMint in order to "expose the utter failure of Jim DeMint to act on behalf of the needs of South Carolina," focusing specifically on DeMint's refusal to support federal funding for the port of Charleston.

Dupree married South Carolina author and historian Jack Bass in 1994; the couple lives in Charleston, South Carolina. KARL FORNES

Conroy, Pat. "Foreword." *Mastering the Art of Southern Cooking.* Layton, Utah: Gibbs Smith, 2012.

Dupree, Nathalie. "Q & A with Nathalie Dupree and Cynthia Graubart, Authors of *Mastering the Art of Southern Cooking.*" Charleston *Post and Courier,* November 7, 2012.

Hagedorn, David. "Nathalie Dupree, Keeping It Juicy." *Washington Post,* March 26, 2008.

Durban, Pam Rosa (b. Rosa Palmer Durban, 1947). Novelist, short story writer, educator. Durban was born in Aiken, South Carolina on March 4, 1947, the daughter of Frampton Wyman Durban, a real estate appraiser, and Maria Hertwig. The writer grew up in Aiken, where her family has lived for generations. In the family tradition, she attended a Catholic grade school, St. Mary Help of Christians. She left Aiken to attend the University of North Carolina, Greensboro, where she earned her bachelor's degree in 1969.

In the 1970s she wrote as a freelancer for *Osceola,* a newspaper published by people associated with Clemson University, followed by a stint as a contributing editor for the *Atlanta Gazette* (1974–1975). In Atlanta she taped interviews with women in a textile mill community and published them as *Cabbagetown Families* (1976). Portions of the book were made into a play called *Cabbagetown: Three Women.* She attended the Writers' Workshop at the University of Iowa, from which she received her M.F.A. in 1979. On June 18, 1983, she married Frank H. Hunter, a photographer. Their son, Wylie, was born in July 1987, and she received a Whiting Writer's Award the same year. She was a founding editor of the magazine *Five Points* and served as its fiction editor from 1996 to 2001. Durban has taught creative writing at the University of New York at Geneseo (1979–1980), Murray State (1980–1981), Ohio University at Athens (1981–1986), and Georgia State University

(1986–2001), where she was awarded an NEA Fellowship in 1998. In 2001 she became the Doris Betts Distinguished Professor of Creative Writing at the University of North Carolina at Chapel Hill.

Throughout the early 1980s Durban published short stories in periodicals, and in 1985 she collected seven of them in *All Set about with Fever Trees, and Other Stories*. The well-received tales are mostly set in the South, and the South Carolina roots are evident. In a Faulknerian way, Durban tries new ways of communicating timeless and impressive experiments in storytelling. *The Laughing Place* (1993), her first novel, is a stylistic triumph with its graceful and poetical narrative voice. It is a story about a woman who returns to her hometown in South Carolina to learn about her birthplace, her father's life, and the family secrets. The novel is a major statement on the southern obsession with the past.

On the publication of her second novel, *So Far Back* (2000), Durban said: "I've been influenced by my upbringing in all sorts of ways, and I became especially aware of that when I was writing *So Far Back*. That book deals with what I see as some fundamental South Carolina attitudes, and I realized as I was writing it that I'm very conversant with them all." The novel is about the last descendant of an old Charleston family and her life up to 1989. Through the diary of an ancestor from the 1830s (with an emphasis on 1837), she discovers how her life is entangled in the family history. For that outstanding novel, Durban was awarded the Lillian Smith Award for Fiction.

In *The Tree of Forgetfulness* (2012), her third novel, Durban focuses on the racially motivated killings of the Lowmans, one woman and two men, who were dragged out of jail by a mob and shot in Aiken County, South Carolina, on Oct. 8, 1926. The case was highlighted with thirty front-page stories in the *New York World*. The novel moves between 1926 and 1943 in order to show the secrecy, the lingering complicity, the denial, and the slow erasure of the murders from the communal memory. In her creation of the right characters, Durban manages to flesh out the haunting past in convincing detail, so it becomes an essential part of our mental make-up today: would we, if we were there as one of the seventeen complicit in the mob violence, have actively participated, have felt guilty, and have tried to forget? Durban excels in small town satire, particularly through Minnie Settles, the help, and "the curious grandchild," who could be a portrait of the author herself.

Durban is working on a book of nonfiction, primarily of a biographical nature, of which the sections "The Old King," "Veterans," "Clocks," and "A Southern Story" have already been published. She is also completing her second collection of short stories, tentatively titled *"Soon" and Other Stories*, which includes the award-winning title story and the highly praised stories "Gravity" and "The Jap Room."

JAN NORDBY GRETLUND

Gretlund, Jan Nordby. "Lines Out across the Gap: An Interview with Pam Durban." *American Studies in Scandinavia* 38, no. 2 (2006): 104–9.

———. "Pam Durban: *So Far Back.*" *Still in Print: The Southern Novel Today*. Ed. Jan Nordby Gretlund. Columbia: University of South Carolina Press, 2010: 58–72.

Reid, Cheryl. "Making Fictions: An Interview with Pam Durban." *Carolina Quarterly* 52 (summer 2000): 61–77.

Edelman, Marian Wright (b. 1939). Lawyer, children's rights advocate, and author. Edelman was born on June 6, 1939, in Bennettsville, South Carolina, the daughter of the Baptist minister Arthur Jerome Wright and Maggie Leola Bowen. She graduated from Marlboro Training High School in 1956; from Spelman College in Atlanta, Georgia, in 1960; and from Yale Law School in 1963.

Edelman became active in civil rights as a student at Spelman College. Following the historic sit-in of four black students at a Woolworth's lunch counter in Greensboro, North Carolina, Edelman and seventy-seven other students were arrested on March 15, 1960, for conducting a sit-in at Atlanta restaurants that served only whites. After graduating from law school, Edelman spent a year—financed by an Earl Warren Fellowship—at the National Association for the Advancement of Colored People Legal Defense and Educational Fund (LDF), where she learned to litigate a variety of civil rights-related cases. From 1964 to 1968 she served as director of the LDF office in Jackson, Mississippi, where she became the first black woman to pass the state's bar exam. During her time in Mississippi, Edelman expanded her horizons beyond civil rights to include the issue of children's rights. In 1965 she helped develop the Child Development Group of Mississippi, which ran Head Start programs for the state's poor children after the state refused to accept federal funds. For three years she prodded federal officials who were being pressured to discontinue the funding by Mississippi's powerful and racist U.S. senators James Eastland and John Stennis.

After four years of protracted struggle, Edelman decided to leave Mississippi. The abject poverty and feudal conditions she had observed in the state affected her profoundly. In 1968 she took a position in Washington, D.C., as the legal counsel for Martin Luther King Junior's planned "Poor People's Campaign." On July 14, 1968, she married Peter Edelman, a legislative aide to U.S. Senator Robert F. Kennedy. They met in 1967 when her future husband accompanied Kennedy to Mississippi and witnessed its poverty firsthand. Their union was the first interracial marriage in Virginia after the U.S. Supreme Court outlawed the state's miscegenation law in *Loving v. Commonwealth of Virginia*. The couple has three sons: Joshua, Jonah, and Ezra.

Edelman founded the Washington Research Project to develop legal strategies to benefit the poor. She continued as the project's director while also directing the

Center for Law and Education at Harvard University, where she had accompanied her husband in 1971. The Washington Research Project ultimately became the Children's Defense Fund (CDF) in 1973. The CDF eventually evolved into one of the nation's strongest and most influential advocates for children in the United States—especially the children of the poor, minorities, and the disabled—and worked to ensure a safe, healthy, and moral start for all children in America.

While she is perhaps best known for her writings on children's issues, Edelman has written on legal issues related to civil rights and has written her autobiography. In her published work, she ranges from policy, to prose, to poetry. The main current of her work is on children and families, with some interesting segues such as a publication on U.S.–Japan relations, co-authored with David Halberstam and Sadako N. Ogata in 1991. Her work has appeared in both scholarly and popular venues both as the sole author and in collaboration with others. Her stature in the field of child advocacy makes hers a sought-after endorsement of other works on children's issues, for which she has written either forewords or introductions.

Works like her autobiography *Lanterns: A Memoir of Mentors* and *The Measure of Our Success: Letter to My Children and Yours* illuminate who Edelman is and how her formative years and time as an activist during one of the most crucial periods of U.S. history are essential to knowing her and to understanding her passion. Her writing career began in the early 1970s. Two of her earliest publications focused on the first twenty years of school desegregation and nonviolent strategies for change. However, since the late 1970s her focus has primarily related to issues regarding children and families. Two of her book-length works, *I'm Your Child, God: Prayers for Our Children* and *Guide My Feet: Prayers and Meditations for Our Children,* are replete with spiritual messages for children and parents and others who love them, from which consolation and inspiration can be drawn. *I Can Make a Difference: A Treasury to Inspire Our Children* argues that children can be agents of change and provides multicultural examples.

As founder of the Children's Defense Fund, Edelman recognizes that the success of children is entwined not only with the health of their nuclear family but also with the positive interconnection of people and communities both locally and globally. Edelman's writings in this policy area, *Families in Peril: An Agenda for Social Change,* a series of lectures given at the W. E. B. Du Bois Institute in 1986, and, more recently, *The Sea is So Wide and My Boat is So Small: Charting a Course for the Next Generation,* respectively identify issues that confronted poor, particularly African American, families in the mid-1980s and the continuing threats to American children in the early twenty-first century. Beyond these books, Edelman has exposed the impact of poverty, educational inequality, and gun violence, among other issues, on America's most vulnerable children. Her publication record crosses disciplinary boundaries, covering medical, legal, and public policy as well as education and religion.

Books such as *Families in Peril*, and *Stand for Children!* translate Edelman's powerful spoken prose and poetics into written form. Although conceived as spoken word, the publication of these speeches as books made Edelman's ideas accessible to wider audiences.

Marian Edelman's work places her as a clarion voice for children's rights, particularly the rights of poor children and children of color. The roots of her South Carolina heritage in faith, family, and caring for the "least of these" infuse her writing. In 2012 she was inducted into the South Carolina Academy of Authors. CARMEN V. HARRIS

Edelman, Marian Wright. *Lanterns: A Memoir of Mentors*. Boston: Beacon, 1999.
————. *The Measure of Our Success: A Letter to My Children and Yours*. Boston: Beacon, 1992.

Edgar, Walter B. (b. 1943). Historian, radio and television host, educator. Anyone living in South Carolina, newcomer or long-time resident, will encounter Walter Edgar in some form or another. Some meet him on ETV Radio by listening to the facts crafted into his one-minute history lessons on *South Carolina from A–Z* or the interviews he conducts with southern specialists on *Walter Edgar's Journal*. Still others first encounter Edgar through the written word as they charge through his monumental *South Carolina: A History* or the landmark, one-volume *The South Carolina Encyclopedia*, a veritable treasure trove of Palmetto State history he edited and managed.

Anyone who has seen, heard, or read Walter Edgar recognizes his distinctive style, redolent of seersucker suits and his signature bowties and a southern accent that is hard to place but pleasing to the ear. A close listening will reveal his Gulf Coast dialect; this is because Walter Bellingrath Edgar was born in Mobile on the coast of Alabama. His accent and lifelong interest in gardening both come from his experiences growing up in that region.

Edgar attended a military prep school in Mobile and then moved on to Davidson College in North Carolina. He wanted to pursue a medical degree, but he did not do well in chemistry. To the dismay of his family, Edgar decided to study history, a topic that held great interest for him but seemed an unprofitable career choice. He spent four years at the University of South Carolina, where he earned his M.A. and then Ph.D. (1969) specializing in colonial history. After a few years in the U.S. Army, including a stint in Vietnam, Edgar decided to remain in the Reserves, which he did until his retirement in 1995 at the rank of colonel.

Walter Edgar came back to South Carolina in 1971 to research the papers of Henry Laurens, a delegate to the Commons House of Assembly and later the Continental Congress. Edgar was hopeful that he would go to Dartmouth next and do research on a post-doctoral fellowship, but a job at the University of South Carolina opened up in 1972, and he settled into the tenure track, marriage, and had children. Edgar said he did not imagine that he would spend the rest of his career in the state, but for forty years, he has been a public fixture at the University of South Carolina, teaching, running the Institute for Southern Studies, and sharing his research through numerous media and print outlets.

Edgar conducted his research using the traditional, pre-internet methods of the historian: he selected and analyzed primary source documents written at the time and saved in archives, and he took notes on index cards, recording what he called "nuggets" or fascinating pieces of information. He verified and validated the data he collected and then synthesized the nuggets into magisterial works. In this regard, perhaps because of his outsider status, Edgar was not wed to the magnolia and moonlight interpretations of South Carolina history that preceded him. With great fervor, he uncovered the stories of Native Americans, women, farmhands, blue collar workers, and African Americans that had previously been excluded from recorded history. He said: "I don't like history behind picket fences. History should be a good story, [but] you don't have to make it up."

By the time that he started working on *South Carolina: A History,* he had filing cabinets full of nuggets: facts and stories he had to sort through to compose what was to become an expansive history of the state. In twenty–three chapters with extensive footnotes, Edgar chronicles every detail worth printing about South Carolina from the time when the area was known as "the land of the Chicora" for the Native peoples who inhabited this region to the tumultuous twentieth century with its troubled race relations. Building on the research of his fellow historians, including Charles Joyner and Vernon Burton, and contributing his own heretofore uncovered facts, Edgar challenged the notion of one culture and one people as the norm for Palmetto State history.

His research continues to this day. From the Cherokee Wars of the colonial period and the Redcoats and Partisans of the Revolution, to the Civil War as seen through the eyes of Mary Chesnut and the emergence of twentieth-century pop stars such as Hootie and the Blowfish, Edgar finds nuggets of historical significance and shares them with his fellow South Carolinians in a multitude of formats.
MAGGI M. MOREHOUSE

Edgar, Walter. *Partisans and Redcoats: The Southern Conflict that Turned the Tide of the American Revolution.* New York: William Morrow, 2001.
———. *South Carolina: A History.* Columbia: University of South Carolina Press, 1998.

————. *South Carolina in the Modern Age.* Columbia: University of South Carolina Press, 1992.

————, ed. *The South Carolina Encyclopedia.* Columbia: University of South Carolina Press, 2006.

Elliott, Irene Dillard (1892–1978). Scholar, educator, community leader. Born in Laurens County, South Carolina, on August 7, 1892, Elliott was the youngest of ten children of James Park Dillard and Elizabeth Irene Byrd. She attended Laurens County public schools, Presbyterian College, and George Peabody College in Nashville, Tennessee. In 1912 she received her bachelor's degree from Randolph-Macon Woman's College in Lynchburg, Virginia. Elliott served as principal of the high school in Cross Hill for two years before returning to Randolph-Macon as an instructor of English. After seven years, she assumed the duties of principal of a small grammar school in Columbia. During this time Elliott pursued her M.A. at the University of South Carolina (USC), which she received in 1921. Dissatisfied with her job, she became determined to earn a Ph.D. She began her doctoral studies in English at the University of North Carolina in 1923 and commenced work on a dissertation, which was later published as *A History of Literature in South Carolina* (1950). In 1924 Elliott became the first woman to receive a Ph.D. from the University of North Carolina.

Elliott accepted an invitation to become the first dean of women at the University of South Carolina, an institution that had recently become fully coeducational. Beginning her work in the fall of 1924, she also served as a full professor until 1935, when ill health forced her retirement. During her years as dean, Elliott helped make smooth what might have been a bumpy process of coeducation. Early in her residence in Columbia, she met Charles Bell Elliott, a member of the USC Law School faculty. They were married on July 30, 1931.

Along with her marriage and work at USC, Elliott became involved in many civic, educational, and cultural organizations. Among these were the American Association of University Women, Phi Beta Kappa, and the Daughters of the American Revolution (DAR). The descendant of Revolutionary War heroes, Elliott established the USC chapter of the DAR and served as the South Carolina state organizing secretary.

With veterans flooding American colleges and universities after World War II, Elliott returned to teaching at the University of South Carolina, where she held the rank of associate professor from 1946 to 1964. She was active in organizing Great Books courses and also engaged in genealogical study. Continued interest in Laurens County led to Elliott's co-editorship of *South Carolina's Distinguished Women of Laurens County: "...Most of Whom Were Redheaded"* (1972).

Elliott showed how difficult it was for a woman of limited financial means to attain the education she desired and to navigate the circuitous route essential to achieving her dreams of becoming a scholar. She never forgot her good fortune or those who helped her. As a dean and professor, she attempted to grant similar opportunities to the young women who came under her tutelage. As testimony to her teaching skills, each year the University of South Carolina awards the Irene D. Elliott Award for Outstanding Teaching. Elliott died in Columbia on April 5, 1978, and was buried in the First Presbyterian Churchyard. MARIAN ELIZABETH STROBEL

Tolbert, Marguerite, Irene Dillard Elliott, and Wil Lou Gray, eds. *South Carolina's Distinguished Women of Laurens County: ". . . Most of Whom Were Redheaded."* Columbia: R. L. Bryan, 1972.

Everett, Percival (b. 1956). Novelist, short story writer, poet, editor, educator. Everett was born at Fort Gordon, Georgia, on December 22, 1956, the son of Percival Leonard, a dentist, and his wife, Dorothy Stinson. He was raised in Columbia, South Carolina, where he graduated from A.C. Flora High School before earning a bachelor's degree in philosophy from the University of Miami in 1977 and—after two years of postgraduate study at the University of Oregon—a master's degree in creative writing from Brown University in 1982.

Everett drew on his experiences as a young African American growing up in Columbia in his first novel, *Suder* (1983), which received laudatory reviews across the United States. Though the novel's black protagonist is a professional baseball player in the Pacific Northwest, much of the narrative is given over to memories of his Carolina childhood. The critical success of *Suder* helped gain Everett the position of professor of English and director of the creative writing program at the University of Kentucky (1985–1989). He then taught at the University of Notre Dame before moving to California in 1992, where he served as a faculty member first at the University of California at Riverside and then at the University of Southern California. In addition to his writing and teaching, Everett has long served as an editor of the distinguished literary journal *Callaloo,* which publishes critical studies of and original works by black writers from around the world.

Despite his long absence from South Carolina, he involved himself in state politics when he unexpectedly spoke out against the presence of the Confederate flag atop the State House while participating in both the Elizabeth O'Neill Verner Awards ceremonies and the Spoleto Festival in 1989. The state resurfaced once again—this time in Everett's imaginary landscape—when he and fellow University of Southern California professor James Kincaid wrote a humor-charged epistolary novel based on their fantasy request to ghost write an account of the accomplishments of the African American people for Senator Strom Thurmond. Pursued by the senator's fictional aide, Barton Wilkes, the two authors, using their real names as pseudonyms in the narrative, are charged with crafting their history, ironically enough, by keeping in mind Thurmond's unique perspective on the subject. *A History of the African-American people (proposed) by Strom Thurmond, as told to Percival Everett and James Kincaid* (2004) is a tour-de-force satire on the politics of race.

Though some of his fiction since *Suder* draws at least partly on southern origins and themes, much of Everett's creative work has more generally focused on his adopted home, the American West—he and his wife, the novelist Danzy Senna, and their two sons live on a ranch in southern California. Nevertheless, these works, such as a parody of the Old West entitled *God's Country* (1994) and contemporary westerns like *Watershed* (1996) and *Wounded* (2005), still offer telling commentary on the problematic status of minority groups in this country. As a black southern writer in exile, Everett might be favorably compared with Oklahoma's Ralph Ellison, with whom he also shares an abiding interest in European and African myth as well as a staunch refusal to limit African American fiction to mere "protest writing." While *Suder*, for example, contains satirical indictments of southern racism, *Erasure* (2002)—favorably reviewed across the United States and abroad—ultimately condemns a publishing industry that favors grim portraits of black ghetto life over stories told by African American authors who try to transcend or ignore racial boundaries. The frustrated writer-protagonist of this novel, a man who has intellectually escaped from the confining notions of race but still finds he must peddle stereotypical images of black life in order to sell his books, clearly bears a close resemblance to Everett.

The protean nature of Everett's career—his dabbling in a host of genres in both fiction and poetry—has made his personal canon difficult to categorize, but he has, especially in recent years, earned his fair share of recognition, including the PEN Center USA Award in Fiction in 2006, the Dos Passos Prize in Literature in 2010, and induction into the South Carolina Academy of Authors in 2011. FARRELL O'GORMAN

"An Interview with Percival Everett." *Callaloo* 28 (spring, 2005): 377–381.

Mack, Tom. "Percival Everett." In *Contemporary Southern Writers*. Edited by Roger Matuz. Detroit: St.. James, 1999.

Starr, William W. "Artists Make Statements at Spoleto." Columbia *State*, June 4, 1989, F1.

———. "Author Everett Prizes Privacy." Columbia *State*, May 29, 1994, F1.

Finney, Nikky (b. Lynn Carol Finney, 1957). Poet, editor, educator. Nikky Finney was born in Conway, South Carolina, on August 26, 1957, the daughter of Ernest A. Finney, Jr., an attorney who became the first African American chief justice of the South Carolina Supreme Court, and Frances Davenport. She took the name

"Nikky" during her high school years in Sumter. She attended St. Jude Catholic School until the mid-1960s, when public schools were integrated in the state. With her older brother, she was among the first to integrate Central School in Sumter.

Finney left Sumter in 1975 to attend Talladega College in Alabama, where she found her calling as a writer. As a child she had started keeping a journal, and at the age of fifteen she had become interested in the black arts movement. In college she spent her time writing and studying literature, especially that of the African American tradition. During her junior year at Talladega, she befriended the poet Nikki Giovanni, who would later play a significant role in her growth as a poet. Finney majored in English in 1979 and won the Whiting Writing Award.

Finney enrolled in the graduate school at Atlanta University to study African American literature but left the program, which did not allow creative writing components in a thesis. Instead she joined Pamoja, a writing collective founded by the writer Toni Cade Bambara. From this workshop came Finney's first book of short poems, *On Wings Made of Gauze*, in 1985. In 1986 Finney moved to Oakland, California, where she made a living from a series of jobs, from photographer, to printer, to workshop instructor.

In 1993 she began teaching creative writing at the University of Kentucky. There she cofounded the Affrilachian Poets, a collective of African American writers in the Appalachian region. In 1995 Finney wrote the script for the PBS documentary *For Posterity's Sake: The Story of Morgan and Marvin Smith*, brothers who were photographers in the 1930s. Her second poetry collection, with photographs, *Rice*, was published in Canada in 1995. *Rice* constitutes an important development in American poetry. The poems are set in coastal Carolina, where Carolina Gold Rice once was a large export crop. Dealing with race, lost values, womanhood, and abuse, the poetry is in plain lyrical words and the imagery is powerfully evocative. Finney emphasizes her ancestry and African lineage, celebrates slaves who rebelled, and delights in the Gullah culture of her home state. PEN American awarded *Rice* the Open Book Award of 1999.

In 1997 Finney was promoted to the rank of associate professor at the University of Kentucky and also published a short-story cycle, *Heartwood*, which is about overcoming racial anger, fears, and prejudice in a small community by relying on the soundness of an individual's duramen or "heartwood." She published her third book of poetry, *The World Is Round*, in 2003. The collection won the Benjamin Franklin Award for Poetry (2004). In these poems Finney emphasizes her African lineage and matriarchal ancestry, celebrates the spirit of anybody who rebels, and convincingly incarnates her delight in the Gullah culture of her home state. Several of the poems are frank about police brutality and honest about same gender sexual relations among the "Southern North American Africans." In spite of the justified sound and fury of the uncompromising political poems, and outraged protests against rocks, guns, flags, and white men, Finney's greatest achievement resides in her ability to breathe true life into universal situations and to create poems that emphasize the importance of having the "charm bracelet of a family."

In 2007 Finney wrote "Heirlooms and Introductions: The Poet Is the Trumpet of the World" as an introduction to a four-hundred-page anthology of contemporary black American poetry, *The Ringing Ear: Black Poets Lean South,* which she edited, featuring "the sound of honey" of 102 poets. In this volume, she included her interview with Lucille Clifton, one of Finney's favorite poets. In 2009 Finney joined other African American women writers to reflect on what had made them writers; in *Shaping Memories,* her essay "Ambrosia" states Finney's main themes, background, and the origin of her ideas.

Head Off & Split (2011) is the title of the collection that won Finney the National Book Award for poetry. Several of the poems are political, and it is no surprise that the collection created interest among people who do not read poetry. Twenty-seven pages parade attacks on the second Bush administration with a sarcastic emphasis on its failure to help victims of hurricanes and flooding. The political poems are rarely among the best, as they are drawn down by the crusading "razor-sharp fins." The "succulent heart" of the collection is in the more private poems on the power of love and the celebration of women in their frustrations and joy. The best poem is "Dancing with Strom," which mixes the private with public life. Only someone who has lived it, and still is able to create a distance to the situation, could express it in words.

The title poem is about heading off from home, 'splitting' in that sense. It is a dramatic ritual of the art of leaving with a script for everybody involved. This is personal, even private, poetry; the interesting result is that the poetry often becomes universally true and relevant for the reader. The poet demonstrates what can never be controlled: "the will of the human heart to speak its own mind," as Finney said in her acceptance speech for the National Book Award.

Nikky Finney was inducted into the South Carolina Academy of Authors in 2013. In that same year, she returned to her home state to take up a faculty position at the University of South Carolina in Columbia; in accepting the appointment as John H. Bennett, Jr. Professor of Creative Writing and Southern Literature, Finney commented, "I feel there are projects waiting for me there, books to write on that home soil, and students to nurture and guide." JAN NORDBY GRETLUND

Dawes, Kwame. "Reading *Rice*: A Local Habitation and a Name." *African American Review* 31 (summer 1997): 269–79.

Finney, Nikky. "Ambrosia." *Shaping Memories: Reflections of African American Women Writers.* Ed. Joanne Veal Gabbin. Jackson: University Press of Mississippi, 2009. 142–51.

———. Foreword to *Good and Bad Hair,* by Bill Gaskins. New Brunswick: Rutgers University Press, 1997.

———, ed. *The Ringing Ear: Black Poets Lean South.* Athens: The University of Georgia Press, 2007.

Kraver, Jeraldine. "'Mobile Images': Myth and Resistance in Nikky Finney's *Rice.*" *Southern Literary Journal* 34 (spring 2002): 134–47.

Fox, William Price (b. 1926). Novelist, short fiction writer, journalist. Fox was born in Waukegan, Illinois, on April 9, 1926, and grew up in Columbia, South Carolina. After serving as a flight officer aboard B-29s in World War II, Fox returned to Columbia to attend the University of South Carolina, graduating in 1950 with a degree in history. He then went to New York City, where he worked as a salesman. During his New York years, he attended Caroline Gordon's creative writing classes at the New School, and she encouraged him to shape his short stories for publication.

Fox's first book of short stories, *Southern Fried* (1962), and its continuance, *Southern Fried Plus Six* (1968), are set in Columbia and its environs, where most of Fox's fictional works take place. Columbia, in Fox's writing, is the place of moonshine stills, barbecue, drive-in movies and restaurants, baseball games, razor fights, torrid summers, and populist politics. In Fox's work, Columbia is a diverse southern city populated by eccentrics, hustlers, and natural comedians, with a peppering of bullies and petty criminals. Their stories are told with high good humor and liberal doses of biting satire. Fox's first two books of stories are remarkably popular, having sold more than one million copies.

Fox's novels, *Moonshine Light, Moonshine Bright* (1967), *Ruby Red* (1971), and *Dixiana Moon* (1981), give full range to his talents for character development, depictions of southern humor, and stinging satirical portraits of the flawed among us, notably hypocritical preachers, and unctuous con men and politicians. These novels display Fox's unique talent for writing the sharp, pointed, economical extended joke or tall tale. His late novel, *Wild Blue Yonder* (2002), returns to Fox's experiences as a high school student and airman during World War II.

In addition to writing fiction, Fox is a journalist of national reputation. He has published articles and features in *Sports Illustrated, Saturday Evening Post, Harper's, Holiday,* and *Golf Digest,* among others. His book *Dr. Golf* (1963) is a rare excursion into contemporary epistolary satire. In the late 1960s Fox wrote screenplays in Hollywood and New York. His screenplay credits include *Southern Fried* (1967), *Off We Go* (1968), and *Cold Turkey* (1970), a movie revered as one of the best comedies of the decade. He also wrote several episodes for the TV series *Beverly Hillbillies,* and a television screenplay, "Fast Nerves," based on his first published short story, for *American Playhouse,* WNET-TV, New York City.

Fox's writing, both fiction and nonfiction, is characterized by his pervasive conviction that humor is a saving attitude and that traditional southern storytelling is a high art form. His humor writing is also characterized by his uncommon talent for hearing and repeating the southern vernacular language, which carries heavy weight in all of his writing.

Fox's teaching career started at the University of Iowa, where he taught creative writing at the graduate level for four years (1968–1973). Then he taught at the University of Iowa School of Journalism from 1974 to 1976. In 1976 he joined the faculty of the English department at the University of South Carolina as writer-in-residence, a position he held until his retirement in 2006. Fox was inducted into the South Carolina Academy of Authors in 2010. CHARLES ISRAEL

Bruccoli, Matthew J., et al., eds. *Conversations with Writers*. 2 vols. Detroit: Gale, 1977–78.

Israel, Charles. "Fact and Fiction in William Price Fox." *Kennesaw Review* (Spring 1988).

Johnston, Carol. "William Price Fox." *Dictionary of Literary Biography*. Vol. 2. *America Novelists since World War II*. Edited by Jeffrey Helterman and Richard Layman. Detroit: Gale, 1978.

Piacentino, Ed. "From Tap Root to Branch: The Humor of William Price Fox." *The Enduring Legacy of Old Southwest Humor*. Baton Rouge: Louisiana State University Press, 2006.

Frank, Dorothea Benton (b. 1951). Bestselling novelist, national public speaker, nonprofit fundraiser. Dorothy Frank and her four siblings were born and reared on Sullivan's Island, South Carolina.

Frank attended Bishop England High School in Charleston, South Carolina, and graduated from General William Moultrie High School in 1969. Her interest in retail apparel took her to Atlanta, Georgia, where she graduated from the Fashion Institute of America in 1972. For a short period she lived in Atlanta and was employed in the Atlanta Apparel Mart by College Town Sportswear. She returned to Charleston in 1973 and became a buyer for Kerrison's Department Store. In 1974 she was hired by Byer California and moved to San Francisco, California. A year later, she relocated to New York City and worked on 7th Avenue for Fire Islander Sportswear, Heralcorp Industries, and Michael Lerner. She retired from the apparel industry in 1985.

In 1983 she married Peter Frank (b. 1947) and moved to Montclair, New Jersey, shortly after the birth of their first child, Victoria Hannah Frank (b. 1985). In 1988, their son, William Richard Frank was born.

While her children were young, Frank became a volunteer fundraiser, organizing events for various nonprofit organizations around the Metropolitan New York area. Past board service includes the Montclair Art Museum, the Whole Theatre Company, the Drumthwacket Foundation, the New Jersey State Council on the Arts, and the New Jersey Cultural Trust. More recently, she has served on the board of trustees of the South Carolina Coastal Conservation League and the parents council of the College of Charleston. At the present time, Frank is a trustee of Bloomfield College (Bloomfield, New Jersey), the Montclair Film Festival (New Jersey), and the South Carolina Historical Society.

Her first novel, *Sullivan's Island* (2000), which debuted on the *New York Times* list at number nine and has been reprinted over twenty-five times, now totals well over one million copies printed in ten languages. Her subsequent novels *Plantation* (2002), *Isle of Palms* (2003), *Shem Creek* (2004), *Pawley's Island* (2005), *Full of Grace* (2006), *Bull's Island* (2006), *The Christmas Pearl* and *Land of Mango Sunsets* (2008), *Lowcountry Summer* (2009), *Return to Sullivan's Island* (2010), *Folly Beach* (2011), and *Porch Lights* (2012) were all *New York Times* bestsellers and may also be found in various foreign languages.

A prolific author of women's fiction, Frank is a disciplined writer who works daily at her craft. She spins yarns—full of southern wisdom and wit—about the beauty, magic, and charm of the Carolina lowcountry. The protagonists of her books, resilient women whose priorities are family and home, cope with fragile and often dysfunctional relationships. For female readers of all ages, she writes about identity and their bittersweet journeys to find themselves through a sense of place. The inspiration for her regional settings is the Carolina lowcountry and its natural beauty. Pat Conroy says that Frank's books "are funny . . . and usually damp with seawater." Frank's latest book, *The Last Original Wife* (2013), conforms to this basic pattern of character development and setting. Feeling isolated in an Atlanta-based social set dominated by second wives, Leslie Carter takes a break from her daily routine and travels to her brother's home in the Carolina lowcountry to reexamine her marriage and her life's goals.

Frank is currently working on a book that incorporates the life of Josephine Pinckney, a novelist, poet, and leading light of the Charleston Renaissance. Pinckney cofounded the Poetry Society of South Carolina (PSSC) with DuBose Heyward, who figures prominently as a character in Frank's novel *Folly Beach*.

Dorothy Benton Frank is the recipient of an honorary doctorate of humane letters from the College of Charleston and a doctorate of fine arts from Bloomfield College. An avid cook, Frank enjoys fly fishing, reading fiction and historical biography, and travelling. She is a frequent speaker on the creative process for students of all ages. Frank divides her time between New Jersey and the Carolina lowcountry. VICKI COLLINS

Dixon, Chris. "Writing Her Way Home." *New York Times,* September 26, 2008.
"Dorothea Benton Frank." *Baker & Taylor Author Biographies* (2000): 1.

Freeman, Grace Beacham (1916–2002). Poet, columnist. Born in Spartanburg, South Carolina on February 18, 1916, Freeman was the daughter of Henry Beacham and Grace Bailey. She attended elementary and high school in the Spartanburg school system and received her undergraduate degree in English, drama, and Latin from Converse College in 1937. In 1993 she received an honorary doctor of letters degree from St. Andrews Presbyterian College.

Freeman taught in the public schools of South Carolina from 1937 through 1942, a period marked by two major events in her life. In 1939 her first adult poetry was published in the *Saturday Evening Post*. On June 11, 1941, she married John Alderman Freeman of Raleigh, North Carolina, whom she had met while visiting relatives in Mars Hill, North Carolina. The Freemans had four children.

In 1952 the family moved to Rock Hill, where John Freeman had accepted a teaching position in the biology department at Winthrop College. From 1954 to 1964 Grace Freeman wrote a column, "At Our House," which was distributed by King Features Syndicate three times a week to newspapers throughout the United States and Canada. In addition to poetry, she wrote plays and radio and television dramas. Her work appeared in literary publications and in the popular press.

Freeman's first collection of poetry, *Children Are Poetry,* was published as a chapbook in 1951. A second chapbook, *Stars and the Land,* was published in 1983. Freeman's first book-length collection, *No Costumes or Masks,* first published in 1975, was honored as the year's Best Book by a South Carolina Poet. A second book, *Midnight to Dawn,* was published in 1981, followed by *Not Set in Stone* in 1986. Later in her life, Freeman published poetic tributes to her parents: *This Woman Called Mother* (1992), for which she received the Fortner Writers Forum Award, and *Remembering a Gentle Father* (1996).

From 1973 until 1986 Freeman participated in the South Carolina Arts Commission's Poet-in-the-Schools program. She served as a poetry therapy consultant to the Gastonia, North Carolina, Mental Health Center from 1973 until 1975. Governor Richard Riley appointed Freeman poet laureate of South Carolina in 1985. She held the title for only one year, relinquishing the role shortly before retiring to North Carolina in 1987. She remained active and involved in community affairs until the time of her death in Asheville, North Carolina, on October 28, 2002, following a brief illness. JULIA ARRANTS

Bigham, Wendy. "Freeman, Former Poet Laureate of South Carolina, Dies at 86." Rock Hill *Herald,* October 30, 2002, B1, B4.
"Distinguished Alumna Award: Dr. Grace Beacham Freeman." *Converse Bulletin* (spring 2002): 24.

Gibbes, Frances Guignard (1870–1948). Playwright, poet. Gibbes was born in Columbia, South Carolina, on October 12, 1870, the daughter of Wade Hampton Gibbes and Jane A. Mason. Inspired by her "urge to write," in 1895 she became the first woman to enroll in South Carolina College (later the University of South Carolina), two years after the general assembly mandated that women should be allowed to attend the school as special students. She attended classes until 1899 but did not earn a degree.

Gibbes published her first work, *Book of Poems,* in 1902. Her first play, *Jael,* was published in 1922 and won the Town Theatre literary prize that year. *Jael* was followed by *Hilda* (1923), *The Face* (1924), *Up There!* (1932), and *Dawn in Carolina* (1946). Her best-known work was *The Face,* produced in Columbia, New York, Mississippi, and Palm Beach, Florida. Gibbes received numerous awards for her plays. According to a review in the *Times Literary Supplement* (December 13, 1923), she produced works that were "worthy of the Elizabethan tradition of poetic drama."

Gibbes traveled extensively throughout her life. In 1925 she went to France with her husband, Oscar Lovell Keith, professor of romance languages at the University of South Carolina. This excursion, with several university students and Columbia community members, was the first Summer School Abroad program at the University of South Carolina. Gibbes and Keith had one daughter, Frances Gibbes Keith, born in 1913. Gibbes died on October 4, 1948, and was buried in Elmwood Cemetery, Columbia. MARY BASKIN WATERS

Gibbes, Frances Guignard. Papers. South Caroliniana Library, University of South Carolina, Columbia.

Gilbreth, Frank B., Jr. (1911–2001). Novelist, newspaper columnist. Gilbreth was born in Plainfield, New Jersey, on March 17, 1911, the fifth child and eldest son of Frank and Lillian Gilbreth, a pair of nationally known engineers and efficiency experts. After attending St. Johns College for a year, Gilbreth went on to the University of Michigan where he was editor of the university's newspaper, the *Michigan Daily.* He graduated in 1933 with a bachelor of arts degree. He then worked for the *New York Herald Tribune,* the *Charleston News and Courier, Buenos Aires Herald,* and the Associated Press. During World War II, Gilbreth served in the Pacific as a naval officer and aerial photographer. He left the navy as a lieutenant commander and was awarded a Bronze Star and two Air Medals for his service.

Gilbreth is best known as the coauthor of *Cheaper by the Dozen.* Published in 1949, this book was Gilbreth's collaboration with his older sister, Ernestine Gilbreth Carey, about their childhood as two of twelve children in a house managed like a factory. Translated into thirty languages, *Cheaper by the Dozen,* along with its sequel, *Belles on their Toes,* was a bestseller and was made into a successful film. Released in 1950, the motion picture of *Cheaper by the Dozen* starred Clifton Web as the eccentric father and Myrna Loy as his steadfast wife. Subsequently, Gilbreth wrote several additional books, including *Innside Nantucket* (1954), about a family-run boarding house, and *Time Out for Happiness* (1971), a biography of his parents.

In 1947 Gilbreth returned to Charleston and joined the staff of the *News and Courier*. For his popular column, "Doing the Charleston," Gilbreth wrote under the pseudonym Ashley Cooper. The column became one of the longest running in American newspaper history. He also assembled a brief dictionary of "Charleston-ese," which amusingly discussed the port city's famous drawl. Selections from his column were published in *Ashley Cooper's Doing the Charleston* in 1993. Gilbreth also worked as assistant publisher of the paper and as vice president of the Evening Post Publishing Company. The final "Doing the Charleston" ran in 1993, and in 1998 Gilbreth was inducted into the South Carolina Academy of Authors.

Gilbreth was married to Elizabeth Cauthen from September 9, 1934, until her death in 1954, and to Mary Pringle Manigault from June 4, 1955 until the time of his death. He had a daughter from his first marriage and a son and a daughter from his second. Gilbreth died in Charleston on February 18, 2001, and was buried in Magnolia Cemetery. At the time of his death, Mayor Joseph P. Riley, Jr. eulogized Gilbreth as an "extraordinary force in the Charleston community for two genera-tions." R. F. STALVEY

Gilbreth, Frank B., Jr. *Ashley Cooper's Doing the Charleston*. Charleston: Post and Courier, 1993.
Rowe, Charles R. "Author, Columnist Gilbreth Dies." Charleston *Post and Courier*, February 19, 2001, 1A, 15A.

Gilman, Caroline Howard (1794–1888). Novelist, poet, editor, publisher. Born in Boston, Massachusetts, on October 8, 1794, Gilman was the daughter of Samuel Howard, a prosperous shipwright, and Anna Lillie. An orphan by age ten, she was raised in part by an older sister. Her childhood consisted of frequent moves until the family finally settled in Cambridge. There, a few years later, she met Samuel Gilman, a graduate of the Harvard Divinity School. In 1819 they married and moved immediately to Charleston, South Carolina, where he had been offered a position as minister to a Unitarian congregation. Their marriage produced seven children, with two sons and their youngest daughter dying in infancy.

For Gilman, Charleston was her first permanent home and, even though she retained much affection for the North, she soon came to see herself as a southerner. As hostilities between the two regions increased, Gilman felt compelled to try to reconcile these differences in her writing. From an early age, she had been com-posing and publishing verse. From 1832 to 1839, as a wife and mother, she turned her attention to publishing and editing a newspaper for young readers and their families called the *Rose-Bud* or *Southern Rose-Bud* and, finally, the *Southern Rose*. One of the first publications of its kind, it became hugely popular, especially with women.

In this publication Gilman serialized much of her work, including the novels *Recollections of a Housekeeper* (1834) and *Recollections of a Southern Matron* (1836), both chronicles of domesticity that attempted to show the similarities between households of the North and South, while also stressing the importance of home and hearth. Gilman believed in the power of the family and in women as its moral center. She was convinced that a wife's most important duty was to act with deference in relations with her husband in order to secure domestic tranquility. Gilman counseled women to hold their tongues and, if necessary, to maintain self-control "almost to hypocrisy." She hoped that in attracting both northern and southern readers to her work, she could somehow extend the peace and tranquility of the home to the entire fractious nation. It was a simplistic notion that, like her growing popularity as a writer, would not last beyond the war.

In the mid-nineteenth century Gilman was a well-loved and prolific author. Between 1835 and 1860, she edited the *Letters of Eliza Wilkinson During the Invasion of Charleston* (1839); produced another novel, *Love's Progress* (1840); published eleven collections of verse, stories, sketches, and "oracles" (used in popular family parlor games); and wrote a tribute to her husband after his death in 1858.

With the firing on Fort Sumter, Gilman surrendered her allegiance to the North and became a strong southern partisan. In 1862 her home was shelled and she moved to Greenville, where she was active in Confederate volunteer and relief work. On returning to Charleston in 1865, she found most of her possessions and papers either destroyed or stolen.

Gilman spent her last days living with a daughter in Washington, D.C. She published four more books in the 1870s and wrote her last poem at the age of eighty-nine, but she never regained the popularity as a writer that she had enjoyed before the war. She died on September 15, 1888, and was buried beside her husband in the Unitarian cemetery in Charleston. In 1990 she was posthumously inducted into the South Carolina Academy of Authors. ELLEN CHAMBERLAIN

Beasley, Maurine H. "Caroline H. Gilman." In *Dictionary of Literary Biography*. Vol. 73. *American Magazine Journalists, 1741–1850*. Edited by Sam G. Riley. Detroit: Gale, 1988.

Greene, Harlan (b. 1953). Novelist, nonfiction writer, archivist. Born on June 19, 1953 in Charleston, South Carolina, Greene is the son of Holocaust survivors Samuel and Regina Miedzyrzecki Kawer Greene. After their release from a Russian work camp at the end of World War II, Greene's parents moved to Charleston, South Carolina. One of four children, Greene attended St. Andrews High School in Charleston. After graduation, he became a student at Clemson University before transferring to the College of Charleston, where he earned a B.A. in English in 1975.

In 1976 Greene began work as a volunteer in the archives of Charleston's South Carolina Historical Society where he catalogued the papers of DuBose Heyward, a key figure of the Charleston Renaissance and author of *Porgy*. For the next thirteen years, Greene worked in various capacities at the South Carolina Historical Society. Greene left the organization in 1989 and followed his partner, Olin Jolley, to Chapel Hill, North Carolina. During that period, Greene founded and served as the director of the North Carolina Preservation Consortium, an association providing preservation education to libraries and archives. He also taught a preservation course at the University of North Carolina. Greene's partner, Olin Jolley, died in 1996 after a long battle with AIDS.

Returning to Charleston in 1998, Greene served as the manager of special collections at the Charleston County Public Library and later held the position of director of archival and reference services at the Avery Research Center for African American History and Culture in Charleston. Greene is currently the senior manuscript and reference archivist at the College of Charleston's Addlestone Library. He now lives with his partner, Jonathan Ray.

A writer of fiction and nonfiction, Harlan Greene created a body of work that thematically centers on Charleston, homosexuality, and Jewish identity. Dripping in historic details and intricacies, Greene's fiction and nonfiction benefit from the skills and expertise honed in his professional life as an archivist, researcher, and historian.

Greene's first novel, *Why We Never Danced the Charleston* (1984), is a gay fiction cult classic that examines the underbelly of Charleston's gay culture in the 1920s. Greene artfully crafts a southern gothic tale that delves into the depths of Charleston's historic and dark past as seen through the characters Hirsch Hess, Ned Grimke, and an unnamed narrator.

What the Dead Remember (1991) is Greene's coming-of-age story. Set in and around Charleston, the narrative follows an unnamed gay protagonist as he explores his identity, sexuality, and the closeted gay culture of Charleston society. The story ends with the protagonist's diagnosis with AIDS. *What the Dead Remember* was the winner of the 1992 Lambda Literary Award for Gay Men's Fiction.

Departing from the genre of the southern novel, Greene's *The German Officer's Boy* (2005) is a piece of historical fiction based on the events surrounding the controversial figure of Herschel Grynszpan. In 1938, a young Polish Jew shot Ernst vom Rath, a German diplomat. In retaliation for this shooting, the Nazi party launched the Kristallnacht or "Night of Broken Glass"—a destructive and murderous assault on the Jewish community that is considered the beginning of the Holocaust. History paints the vom Rath murder as an act of political aggression. Greene instead follows an alternative theory that vom Rath and Grynszpan were involved in a passionate affair. In a tragic series of events, Grynszpan accidentally shoots and mortally wounds his lover, vom Rath. Greene's tale of passion and tragedy fills a narrative void in the mystery surrounding the events of Ernst vom Rath's death and the legacy of Herschel Grynszpan.

Widely considered an authority on the history of Charleston, and specifically the Charleston Renaissance, Greene has authored several nonfiction works related to this subject matter. *Charleston: City of Memory* (1987) offers up a brief history of Charleston enhanced with photographs by N. Jane Iseley. Greene's 2001 release *Mr. Skylark: John Bennett and the Charleston Renaissance* is a biographical account of John Bennett, a writer, expert on Gullah folklore, and a major figure of the Charleston Renaissance. Extending his writings on that critical period in the city's cultural life, Greene coedited in 2003 *Renaissance in Charleston: Art and Life in the Carolina Lowcountry, 1900–1940*. Working with James Hutchisson, Greene envisioned this collection of essays as a tribute to the artistic flowering of Charleston in the early twentieth century. Also in 2003, Greene co-authored *Slave Badges and the Slave-Hire System in Charleston, South Carolina, 1783–1865* with a Medical University of South Carolina pediatric dentistry professor, Harry S. Hutchins, Jr., and his son Brian E. Hutchins. Their work examined the history of the Charleston slave badge system that permitted slave owners to hire out slaves. In addition to his nonfiction writing, Greene has contributed biographical essays to *Hometowns: Gay Men Write about Where They Belong* (1991) and *A Member of the Family: Gay Men Write about Their Families* (1992). DEBORAH TRITT

"Greene, Harlan." *Literary South Carolina.* Spartanburg, S.C.: Hub City Writers Project, 2004.
"Harlan Greene (1953–)." *Contemporary Gay American Novelists: A Bio-bibliographical Critical Sourcebook.* Westport, Conn.: Greenwood Press, 1993.

Greer, Bernard Eugene (b. 1948). Novelist, poet, educator. Ben Greer was born on December 4, 1948, in Spartanburg, South Carolina, the son of Bernard Eugene Greer, a television newsman, and Margaret Philips. Greer came to the University of South Carolina just as James Dickey and George Garrett were establishing its creative writing program. Greer studied with both of them while working as a prison guard at Columbia's notorious Central Correctional Institution. After graduating with a bachelor of arts degree in 1971, Greer was accepted into the prestigious creative writing program at Hollins College, where he studied poetry and fiction with R. H. W. Dillard and William Jay Smith. After earning his master of arts degree from the Hollins program in1973, Greer left the South and academia and moved to Maine where he worked on a fishing boat. During this first long Maine winter, he began to forge his experiences as a prison guard into his first novel, *Slammer.*

Slammer, published in 1975, was a critical and popular success. It was hailed for its gritty authenticity, and Greer was praised as a writer "with amazing economy of means" and great promise for the future. In his novel, Greer created a prison that contained hopelessness and terror but also courage and compassion.

Greer's second novel, *Halloween* (1978), demonstrated both his versatility and his desire to recreate himself. Avoiding the temptation to capitalize on *Slammer* with another work about political or social issues, Greer merged the southern gothic family novel with a thriller and created a tale of a psychotic killer and disintegrating family. Taking place during a single Halloween night in a southern coastal city, this novel manages to balance the immediate horror of the serial killer with a family that drains the life out of its members. *Halloween* was a commercial success, but some critics missed the gritty reality of *Slammer* and found the new novel stagy and unrealistic. Others saw it as a noble risk, which was not always successful.

In 1979 Greer returned to the University of South Carolina as a faculty member in the English department's creative writing program. Greer's third novel, *Time Loves a Hero* (1986), brought the protagonist, a young southern writer, to a New England island to encounter a wealthy northeastern family. Highly anticipated, this novel represented another radical change of genres.

Loss of Heaven (1988) was Greer's exploration of a traditional southern family facing the political and social changes of the 1960s. With locales ranging from a Trappist monastery to the jungles of Southeast Asia, and characters like Lyndon Johnson, faded French colonial bureaucrats, southern grandmothers, and civil rights marchers, *Loss of Heaven* was compelling, if perhaps overly ambitious.

In the 1990s Greer became involved with journalistic and political writing as well as other nonfiction projects. In *Presumed Guilty: The Tim Wilkes Story* (1995), Greer explored the indictment, trial, and acquittal of a local politician and mused about the meaning of justice. His fascination with politics led him to work for a time with controversial South Carolina political maven Lee Atwater. In the new century, Greer's experiment with forms and genre produced two well-reviewed books of poetry, *A Late Disorder* (2007) and *The Bright House* (2011), along with a play *Little Tin Gods* (2008). In 2006 Greer returned to the setting and subject matter of *Halloween* but adapted it into a detective novel, *Murder in the Holy City*, creating an aristocratic detective from an old Charleston family who pursues a crazed serial killer specializing in killing English professors.

Although Greer's refusal to be typed into one style or genre may have kept him from having the kind of audience that always knows what to expect, it has allowed him to continue to explore and experiment. THORNE COMPTON

Garrett, George. "Ben Greer." In *Dictionary of Literary Biography*. Vol. 6. *American Novelists since World War II, Second Series*. Edited by James E. Kibler. Detroit: Gale, 1980.

Gregorie, Anne King (1887–1960). Historian, editor, educator. Gregorie was born in Savannah, Georgia, on May 20, 1887, the daughter of South Carolina natives Ferdinand Gregorie and Anne Palmer Porcher. Her father was managing plantations in Georgia, but in 1893 returned with his family to Oakland, his father-in-law's plantation near Mount Pleasant. Gregorie lived at Oakland for the next sixteen years, absorbing the area's history, folklore, and myths. She attended the local public school, Victory Point Academy, and obtained a scholarship to Winthrop College, which she entered in 1903 as a sophomore. Gregorie graduated in 1906 with a Bachelor of Arts degree and a lifetime license to teach in the state's public schools. After a year of postgraduate study, she embarked on an eleven-year teaching career that took her to schools in Lynchburg, Chester, and, finally, Christ Church Parish. When her mother died in 1918, Gregorie resigned her teaching position, taking over housekeeping for her father and serving his business, F. Gregorie and Sons, as treasurer. This hiatus lasted until 1923, but the five years rekindled her interest in local history.

In 1925 Gregorie embarked on the process of becoming a professional historian. She entered the University of South Carolina and earned a master's degree a year later. That fall she transferred to the University of Wisconsin as a full-time graduate student but returned to the University of South Carolina in January 1927. She taught freshman history courses, took courses herself, and completed her dissertation, a biography of Thomas Sumter. Gregorie graduated in 1929, the first woman to receive a doctorate from the department of history of the University of South Carolina.

Gregorie spent the next four years teaching at Arkansas College and Alabama College while readying *Thomas Sumter* for publication in 1931. Reviews of *Thomas Sumter* stressed the diligence and research that made the book not just a biography but also a social study of South Carolina's Revolutionary and early-statehood periods. When the Depression ended her teaching career in 1933, Gregorie returned to Mount Pleasant and wrote twenty-one entries for the *Dictionary of American Biography*. Economically independent through judicious investments of savings and monies earned for her writings, Gregorie began working for the Civil Works Administration, repairing and transcribing historical records. In 1936 she became the director of the South Carolina Historical Records Survey, a Works Projects Administration agency that inventoried records in courthouses, capitols, and churches nationwide. By the time that the project was suspended in 1941, Gregorie had compiled forty-six county records inventories and published fourteen. Her final task for the agency involved drafting the first disaster preparedness plan for cultural institutions and records in South Carolina; thereafter, she turned in earnest to historical writing and editing.

Gregorie's major work for the American Historical Association, *Records of the South Carolina Court of Chancery, 1671–1779,* was published in 1950. Four years later *The History of Sumter County* earned an award of merit from the American Association for State and Local History. Gregorie served as editor of the *South Carolina Historical Magazine* from 1948 until 1958. Lastly, Gregorie fulfilled her life's dream by completing a volume on her adopted home, *Christ Church Parish, 1706–1959,* which was published posthumously in 1961. As a historian, Gregorie demonstrated the validity of good local history and the importance of local records. Her heritage and training enabled her to present South Carolina's history with intimacy and insight enriched with anecdotes and tradition. She died on December 4, 1960, and was buried in the Christ Episcopal Churchyard, Mount Pleasant. ROBERTA V. H. COPP

Copp, Roberta V. H. "Of Her Time, Before Her Time: Anne King Gregorie, South Carolina's Singular Historian." *South Carolina Historical Magazine* 91 (October 1990): 231–46.

Surles, Flora Belle. *Anne King Gregorie.* Columbia: R. L. Bryan, 1968.

Grosvenor, Vertamae (b. 1938). Writer, culinary anthropologist. Grosvenor was born to Frank and Clara Smart on April 4, 1938, in Fairfax, Allendale County, South Carolina. When she was ten, her family moved from the South Carolina lowcountry, where Grosvenor spoke Gullah, to Philadelphia. By that time, she had developed an interest in food and cooking. After high school, Grosvenor went to Paris and traveled throughout Europe. She has been married twice and has two daughters.

A woman with varied interests, Grosvenor is best known as a writer and culinary anthropologist. During her travels abroad, she became interested in the African diaspora and how African foods and recipes traveled and changed as a result of it. Her first book, *Vibration Cooking; or, The Travel Notes of a Geechee Girl,* was published in 1970. It is a unique combination of recipes, reminiscences, and stories from family and friends. It shows Grosvenor's strong devotion to these people as well as her growing interest in Afro-Atlantic foodways and culinary history: "A bowl of collard greens does for me what a bowl of chicken soup does for others." This interest has been further developed in *Vertamae Cooks in the Americas' Family Kitchen* (1996) and *Vertamae Cooks Again* (1999), and in her cooking series, *Seasonings,* for public radio and *Americas' Family Kitchen* on the Public Broadcasting Service (PBS).

Grosvenor's other interests have led her in several directions. She has written for such varied publications as *Ebony,* the *New York Times,* the *Village Voice, Essence, Life,* and the *Washington Post.* In 1972 she published a history of black servitude in the United States and England, *Thursdays and Every Other Sunday Off: A Domestic*

Rap. She has also been an editor for *Elan Magazine* and served on the Literary Task Force for the South Carolina Arts Commission. She has lectured throughout the Americas, catered celebrity affairs, and been a guest on many television shows. She has acted on Broadway and in the movies *Daughters of the Dust* and *Beloved.* She is perhaps best known, however, as a regular contributor to National Public Radio (where she has been a commentator on *All Things Considered*) and PBS.

Throughout her career, Grosvenor has continued her loving explorations of lowcountry culture. She was a writer in residence for the Penn Center on St. Helena Island and worked on the National Geographic Explorer documentary, *Gullah.* She won an Emmy for "Growing Up Gullah," a story for the Washington, D.C., program, *Capitol Edition.* She has combined her love of theater and cooking in the folk opera, *Nyam,* which is Gullah for "eat."

She lives now in a small bungalow on a former rice plantation in Jasper County.
KATHY A. CAMPBELL

Grosvenor, Vertamae. *Vibration Cooking; or, The Travel Notes of a Geechee Girl.* Garden City, N.Y.: Doubleday, 1970.

Hayes, Terrance (b. 1971). Poet, educator. In his award-winning 2010 collection, *Lighthead,* Terrance Hayes explains through verse the essence of poetry: "Not what you see, but what you perceive: that's poetry. Not the noise, but its rhythm; an arrangement of derangements; I'll eat you to live: that's poetry." This quote summarizes the power of Hayes's own verse: contradictions of images, voices, and themes explode within the subtle beauty of each poem. At this point in time, Hayes stands at the crux of a new wave of American poetry, one that simultaneously plays with and challenges forms and styles to create a liberated voice that is unique, fun, and deep.

Hayes was born in Columbia, South Carolina, on November 18, 1971. He was both an athlete and creative writer while in high school, earning him a scholarship to Coker College in Hartsville, South Carolina. There he majored in English with a minor in fine arts and garnered recognition as an Academic All American. He graduated in 1994. During his senior year at Coker, he was turned on to poetry by a professor, and he decided to pursue that passion in graduate studies at the University of Pittsburgh in 1997. He is married to fellow poet Yona Harvey, and they have two children.

Critically, Hayes has been received remarkably well for such a young poet. His first collection, *Muscular Music,* was published in 1999 and won the Whiting Writers' Award that same year and the Kate Tufts Discovery Award in 2000. His second collection, *Hip Logic,* was published in 2001 and won the National Poetry Series Award while becoming a runner-up for both the *Los Angeles Times* Book Award and the James Laughlin Award (2001). His third collection, *Wind in a Box,* was published in 2005 and won the Pushcart Prize (2006). Hayes garnered a National

Endowment for the Arts fellowship following *Wind in a Box*. His fourth collection to date, *Lighthead*, was published in 2010 and won the National Book Award that same year. The latter three also display his visual art on the covers. According to the National Book Award website, this recent collection represents where Hayes has arrived in his art: "With one foot firmly grounded in the everyday and the other hovering in the air, his poems braid dream and reality into a poetry that is both dark and buoyant."

In his earlier poetry, Hayes frequently chose subjects—popular culture, music, sports, racism—and explored how each shapes black identity. More recently, however, he has moved beyond those concerns to more universally existential matters. A good example of this latest shift is the poem "Woofer (When I Consider the African American)" from the collection *Wind in a Box*: "When I consider the much discussed dilemma of the African-American, I think not of the diasporic middle passage, unchained, juke, jock, and jiving sons and daughters of what sleek dashikied poets and tether fisted Nationalists commonly called Mother Africa." Here he takes the common flash words and concepts associated with the Harlem Renaissance and the Black Power Movement, flips them around, and dismisses them. He argues that identity is not always constructed against the enormous backdrop of historic injustices and militancy. Instead, the speaker relates more to the subwoofers bumping upstairs of his girlfriend's parents' house, ushering him into a rite of passage both sexual and cultural. This woofer, the instrument of a post-civil rights generation, symbolizes the new African American according to Hayes, as the speaker admits at the poem's closing: "When I consider the African-American I think of a string of people connected one to another."

Similarly, "The Avocado," in the collection *Lighthead*, narrates a luncheon with a civil rights spokesman. While quoting key phrases from this man, the speaker in the poem concentrates on the guacamole on the table in front of him, a potential assuagement for his ever-growing hunger. Indeed, the shift in focus within the poem makes the speaker think about the mundane everyday struggle that African American pathfinders had to endure to make changes. After all, was not Rosa Parks just tired and reluctant to give up her seat? In this poem, the speaker shows that action and protest may emerge from a minor spark that in turn fosters the most profound response.

Another important theme in his work is that black identity can be revised. Hayes achieves this revision through carefully crafted mimicry and pastiche. To signal this theme, he often employs the color blue or a dedication line. For Hayes, the word "blue" represents the revision of traditional expression, a riff of sorts. He experiments in these "blue" poems with the voices, rhythms, and rhymes associated with each artist or person he reacts to: "Blue Baraka" (after Amiri Baraka), "Blue Bowie" (after David Bowie), "Blue Seuss" (after Theodore Giesel or Dr. Seuss),

"Blue Strom" (after Strom Thurmond), and "Blue Terrance" (after himself). These revisions move African American poetry to new heights. *Lighthead*, more than his other work, celebrates the new altitudes Hayes has climbed, riffing once again on subjects of identity, race, and history. He writes poems playing with the tonal characteristics of Gwendolyn Brooks, Tupac Shakur, and Wallace Stevens, creating imagery that both alludes to each of these artists and, in turn, reinvents them.

Stylistically, Hayes offers tremendous variety. Beyond the blue poems and other homages, Hayes writes many prose poems, monologues, and abecedarians. His ability to create and expand form is perhaps his greatest achievement. He remarks on his webpage, "There are recurring explorations of identity and culture in my work and rather than deny my thematic obsessions, I work to change the forms in which I voice them. I aspire to a poetic style that resists style." Like a gifted quick-change artist, Hayes puts on different outfits to entertain and amaze the public. Intellectually, these forms offer new territory for students and scholars to examine and enjoy.

Following a short stint at Xavier University of New Orleans from 1999 to 2001, Hayes resettled in Pittsburgh and became a professor of creative writing at Carnegie Mellon University. Hayes has asserted, "The dimensions of culture remain at the center of my professional and personal goals, permeating not only the themes of my work, but my relationships with audiences, colleagues and students." Any reader of his work certainly appreciates and notices these dimensions. For these reasons and others, he was inducted into the South Carolina Academy of Authors in 2013. MATTHEW L. MILLER

Hayes, Terrance. *Hip Logic.* New York: Penguin, 2002.
——-. *Lighthead.* New York: Penguin, 2010. Print.
——-. *Muscular Music.* Pittsburgh: Carnegie Mellon University Press, 2005.
——-. *Wind in a Box.* New York: Penguin, 2006.

Hayne, Paul Hamilton (1830–1886). Poet, editor, essayist. Hayne was born as the only child of a prominent Charleston, South Carolina family on January 1, 1830, and named for his father, a navy lieutenant who died when Hayne was only one year old. He was brought up by his mother, Emily McElhenney, the daughter of a Presbyterian minister, and his uncle, U.S. Senator Robert Young Hayne. The uncle died in 1839 after having decisively influenced his nephew, who wrote an admiring sketch of Robert Hayne in 1878.

Hayne graduated from the College of Charleston in 1850, studied law under James Louis Petigru, and was admitted to the bar, but found the legal profession disagreeable. Already in 1845 Hayne had published poems in the *Charleston Courier* under the pseudonym "Alphaeus," and in 1848 he contributed to the *Southern*

Literary Messenger. He became the manager of the short-lived *Southern Literary Gazette*, a weekly, and wrote for several journals including *Graham's Magazine*.

On May 20, 1852, Hayne married Mary Middleton Michel, the daughter of a Charleston physician. They had one son. Before the war he published three volumes of poetry, which were representative of the literary taste of the time: *Poems* (1855), with the ambitious poem "The Temptation of Venus"; *Sonnets, and Other Poems* (1857); and *Avolio: A Legend of the Island of Cos* (1860), the title poem of which is an involved narrative effort. His poems were from the start devoted to the universal. The best early work is in the versatile sonnets where the Elizabethan heritage is obvious. In April of the following year, at the urging of William Gilmore Simms and Henry Timrod, Hayne became the editor of *Russell's Magazine*, which he made a successful periodical. It was the last important literary magazine founded in the South before the war.

Long before the war, Hayne supported South Carolina's withdrawal from the Union. In the fall of 1851, for example, he wrote for the unsuccessful secession organ the *Palmetto Flag*. He later wrote poetry in support of the Confederacy, especially in 1862, mostly on the themes of family, native land, and death. Some poems are rousing, such as his "Vicksburg: A Ballad," "Charleston," "Beyond the Potomac," and "My Mother Land." He served as an aide-de-camp to South Carolina Governor Francis Pickens, but his health put a stop to this active involvement after only four months. After the war he was ruined and his Charleston home and library burned, so in 1866 he moved to a small plot of barren pineland and a cabin at Grovetown near Augusta, Georgia. It was here at Copse Hill in his reduced circumstances that he wrote some of his best poetry, such as "South Carolina to the States of the North," protesting the exploitation of the South during Reconstruction.

During the last decades of his life, Hayne published additional volumes of poetry: *Legends and Lyrics* (1872); *The Mountain of the Lovers: with Poems of Nature and Tradition* (1875) with "Aspects of the Pines"; and *Poems: Complete Edition* (1882, republished by BiblioLife, 2009) with the lyrical poems "The Mocking-Bird" and "A Dream of the South Winds." In these poems Hayne became a subtle interpreter of nature in her southern aspects.

Hayne lived by selling his poems or essays, mainly to northern journals, such as *Appleton's Journal* and *Lippincott's Magazine*. He was an eclectic critic who judged by personal taste rather than aesthetic standard. Hayne rejected Walt Whitman's free verse and ideas but recognized the genius of Edgar Allan Poe at an early date. He edited *The Poems of Henry Timrod* (1873) and added "A Memoir"; in youth they were classmates at Christopher Cotes's school in Charleston and had remained friends.

Hayne corresponded with the best writers in the nation and in Europe and was, as one of few in the post-Reconstruction South, respected in academia as a refined poet and cultured man of letters. In this sense Hayne was a vital link between the culture of the antebellum and postbellum South. The year before his death he wrote a reminiscing essay for the *Southern Bivouac* (Louisville) on "Ante-Bellum Charleston," which offers an account of a golden time in the city's intellectual and cultural life. He died at Copse Hill on July 6, 1886, and was buried in Magnolia Cemetery in Augusta, Georgia. Duke University Libraries have a considerable collection of Hayne manuscripts; Librivox recorded "Freshness of Poetic Perception: Paul Hamilton Hayne's Poetry" in 2012. JAN NORDBY GRETLUND

Hayne, Paul Hamilton. *A Man of Letters in the Nineteenth-Century South: Selected Letters of Paul Hamilton Hayne.* Edited by Rayburn S. Moore. Baton Rouge: Louisiana University Press, 1982.

Hubbell, Jay B. *The South in American Literature, 1607–1900.* Durham: Duke University Press, 1954.

Moore, Rayburn S. *Paul Hamilton Hayne.* New York: Twayne, 1972.

Parks, Edd Winfield. *Ante-Bellum Southern Literary Critics.* Athens: University of Georgia Press, 1962.

Heyward, DuBose (1885–1940). Novelist, librettist. Heyward was born in Charleston, South Carolina, on August 31, 1885, the son of Edwin Watkins Heyward and Jane Screven DuBose. Both parents were dispossessed aristocrats from the upstate who had come to Charleston to better their opportunities. Joining the once powerful families in Charleston that had been reduced to genteel poverty by the Civil War, "Ned" Heyward eked out a living in a rice mill then died in a tragic industrial accident when DuBose was not quite three. Thrown on her own resources, Janie, as she was called, took in sewing, ran a boardinghouse on Sullivan's Island, and wrote down Gullah folktales she had heard as a little girl and performed them for local arts groups. This immersion in the Gullah world worked its way into Heyward's imagination as he was growing up, but his hopes for a career in the world of art were forestalled repeatedly by a series of illnesses—the most devastating of which was polio—which left him weakened and directionless.

Without a college education, he took the only honorable route open to him, as a Heyward, and went into the insurance business with a partner. The agency was successful, and once Heyward solidified his financial base, he gave more time to his first love, poetry writing. In 1920, with John Bennett and Hervey Allen, he founded the Poetry Society of South Carolina, an organization that initiated the great southern literary renaissance of the early twentieth century. Having met such literary luminaries as Carl Sandburg and Amy Lowell, Heyward gained entry to the New Hampshire artists' retreat, the MacDowell Colony, where he met his future wife, Dorothy Hartzell Kuhns, a playwright. Shortly after their wedding in New York on September 22, 1923, she convinced him to throw over the insurance business for full-time writing. At her instigation, and calling on the encyclopedic knowledge about Gullah culture possessed by his mentor, John Bennett, Heyward threw caution aside and wrote *Porgy* (1925), a novel about African American life in Charleston. Revolutionary for its time, the book changed literary depictions of blacks in the United States forever, because in it a white southerner presented African Americans in an honest and realistic way, as opposed to the stereotyped portrayals found in minstrelsy and antebellum narratives. Heyward was mildly ostracized from some quarters of Charleston society for the book, but he took his licks with characteristic grace and self-deprecating humor. Regardless, he was by then enthralled with the New York literary world, who lionized him for his courage in writing *Porgy*. The artists of the Harlem Renaissance feted him, and with Dorothy's considerable assistance in stagecraft, brought a nonmusical version of *Porgy* to the theater, in the process creating important dramatic roles for African American actors and raising public awareness of their talents. The play forever ended the vaudevillian character of most African American stage works at the time and catapulted Heyward on a trajectory that was to take him up to the highest literary levels.

If to many Charlestonians the novel *Porgy* presented an unorthodox stand on race relations, then *Mamba's Daughters* (1929) must have seemed the work of a lunatic. In its pages, a white man carries the suitcase of a black girl (albeit in New York), who goes on to perform to a packed house in a hybrid native opera that enfranchises both its black and its white audience. How accurate Heyward's prophecy turned out to be, for six short years later the innovative opera *Porgy and Bess* made its debut. Heyward had a large role in the composition and production of the opera: he authored the lyrics (alone or with Ira Gershwin) to half its songs; he collaborated with George Gershwin on the script and wrote the libretto (the sung dialogue) by himself; and he assisted with rehearsals and all manner of production details. When it opened, however, *Porgy and Bess* was in relative terms a critical and financial failure. Heyward beat a hasty retreat away from New York and back to Charleston. His works since *Mamba* had taken a decided turn toward more overt social criticism of the South, but he also spent his remaining years fostering local playwriting talent as resident dramatist of the Dock Street Theatre, newly restored in 1937. Charleston welcomed him home, but largely as a prodigal son. *Porgy and Bess*, the work that brought him—and his city—unprecedented fame was not performed in Charleston until the South Carolina Tricentennial in June 1970. Heyward died on June 16, 1940, in North Carolina and was buried in St. Philip's Churchyard, Charleston. He was posthumously inducted into the South Carolina Academy of Authors in 1987. JAMES M. HUTCHISSON

Durham, Frank. *DuBose Heyward: The Man Who Wrote "Porgy."* Columbia: University of South Carolina Press, 1954.

Greene, Harlan. "Charleston Childhood: The First Years of DuBose Heyward." *South Carolina Historical Magazine* 83 (April 1982): 154–67.

Hutchisson, James M. *DuBose Heyward: A Charleston Gentleman and the World of Porgy and Bess.* Jackson: University Press of Mississippi, 2000.

Slavick, William. *DuBose Heyward.* Boston: Twayne, 1981.

Hoagland, Jimmie Lee (b. 1939). Journalist. A two-time Pulitzer Prize winner, Jim Hoagland was born on January 22, 1940, in Rock Hill, South Carolina, the son of Lee Roy Hoagland, Jr. and Edith Irene Sullivan. He attended public schools there before entering the University of South Carolina, where he graduated cum laude in 1961 with a degree in journalism. He worked briefly as a sports writer for the *State* and the *Columbia Record* before winning a scholarship to study French at Aix-en-Provence in southern France. After serving two years with the United States Air Force in Europe, Hoagland worked as copy editor on the international edition of the *New York Times* in Paris from 1964 to 1966.

Hoagland joined the *Washington Post* in 1966 as a metro reporter. But it is in international reporting and commentary that Hoagland has made his mark. He was assigned to Nairobi in 1969 as the *Post*'s correspondent in Africa. For nearly two years he covered colonial wars, the revolution in Rhodesia (now Zimbabwe), and apartheid in South Africa. Hoagland's reporting on apartheid was the basis for his first Pulitzer—for international reporting—in 1971 and also for his book *South Africa: Civilizations in Conflict* (1972). Hoagland became the *Post*'s Middle East correspondent in 1972, covering the Arab world, Israel, and Iran. He moved to Paris in 1976 to cover France, Italy, and Spain. In 1978 he became diplomatic correspondent on the *Post*'s national staff in Washington and in 1979, foreign news editor. Hoagland's second Pulitzer Prize—for distinguished commentary—was awarded in 1991. As associate editor / senior foreign correspondent for the *Post*, he continues his twice-weekly commentary on international affairs. In 2002 he was awarded the Cernobbio-Europa Prize by the European press for his commentary on the aftermath of the September 11, 2001, terrorist attacks on New York City.

"My strength as a foreign correspondent," Hoagland once said, "was that I conveyed a sense of place, a sense of adventure." He lives in Washington, D.C., with his wife, Jane Stanton Hitchcock. TOM MCLEAN

Hospital, Janette Turner (b. 1942). Novelist, short story writer, educator. "All of my writing career is about how human beings negotiate dark matter," Hospital maintains. "I am extremely interested in how people negotiate catastrophe, not because I'm morbidly interested in it but because I'm interested in the secret of resilience, that's what I'm always exploring in the stories and the novels." Precariousness pervades her writing, which is filled with "absent fathers, abandoned wives, troubled children, isolated adults, catastrophic, unrecoverable loss and the subsequent struggle for psychological survival."

Much of Hospital's writing is set in Australia though she has lived most of her life outside her native country, residing in Canada, India, and the United States. Born in Melbourne, Queensland, Australia, in 1942 to Adrian C. Turner and Elsie (Morgan) Turner, she moved to Brisbane in 1950 with her family. Raised in Brisbane in a strict religious fundamentalist Pentecostal household, Hospital felt silenced as a child and unable to ask questions about her parents' authority or about the irrationality of biblical stories she was told. Ostracized and bullied at school because of her "otherness," she eventually invested her work with an outsider's perspective. She became a writer by chance: "I became a writer by accident and from a dearth of options. It never occurred to me that a writer was something you could become. Nor did it occur to any teacher at my elementary or high school. I don't think my teachers, any more than I, knew of any living writers. My writing powers were always warmly praised, and then I would be told: You must become an English teacher." She taught high school English in Brisbane's outback from 1963 to 1966 and married Clifford G. Hospital, a professor, on February 5, 1965. Hospital graduated from the University of Queensland, St. Lucia, Australia (B.A., 1965); Queen's University, Kingston, Ontario, Canada (M.A., 1973); and the University of Queensland, Australia (D.Litt, 2003). She worked as a librarian at Harvard University Libraries in Cambridge, Massachusetts from 1967 to 1971, taught English at St Lawrence College and Queens University from 1973 to 1982, and served as writer-in-residence at numerous universities in North America and Australia. She also taught writing to men in maximum- and medium-security penitentiaries in Kingston, Ontario, Canada.

Although her entry into published writing came well into her third decade, she was immediately successful. Her first short story "Waiting" was published in the *Atlantic Monthly* in 1978 when she was 35, and it won the "Atlantic First" award, which led to the subsequent publishing of her first book. Hooked on the excitement of creating a world, Hospital called the compulsion the "God Itch." Her short stories have appeared in *Canadian Forum, Commonweal, North American Review, Queen's Quarterly, Saturday Night,* and *Yale Review.* Her first novel, *The Ivory Swing,* published in 1982 won a $50,000 Canadian prize for debut fiction after she radically pruned perhaps a third of it on her editor's recommendation. In response to that act, she confessed that she felt demolished and outraged because she had "spent months honing [her] cultural vignettes, [her] insights: I revised endlessly to achieve the most finely nuanced portrait of South Indian life." Her subsequent novels are *The Tiger in the Tiger Pit* (1983), *Borderline* (1985), *Charades* (1988) *The Last Magician* (1992), *Oyster* (1996), *Due Preparations for the Plague* (2003), and *Orpheus Lost* (2007). Hospital's treatment of memory and the search for origins have prompted some readers to compare her novels to the work of Marcel Proust. Her four collections of short stories are *Dislocations* (1986), *Isobars* (1990), *North of Nowhere, South of Loss* (2003) and *Forecast: Turbulence* (2011). Her stories are inspired by real events gathered from her habit of reading the *New York Times* every day: "Indeed, I don't think fiction can hold a candle to the *New York Times* when it comes to dark things happening on the world stage, but the artist's job is to try to figure out what it was like in the minds of the people involved." Nevertheless, through her "glimpses [of] the intimate lives of students and their family circumstances," Hospital has let this type of information spur her imagination as well. Besides poetry and literary fiction, she used the pseudonym Alex Juniper to publish *A Very Proper Death* (1990), a work of detective fiction.

In the late 1990s Hospital moved to South Carolina to direct the Master of Fine Arts in Creative Writing program at the University of South Carolina in Columbia. While at USC, Hospital created Caught in the Creative Act, an annual visiting writers' series that brought luminaries such as Joyce Carol Oates and Salman Rushdie to Columbia. After retiring from USC, Hospital sent an email to her former creative writing students from her temporary assignment as an adjunct professor at Columbia University in New York. Perceived as critical of her former charges and the quality of USC's creative writing program in general, the communication caused quite a stir in South Carolina and elsewhere after it was widely circulated and published online.

Hospital won the 2003 Patrick White Award, an annual Australian literary award, for lifetime literary achievement; in 2014 she was inducted into the South Carolina Academy of Authors. REBECCA TOLLEY-STOKES

Brandhorst, Craig. "Caught in the Act: Leaked Email Snares Prominent Professor." *Free-Times*, November 11, 2010.

Greiner, Donald J. "The 'God Itch': An Interview with Janette Turner Hospital." *Critique: Studies in Contemporary Fiction* 48 (Summer 2007): 331–43.

Romei, Stephen. "Janette Turner Hospital's Dark Matter." *The Australian*, October 22, 2011.

Humphreys, Josephine (b. 1945). Novelist. Born in Charleston, South Carolina, on February 2, 1945, Humphreys is the daughter of William Wirt Humphreys, a longtime director of the Charleston Development Board, and Martha Lynch. She attended schools in Charleston and enrolled at Duke University, where the author Reynolds Price served as her mentor. After receiving her bachelor of arts degree in English in 1967, she went on to Yale University, where she earned a master of arts degree the following year. On November 30, 1968, she married the attorney Thomas A. Hutcheson. She studied at the University of Texas at Austin from 1968 to 1970, returning to Charleston to teach at Baptist College (now Charleston Southern University) from 1970 to 1977. She has two sons, Allen and William.

Drawing praise for its finely honed language and strong characters, Humphreys's first novel *Dreams of Sleep* (1984) won the Ernest Hemingway Prize for a first book of fiction. The story concerns Alice Reese and her husband Will (a Charleston gynecologist), who have two daughters. When Alice learns that Will is having an affair with his receptionist, she hires Iris Moon as a babysitter to allow herself time away from home. Iris, a teenager from a troubled home but mature beyond her years, idealizes the Reese family and becomes an unlikely catalyst in saving the marriage.

Humphreys's second novel, *Rich in Love* (1987), also depicts a family in crisis and a precocious teenager, in this case the lively narrator Lucille Odom, who Humphreys acknowledged to be modeled after Iris Moon. Lucille's mother abandons her and her father, her pregnant sister Rae returns home to Charleston unhappily married, and Lucille breaks up with her boyfriend. Out of these troubled relationships comes some resolution in Lucille's increased independence and her realization that she is "rich in love." The 1992 film adaptation of the novel starred Katherine Erbe, Albert Finney, and Jill Clayburgh.

Although Humphreys makes no attempt to capture the exact geography of Charleston, her first two novels bring the city to life, touching on its beauty, traditions, and troubled past as it clashes with the new developments on its fringes. Her third novel, *The Fireman's Fair* (1991), also takes the Charleston environs as its setting. Here Humphreys writes from the point of view of bachelor Rob Wyatt, who at age thirty-five decides to quit his law practice. He then meets Billie Poe, a refugee from a bad marriage and also a breath of fresh air for Rob. Billie, as does Iris in *Dreams of Sleep,* has a maturity that belies her age.

In 1994 Humphreys collaborated with the pseudonymous Ruthie Bolton on *Gal: A True Story,* an account of Ruthie's deeply troubled childhood and near miraculous escape into a stable life in Charleston. In that same year, she was inducted into the South Carolina Academy of Authors.

Nowhere Else on Earth (2000), as does Humphreys's previous work, concerns a family in crisis, but in this case the threat derives from racial violence, and the setting is Scuffletown, North Carolina, at the end of the Civil War. The narrator, Rhoda Strong, is another of the author's memorable and enduring women. For her significant contribution to southern letters, Humphreys won the 2012 Thomas Wolfe Prize at UNC-Chapel Hill. KEN AUTREY

Magee, Rosemary M. "Continuity and Separation: An Interview with Josephine Humphreys." *Southern Review* 27 (Autumn 1991): 792–802.

Hunter-Gault, Charlayne (b. 1942). Journalist, civil rights activist. Charlayne Hunter-Gault was born on February 27, 1942, in Due West, South Carolina, the daughter of Charles and Althea Hunter. Raised in Covington, Georgia, then Atlanta,

Hunter-Gault attended Wayne State University in Detroit, Michigan, before a judge allowed her and a male classmate to desegregate the University of Georgia. In 1963 she became the first African American woman to graduate from the school. It was the first of many firsts for one of the nation's groundbreaking minority journalists. After a fellowship, she joined WRC-TV in Washington, D.C., as a reporter and news anchor. She worked as the "Talk of the Town" reporter for the *New Yorker* magazine from 1963 to 1968. She joined the reporting staff of the *New York Times* in 1968, creating the newspaper's Harlem bureau and convincing the newspaper's editor to use the term "black" instead of "Negro."

She joined public television's *The MacNeil/Lehrer Report* in 1978 as a correspondent, winning many national awards for her reporting on "Apartheid's People," a special series on the struggle for civil rights in South Africa. Later she worked for National Public Radio as the chief African correspondent and joined CNN in 1999 as the news network's Johannesburg bureau chief and correspondent. She resigned from the latter position in 2012 to pursue independent projects, including *To the Mountaintop: My Journey through the Civil Rights Movement*, a memoir geared toward young adults.

Her 1992 book, *In My Place*, is a memoir of her growing up in the South and recounts her experiences at the University of Georgia; in 2011, she donated her papers to the library of the school that had at one time resisted her admission. She married twice, first to Walter Stovall in 1963, then to Ron Gault in 1971. The marriages produced a daughter and a son, respectively. ALAN RICHARD

Hunter-Gault, Charlayne. *In My Place*. New York: Farrar Straus Giroux, 1992.

Hyer, Helen von Kolnitz (1896–1983). Poet, writer. Hyer was born on December 30, 1896, in Charleston, South Carolina, to George von Kolnitz and Sarah Holmes. She attended Simmons College from 1917 to 1918 and married Edward Hyer in 1921. The couple had four daughters. From childhood she had a love of poetry and memorized poems from a book of nineteenth-century English verse, reciting them to visitors at her grandparents' home in Mount Pleasant. At Ashley Hall in Charleston, one of her poems was selected as the school song. Hyer won youth poetry prizes as well. Her first poem appeared in *Romance* when she was seventeen; she then was published several times in *Adventure Magazine*.

Hyer joined the Poetry Society of South Carolina in 1920. Although younger than most group members, she impressed her peers. "What really burnt them up was our first poetry contest," Hyer recalled. "I won it; they didn't think a young girl should win." Her first poetry collection, *Santee Songs*, was published in 1923. That volume was followed by *Wine Dark Sea* (1930), *The Wimp and the Woodle, and Other Stories* (1935), *Danger Never Sleeps* (1970), and *What the Wind Forgets a Woman's Heart Remembers* (1975). During her more than fifty years of writing poetry, Hyer's work also appeared in magazines such as *Poet Lore, Argosy,* and the *Christian Science Monitor.*

In 1974 Hyer became South Carolina's second poet laureate—a fitting honor for a writer whose work reflects a deep love for her state. Frequent topics of Hyer's verse include Confederate heroes, South Carolina history, and southern romance. Tennyson and his theme of Camelot was one of her poetic inspirations; Hyer often recreated that magical myth in the familiar world of Carolina's lowcountry. Her attention to the outdoor sounds of South Carolina earned recognition as well. The lyrics of her poem "Santee Lullaby" were used by composer Jim Clemens in his choral arrangement "The Tidelands of Georgetown." Hyer's words became part of the first movement, "River Lullaby," premiered by Georgetown's Indigo Choral Society in 2003.

Hyer's more serious compositions were balanced with playful poems. In 1968 a limerick of hers won the Poetry Society's prize: "A lady who lived just to borrow, / Moved next to us, much to our sorrow. / We fulfilled all her wishes, / Now she has all our dishes— / To our sorrow, we'll borrow, tomorrow." Another playful poem, "Portrait of Two Ancient Ladies," jests: "Her waist is small, her shoes are tight, / She wears black silk and diamond broaches, / Her parlor's full of Hepplewhite / Her kitchen's full of roaches."

Hyer cared about spreading a love of poetry in South Carolina, particularly among the state's young people. She fulfilled her role of poet laureate well, traveling and giving poetry readings, allowing many to hear the musical rhythms of her verse firsthand. She died in Beaufort on November 14, 1983, and was buried in Charleston's Magnolia Cemetery. AMY L. WHITE

Allen, Paul Edward. "Helen von Kolnitz Hyer: South Carolina Poet Laureate." *South Carolina Review* 9 (November 1976): 115–18.

Starr, William. "At 81, Helen Hyer Hops around the State Talking about Poetry." Columbia *State,* May 7, 1978, E1, E2.

Ioor, William (1780–1850). Playwright, physician, farmer. South Carolina's first dramatist, William Ioor, was born on January 4, 1780, in St. George's parish, near old Dorchester, South Carolina, the descendant of French Huguenots who immigrated to Berkeley County from Holland. By his twentieth birthday, Ioor had received a diploma in medicine at the University of Pennsylvania and by 1801 had returned to Dorchester to practice. He married Ann Matthews, a relative of John Matthews (or Mathewes), the third governor of South Carolina, and with her had nine children. Between 1800 and 1803, during the rise of the Democratic-Republican Party in the state, he served as a representative of St. George in the General Assembly and, inspired by his political involvement, wrote the plays on which his reputation rests: *Independence* and *The Battle of Eutaw Springs.*

Independence; or Which Do You Like Best, the Peer or the Farmer? is the first play written and produced by a native of South Carolina. It premiered at the Charleston Theatre, then on the corner of Broad and New Streets, on March 30, 1805, and was printed the same year by G.M. Bounetheau. Though set in England, adapted from an English novel (*The Independent* by Andrew McDonald), and indebted to the conventions of English pastorals and comedies, the play illustrates distinctly American themes and, in its protagonist Charles Woodville, a distinctly American character: the independent farmer. A farmer himself, Ioor embodied in Woodville the values of Jeffersonian Democrats: a preference for rural over urban pleasures, a commitment to hard work and financial autonomy, honesty, piety, and a refusal to relinquish his land—in this case, to the rich and scurrilous Lord Fanfare.

In Fanfare and his lawyer, Whittington, Ioor presents other recognizable and decidedly negative types: the peer and the lawyer. As a representative of English nobility, Fanfare is greedy, adulterous, and duplicitous. In the play's most memorable and bizarre scene, he is brought before Lucifer and his devils—later revealed as Woodville and others—and made to beg forgiveness for "intriguing with a married woman." Meanwhile, as his agent, Whittington pretends to assist Fanfare in acquiring Woodville's small farm while all the while scheming to purchase Fanfare House. As critic Charles Watson has pointed out, their attempts to buy out Woodville parallel contemporaneous campaigns by wealthy South Carolina landowners to consume small farms and unite old homesteads in the state's lowcountry. This scheme comes to no avail: by the play's end, Fanfare has fled the countryside for London, Whittington has been revealed as the "prince of rogues," and Woodville not only has won the hand of Fanfare's daughter Louisa but also has been reunited with his own father and therewith his financial legacy.

Ioor's second play, *The Battle of Eutaw Springs*, appeared the same year—1807—as his open declaration of allegiance to the Democratic-Republican Party. Written during the politically tumultuous period precipitating the War of 1812, the play was dedicated on its cover to "the Republicans of South Carolina in general" and intended, as Ioor wrote in a letter to the Charleston *City Gazette*, to "exalt the American character, and, possibly, depress that of the British government." It premiered at the Charleston Theatre on January 10, 1807, was printed "for the author" later that year, and was reprised for one performance the next season. A troupe connected to the Charleston Theatre performed the play in Richmond on September 27, 1811, and again at the Southwark Theatre in Philadelphia on June 9, 1813.

The Battle of Eutaw Springs is the first play to dramatize Revolutionary War combat occurring in the southern colonies. The eponymous 1781 battle was in fact the turning point of the war in the Carolinas: at Eutaw Springs, about fifty miles northwest of Charleston, forces led by American General Nathanael Greene (and aided by those of Generals Francis Marion and Thomas Sumter) engaged

British troops and eventually trapped them in an abandoned mansion. Though the American forces suffered more casualties, the skirmish led to British Colonel Alexander Stewart's retreating to and ultimately surrendering Charleston.

In General Greene, Ioor finds both his protagonist and raisonneur. In his opening soliloquy, Greene prays for the freedom "of these Southern States from foreign domination" and with the other generals swears to "complete the glorious work" of not just "Washington, Adams, Hancock [and] Franklin" but of South Carolina heroes "Laurens, Gates, Rutledge [and] the Pinckneys." When later he despairs that his reconnaissance parties are lost, his troops starving, and his foe elusive, he is visited by the spectacular "Genius of Liberty," who descends from the flies "drawn by the American Eagle, the American Flag in her hand" and promises that America will soon become "a great, free, powerful, and, I hope, virtuous nation." Duly galvanized, Greene leads his troops to victory at Eutaw Springs and then to Charleston, where he proclaims to the citizenry that "WE ARE FREE!!!"

The actual battle occupies very little of the play; most of the action follows politically emblematic secondary characters. The most significant is Jonathan Slyboots, now considered the prototype of the Southern gentleman. A devout Whig, Slyboots saves young Emily Bloomfield from the wicked "Tory plunderers" who have destroyed her home and killed her family. He is rewarded in the play's closing moments with the honor of giving Emily away at her marriage to her fiancé, General Greene himself, while the Genius of Liberty presides approvingly from above. Slyboots also harbors a fugitive British sailor, Queerfish, who complains of having been press-ganged into military service. Hearing his story, Slyboots acknowledges that all natives "of the hospitable and charitable state of South Carolina" should treat every such "child of sorrow" as a brother.

Queerfish was played at the premier by popular Charleston comic actor Thomas Sully—very likely a friend of Ioor's. The character provides more than comic relief. Indeed, his account of being forcibly conscripted would have immediately called to mind one of the most heated topics of the day: the British impressment of American seamen. While cowardly and foppish, owing to his Britishness, Queerfish would have endeared himself to audiences by observing, "I don't much admire this fighting against our own dear countrymen"; furthermore, at the end, he announces that he will "go to Gen'ral, get a discharge—become an AMERICAN CITIZEN."

Following the productions of his plays, Ioor moved to Savannah, Georgia, where he practiced medicine for fifteen years before retiring to the Greenville District in the upstate of South Carolina, where he and his family had summered. He died on July 30, 1850, at his residence near Pelzer and is buried alongside his wife in the Springwood Cemetery in Greenville. JON TUTTLE

American Plays Printed 1714–1830: A Bibliographical Record. Ed. Frank Pierce Hill. Stanford: Stanford University Press, 1934.

Ennis, Daniel J. "William Ioor." In *Southern Writers: A New Biographical Dictionary.* Edited by Joseph M. Flora and Amber Vogel. Baton Rouge: Louisiana State University Press, 1996.

Watson, Charles S. *Antebellum Charleston Dramatists.* Tuscaloosa: University of Alabama Press, 1976.

———. *The History of Southern Drama.* Lexington: University Press of Kentucky, 1997.

Jackson, Dot (b. Dorothea Mauldin Jackson, 1932). Investigative reporter, columnist, editor, novelist. Dot Jackson was born in 1932 in Miami, Florida, to William Walter Woodin Mauldin and Doretta Eulalia Thode, who were both born and reared in the Appalachian area of the Keowee River Valley of South Carolina. Jackson's only sibling, Walter Wilds Mauldin, died in a plane crash on his twenty-first birthday during the battle of Iwo Jima. Her mother, a teacher and professional artist, was an offspring of the German Colonization Society that founded Walhalla, South Carolina. Her father worked on a small truck farm in Florida during the Depression and helped build dams for the Tennessee Valley Authority. Jackson felt a personal sense of "place" when the Mauldins moved temporarily to Hot House Township in Cherokee, North Carolina. The family subsequently returned to the Everglades area where her father worked to build a base for naval blimps.

Dot Jackson received a music scholarship from the University of Miami where she also studied dance but dropped out her junior year to marry psychologist Bill (Willy) Jackson, whose parents were from Grand Cayman Island. They had three children—Frederick Walter, Thomas Julian, and Johanna Katharine. Tom died during his senior year in college; both Fred and Katharine live in the mountains of North Carolina. Jackson belonged to a "small but inept ballet group led by an elderly Russian woman"; she also served a lengthy time on the substitute teacher circuit.

From earliest childhood, Dot Jackson was aware that her family revered Ben Robertson, one of their cousins who became a war correspondent and worked with Edward R. Murrow. After his last furlough home, he wrote *Red Hills and Cotton,* a family history of life in the Carolina hills. It became a bestseller when it was published in 1942. Ben died the next year when his plane, bound for London, crashed.

Jackson and her family moved to Charlotte in 1962 and lived there for over twenty years. She worked as a proofreader, copy editor, reporter, and columnist for the *Charlotte Observer.* She also wrote for the *Greenville News* and *Anderson Independent Mail.* Her investigative reporting included murder trials, snake-handling churches, and environmental battles. Jackson's work earned her two Pulitzer Prize nominations and the award for National Conservation Writer of the Year. She also won an Alicia Patterson Fellowship to study the economics of southern Appalachia.

Dot Jackson co-authored, with Frye Gaillard, *The Catawba River* (1983), illustrated by Don Sturkey and published by Gardner Webb College Press. With Michael Hembree, she co-authored *Keowee: The Story of the Keowee River Valley in Upstate*

South Carolina (1995). She provided commentary in two films by Neal Hutcheson: *The Last One,* about Popcorn Sutton and his last moonshine run, and *The Outlaw Lewis Redmond,* featuring the upcountry's most wanted nineteenth-century outlaw. In late 1984, Dot Jackson moved to Pickens County, where her ancestors lived for over 200 years, to work on a project for the *Anderson Independent Mail.* Her stellar career in journalism, which earned her membership in the North Carolina Journalism Hall of Fame, was followed by the publication of *Refuge: A Novel,* published in 2006 by the Novello Festival Press of Charlotte. Jackson noted that after years of working for newspapers, writing fiction took a "different set of muscles." This regional tale with a thick local accent uncovers family secrets about Mary Seneca ("Sen") Steele, a determined and independent woman from Charleston who leaves an abusive husband and flees to the Appalachian Mountains. Sen and her two young children, Pet and Hugh, settle into an abandoned family homestead, discover the hardships of rural mountain life, and learn how to grow crops and care for livestock. She discovers strong ties to her paternal kinfolk, especially her cousin Ben Aaron, with whom she falls in love and bears a child.

In 2010 Dorothea Mauldin Jackson was inducted into the South Carolina Academy of Authors during a ceremony at the University of South Carolina Upstate in Spartanburg. Jackson is the cofounder and on-site manager of the Birchwood Center for Arts and Folklife, her current refuge in the Blue Ridge Mountains of South Carolina. Fundraising for Birchwood, she says, is "an honest cause on behalf of the southern Appalachian culture because we have some near-sacred skills and arts and traditions that need and deserve to live. I want to see it [the center] evolve into a self-sufficient and secure entity, with the old house repaired and safe to use as studios and a discussion parlor ... comfortable accommodations for teachers and students to stay here and work." VICKI COLLINS

"Dot Jackson." *Contemporary Authors Online.* Detroit: Gale, 2007.
Fisher, Ann H. "Refuge." *Library Journal* 131.11 (2006): 57.

Jakes, John (b. 1932). Novelist. Jakes was born on March 31, 1932, in Chicago, Illinois, the son of John Adrian Jakes and Bertha Retz. Jakes is a nationally known, bestselling novelist and historian. He and his wife, Rachel Ann Payne Jakes, live most of the year on Hilton Head Island. As an eighteen-year-old freshman at Northwestern University, Jakes sold his first short story for $25 and has been a commercial writer ever since. On June 15, 1951, he married Rachel Ann Payne. The marriage produced four children.

Jakes received his bachelor of arts degree from DePauw University in 1953 and a master of arts degree in American literature from the Ohio State University in 1954. He worked for several pharmaceutical and advertising companies during the 1950s and 1960s. At the same time he was producing two hundred short stories while writing at night. In 1973 he began composing the *Kent Family Chronicles*, which eventually ran to eight volumes, depicting American history in the age of the Revolution through the eyes of one fictional family. All eight books became national bestsellers. Between 1982 and 1987, Jakes published his Civil War trilogy–*North and South, Love and War*, and *Heaven and Hell*–that featured the fictional South Carolina family of Orrie (Horry) Main. Sixty million copies of these eleven novels are currently in print.

More recent novels have included *California Gold, Homeland*, and *American Dreams*. In 2002 Jakes published *Charleston*, his first full-length historical novel based on the history of his adopted state. The novel chronicles the history of the city and, through it, the history of the state and the old South, from the seventeenth century through the Civil War.

Jakes holds honorary degrees from five universities, including his alma mater, the Ohio State University. He has been a research fellow of the department of history at the University of South Carolina, and in 1996, he became the tenth living inductee of the South Carolina Academy of Authors. Two of his novels, *North and South* (1982) and *Homeland* (1993), were nominated for the Pulitzer Prize. In 2002 he received the prestigious Cooper Medal from the Thomas Cooper Library at the University of South Carolina.

Jakes has been a lifelong devotee of local theater as an actor, director, and scriptwriter of dramas and musicals. He was an early and regular benefactor of the Self Family Arts Center on Hilton Head Island. He is also an expert on the life and works of Charles Dickens. His stage adaptation of *A Christmas Carol* has been produced on Hilton Head and in theaters in Alabama, Ohio, and Florida. Jake completed a fifty-minute touring version of the play in 2005. He wrote a musical adaptation of *Great Expectations*, which has been produced on Hilton Head and in Connecticut. LAWRENCE S. ROWLAND

Joyner, Charles W. (b. 1934). Historian, folklorist, filmmaker, musicologist. Charles Joyner's relationship to South Carolina began in the 1730s when his first ancestors came to the Horry County area. His own experiences growing up in the Grand Strand have informed his writings and scholarly work. As a teenager, Joyner worked summer jobs in Myrtle Beach and took note of the unique musical forms (beach music) and dance styles (the shag) of the area. Recalling a time when he was fourteen, Joyner said: "I stood by the jukebox at the Myrtle Beach Pavilion, patting my foot to the hypnotic beat, observing a provocative ballet of poise and sublimated passion called 'the shag,' with the darkening Atlantic in the background." In his numerous publications, presentations, and films, Joyner has documented this fascination with local culture, southern identity, and regional history. "Miss Petey," a Gullah woman and one of his first tutors of southern culture, taught Joyner to place the South, and particularly the lowcountry, within the histories of three continents: North America, Europe, and Africa. This broadening of the South into a global context has been at the heart of Joyner's research: what he calls "asking large questions in small places."

Joyner attended Myrtle Beach High School and earned his baccalaureate in history and English from Presbyterian College in Clinton, South Carolina. After two years in the U.S. Army, Joyner continued his education at the University of South Carolina, where he earned his Ph.D. in history. Employing the skills of an historian, he wrote his first nonfiction pieces at USC about major figures in America at the beginning of the twentieth century. Rather than stay within the more rigid constraints of historical investigation, Joyner began exploring folk life in his beloved Grand Strand, employing a different set of skills and methods that involved fieldwork. Joyner supplemented his "academic income by performing concert-lectures of folk songs" that he had recorded from the Appalachians to the Carolina lowcountry, from the United States to Ireland and England—these recordings span over two decades, from 1989 to 2011. He continued building these skills and interests through his next Ph.D., at the University of Pennsylvania, where his doctoral specialization was folklore. In all of his scholarly products—publications, fieldwork, films, musical performances, and lectures—Joyner has continued to intertwine the skills of an historian with that of a folklorist.

Before joining the faculty at Coastal Carolina University, Joyner held a post-doctoral fellowship at Harvard University where he studied comparative slave societies, and later he returned as an associate of the Du Bois Center. Twice, he has been a Fulbright lecturer in New Zealand. In addition, he has lectured at numerous venues around the world including Australia, Europe, South America, and the Caribbean. Presbyterian College awarded Joyner an honorary doctor of humane letters, along with its highest alumni award, the "Gold P," which recognized Joyner's outstanding lifetime accomplishments. The South Carolina Humanities Council awarded Joyner the Governor's Lifetime Achievement Award, also recognizing his significant impact on the humanities in the state. He has been honored with the Ambassador of Peace Award given by the Ba'hai Center. In addition, in 2004, he was chosen for the roster of Distinguished Lecturers for the Organization of American Historians, and that same year, he was elected president of the Southern Historical Association. In 2012, he was inducted into the state's literary hall of fame by the Board of Governors of the South Carolina Academy of Authors, an organization that recognizes the state's distinguished writers. His latest accolade comes from CCU where he was awarded the first University Medallion, acknowledging his significant community and scholarly contributions.

Joyner has published numerous books, co-edited many more, frequently contributed chapters, and written articles for such scholarly journals as the *Southern Quarterly, Callaloo,* and the *American Historical Review.* Two of his works, *Folks Songs of South Carolina* (1971) and *Ain't You Got a Right to the Tree of Life? The People of John's Island, South Carolina—their Faces, their Words, and their Songs* (1994), provide documentation of a mostly forgotten folk history. Through photographs, oral histories, field recordings, and contextual essays, these works seek to illuminate an African American history in small places. His book *Remember Me: Slave Life in Coastal Georgia* (1989/2011) recounts in pithy detail and beautiful prose the history, music, and culture of the African Americans of St. Simons and Sapelo islands. In *Shared Traditions: Southern History and Folk Culture* (1999), Joyner investigates the diverse peoples and traditions that bring unity in diversity to southern cultures and South Carolina in particular.

His most important book, *Down by the Riverside: A South Carolina Slave Community,* a seminal study of rice plantations along the Waccamaw River, was the 1985 winner of the National University Press Book Award for "the best book in the humanities published by a university press," as well as the co-winner of the Chicago Folklore prize. Asking large questions in small places, specifically All Saints Parrish on the Waccamaw, Joyner describes slave life as if he had been a first-hand observer. He brilliantly combines the skills of the historian and folklorist as he describes the foodways of the slaves: "On the Waccamaw rice plantations slaves ate the grains, fruits, vegetables, and meats of the New World environment; but to those foodstuffs slave cooks applied an African culinary grammar—methods of cooking and spicing, remembered recipes, ancestral tastes."

Joyner is Distinguished Professor Emeritus of Southern History and Culture at Coastal Carolina University in Conway, South Carolina. He was the first Burroughs Distinguished Chair in Southern History and Culture, as well as the director of the Waccamaw Center for Historical and Cultural Studies, two positions he held until his retirement in 2006. Chaz Joyner is a South Carolina treasure who has uncovered and documented our united realities and presented the historical facts with the skill of a master storyteller. MAGGI M. MOREHOUSE

Joyner, Charles. *Down by the Riverside: A South Carolina Slave Community.* Urbana and Chicago: University of Illinois Press, 1984.

———. "A Region in Harmony: Southern Music and the Soundtrack of Freedom." Presidential Address, Southern Historical Association, Nov. 2005, Atlanta, Georgia, reprinted in *Journal of Southern History* 72 (February 2006): 3–38.

———. *Remember Me: Slave Life in Coastal Georgia.* Athens: University of Georgia Press, 1989.

———. *Shared Traditions: Southern History and Folk Culture.* Urbana and Chicago: University of Illinois Press, 1999.

Kidd, Sue Monk (b. 1948). Novelist, memoirist. Born in Albany, Georgia, on August 12, 1948, Kidd was raised in the tiny Georgia town of Sylvester. She credits the stories told to her by her father and the African American women who worked in her family's home, along with the writings of Henry David Thoreau and Kate Chopin, as being influential on her development as a writer. Kidd graduated from Texas Christian University in 1970 with a degree in nursing and pursued a career as a registered pediatrics nurse during her twenties. Also at this time, Kidd met and married theologian Sanford Kidd, with whom she had two children: Bob and Ann. Although she has kept a journal throughout her life, and took classes in fiction writing while her husband was teaching at Anderson University in Anderson, South Carolina, Sue Monk Kidd's first major publication was a spiritual memoir in *Guideposts* that was reprinted in *Reader's Digest*. Subsequently, Kidd published a number of articles and essays of spiritual memoir and became a contributing editor to *Guideposts*.

Kidd published her first book, *God's Joyful Surprise: Finding Yourself Loved*, in 1988. This spiritual memoir delves into Kidd's personal faith as a Christian and her relationship with God. Another memoir, *When the Heart Waits: Spiritual Direction for Life's Sacred Questions*, was published in 1990. It further explores her Christian faith. Kidd's bestselling third memoir, *Dance of the Dissident Daughter: A Woman's Journey from Christian Tradition to the Sacred Feminine*, published in 1996, marks a departure from the subject matter of Kidd's first two books toward a more feminist perspective—a transition that would come to fruition in *The Secret Life of Bees*.

In the 1990s, Kidd also began to focus on writing short fiction. She was awarded a South Carolina Fellowship in Literature from the South Carolina Arts Commission in 1994 and South Carolina Academy of Authors Fellowships in Fiction in 1994 and 1996. After taking graduate courses in writing at Emory University in Atlanta, Kidd expanded a short story published in 1993 into her first novel, *The Secret Life of Bees*. Published by Viking in 2002, Kidd's overwhelmingly successful transition into book-length fiction was born from her childhood in Sylvester, Georgia; nurtured by her experiences with segregation and the civil rights movement; and brought to fruition through her unique feminist perspective. Set in Tiburon, South Carolina, in 1964, the novel tells the intertwined stories of fourteen-year-old Lily Melissa Owens, who is white and struggling to discover the past of the mother she saw killed; and Rosaleen, Lily's African American caretaker whose determined attempt to vote results in her savage beating at the hands of three white men. Lily and Rosaleen hitchhike to Tiburon, where they are taken in by the Boatwright sisters, under whose beneficent influence and guidance Lily and Rosaleen come to terms with both the present and the past. The novel spent more than two years on the *New York Times* bestseller list and has been published in thirty-five countries. It won the 2003 SEBA Book of the Year Award, the 2004 Book Sense Book of the

Year Award for a paperback, and the 2005 Southeastern Library Association Fiction Award. In 2008 *The Secret Life of Bees* was adapted into a major motion picture by Fox Searchlight starring Dakota Fanning and Queen Latifah and directed by Gina Prince-Blythewood.

Kidd's second novel, *The Mermaid Chair*, was published by Viking in 2005. Set on a South Carolina barrier island, the novel tells the story of Jessie Sullivan, a married woman who falls in love with a Benedictine monk. A *New York Times* bestseller, the book has been translated into twenty-four languages. It won the Quill Award in General Fiction in 2005 and was adapted into a television movie by Lifetime in 2006.

Guidepost Books published *Firstlight*, a collection of Kidd's early writings, in 2006. This collection of spiritual essays, stories, and meditations was for Kidd an opportunity to return to her beginnings as a writer and to reflect on her career. In the introduction, she writes, "A significant portion of my life can be understood as spiritual quest and the articulation of that experience."

The theme of the spiritual quest is central to Kidd's book, *Traveling with Pomegranates: A Mother-Daughter Story*, co-authored with her daughter Ann Kidd Taylor and published by Viking in 2009. This shared memoir, which appeared on the *New York Times* bestseller list, chronicles both women's physical expedition to Greece and France and their spiritual journeys to rediscover themselves and each other. Her third novel, *The Invention of Wings* (2014), re-imagines nineteenth-century Charleston with a special focus on women's rights pioneer Sarah Grimke. Kidd received the Order of the Palmetto, South Carolina's highest civilian honor in 2006; she was inducted into the South Carolina Academy of Authors in 2011.
ANDREW GEYER

"*Firstlight*: The Early Inspirational Writings of Sue Monk Kidd." *Publishers Weekly* 253.26 (2006): 47.
Frykholm, Amy Johnson. "Breaking Away." *The Christian Century* 124.9 (2007): 36.
Morey, Ann-Janine. "The Secret Life of Bees." *The Christian Century* 120.4 (2003): 68.
"A Winning Exchange." *Poets & Writers Magazine* 37.1 (2009): 160.

Kilgo, James Patrick (1941–2002). Essayist, novelist, educator. Born on June 27, 1941, in Florence County, South Carolina, Kilgo was the son of John Simpson Kilgo and Caroline Lawton. He grew up in Darlington, attending St. John's Grammar and High School from first grade through graduation. He received his undergraduate degree from Wofford College in 1963 and then attended graduate school at Tulane University, earning his M.A. in 1965 and the Ph.D. in 1972. While working at Lake Junaluska, North Carolina, during the summer of 1961, Kilgo met Jane Guillory, a coworker from Memphis, Tennessee. They were married on August 27, 1963. The marriage produced three children.

While writing his doctoral dissertation, Kilgo moved to Athens, Georgia, to accept a teaching position in the English department at the University of Georgia. On completion of the dissertation, he was offered a position on the English faculty at Georgia, where he played a pivotal role in the development of the university's creative writing program. He remained at Georgia until his retirement in 1999, when he devoted himself full-time to writing.

Kilgo's writing grew out of observations recorded in his private journals, from which developed his personal narrative style. Much of his early work consisted of reflections on the outdoor life and his hunting experiences. When he was in his late thirties, he was asked to write a series of outdoor columns for the *Athens Observer,* a fledgling weekly newspaper. The resulting columns formed the foundation for what would be Kilgo's first book of essays, *Deep Enough for Ivorybills* (1988). A second book of essays, *Inheritance of Horses,* followed in 1994.

Kilgo's novel, *Daughter of My People* (1998), a fictionalized retelling of a story retrieved from the hidden lore of his own family, was a finalist for the Lillian Smith Award for fiction and the Stephen Crane Award for first novel, and it was the winner of the Townsend Prize, awarded by Georgia Perimeter College and the *Chattahoochee Review. The Hand-Carved Crèche and Other Christmas Stories* (1999) is a collection of holiday stories and memories gleaned from the author's Darlington childhood and the traditions that shaped it. In addition, Kilgo's essays have appeared in numerous publications, including the *Georgia Review, Gettysburg Review,* and *Sewanee Review.*

"You can't write unless you have a story to tell," said Kilgo. He stressed that it must be the writer's story, not necessarily a lived story, but one that engages the writer's passion. He died of cancer on December 8, 2002, in Athens, Georgia. JULIA ARRANTS

Obituary. Columbia *State,* December 12, 2002, B4.

King, Susan Petigru (1824–1875). Novelist, short story writer. King was born on October 23, 1824, in Charleston, South Carolina, the fourth child of the lawyer James Louis Petigru and Jane Amelia Postell. "Sue" Petigru received a finishing-school education at Madame Talvande's School in Charleston and at Madame Guillon's in Philadelphia. While decidedly intelligent and talented, she possessed an independent spirit and fun loving personality; she was also reportedly quick tempered, rebellious, flirtatious, and indiscreet. At the age of eighteen, on March 30, 1843, she married a young local lawyer, Henry Campbell King. A thinly disguised account of their unhappy marriage is presented in "A Marriage of Persuasion," a story in her third book, *Sylvia's World: Crimes Which the Law Does Not Reach.* The marriage produced one child, Adele, before Henry King was fatally wounded at the Battle of Secessionville in 1862.

Susan Petigru King's first book, *Busy Moments in the Life of an Idle Woman*, which contained four short stories and a novella, was published to critical acclaim in late 1853. She followed with *Lily* in 1855 and *Sylvia's World* in 1859. *Gerald Gray's Wife*, completed in 1863 and published the next year, was an extensive and incisive critique of marriage as a joyless liaison of entrapment and an endless struggle of competing wills. Her last known published work, "My Debuts," appeared in *Harper's Magazine* in 1868. In her writing, Susan Petigru King perceived herself to be an American William Makepeace Thackeray. She wrote realistically and satirically about the manners and mores—the sexual politics and unhappy unions—of the Charleston and lowcountry plantation elite in the divorce-prohibited South Carolina that she knew well. A contemporary critic in 1870 observed that "Mrs. King despises foolish sentimentalism and shows up human vice in all of her books. . . . All of her characters are true to nature." The historians Jane and William Pease argue that "King's novels are differentiated by their critical perspective on women's position, their exploration of themes of failure and frustration, and their focus on the drawing room and ballroom rather than the kitchen and nursery."

After the war, King tried unsuccessfully to support herself as a writer, and by 1867 she was working in Washington, D.C., as a government clerk. On August 17, 1870, she married the Republican boss of Charleston County, U.S. Congressman Christopher Columbus Bowen. A native Rhode Islander eight years her junior, Bowen was an unsavory but wily character who was turned out of Congress in 1872. The couple returned to Charleston, where Bowen served a term as county sheriff. Largely shunned by family members and polite society alike, King became lonely and unhappy. She died of typhoid pneumonia in Charleston on December 11, 1875, and was buried in the churchyard of St. Michael's Episcopal Church. In 1994, King was posthumously inducted into the South Carolina Academy of Authors. THOMAS L. JOHNSON

Helsley, Alexia Jones. "Henry Campbell and Susan Petigru King." *Proceedings of the South Carolina Historical Association* (2001): 11–18.

Pease, Jane H., and William H. Pease. *A Family of Women: The Carolina Petigrus in Peace and War.* Chapel Hill: University of North Carolina Press, 1999.

Scafidel, J. R. "Susan Petigru King: An Early South Carolina Realist." In *South Carolina Women Writers: Proceedings of the Reynolds Conference, University of South Carolina, October 24–25, 1975.* Edited by James B. Meriwether. Spartanburg, S.C.: Reprint Company, 1979.

Lane, John (b. 1954). Poet, environmentalist, educator. John Lane was born in Southern Pines, North Carolina, and he is currently a professor of English and environmental studies at Wofford College in Spartanburg, South Carolina. Lane is the author of nearly a dozen books of essays, poetry, and non-fiction, as well as the coeditor of five volumes of nature essays. In addition, he has published several chapbooks and pamphlets of both poetry and prose; and his poetry, essays, and other short prose pieces have appeared in magazines and journals, both regional and national. He is also involved in several online and digital projects, and his work has received wide critical attention.

Lane earned his B.A. from Wofford College in 1977 and his M.F.A. from Bennington College in 1995. From the late 1970s to the late 1980s, Lane lived variously in the Pacific Northwest, Oklahoma, Virginia, South Carolina, and North Carolina, working both in and out of the academy. In the late 1980s he was invited back to Wofford to teach creative writing; he settled into this position and was eventually awarded tenure in 1999. When Wofford created an environmental studies major in 2008, Lane served as the program's interim director, and he is currently the director of Wofford's Glendale Shoals Environmental Studies Center. Lane is an avid kayaker and outdoorsman, and his love of nature and the wilderness infuses nearly every aspect of his writing and teaching.

Lane's work has garnered numerous awards, including an NEA Poetry Apprentice Grant in 1979, a University of Virginia Hoyns Fellowship in Poetry (1980), a South Carolina Arts Commission Individual Arts Fellowship (1984), and the Phillip D. Reed Memorial Award for Outstanding Writing on the Southern Environment (2001). In addition, in 2008 Lane had the honor and distinction to have his literary papers acquired by the Sowell Family Collection in Literature, Community, and the Natural World at Texas Tech University. In 1995 Lane cofounded the Hub City Writers Project in Spartanburg, dedicated to promoting and publishing high-quality southern-oriented writing. This organization has since published more than four hundred authors and has received several notable accolades, including the Elizabeth O'Neill Verner Award for the Arts, the South Carolina Governor's Award for the Humanities, and three first-place Independent Publisher Book Awards.

Lane has always been a prolific writer, producing works in several different genres, including poetry, nonfiction, fiction, drama, and screenplay. Lane's early reputation as a writer was founded on his poetry, but in recent years his repute has been based on his accomplishments as a nonfiction writer, especially in the realm of personal narrative and nature writing. His major titles in this genre include *Waist Deep in Black Water* (2002), *Chattooga: Descending into the Myth of Deliverance River* (2004), *Circling Home* (2007), and *My Paddle to the Sea* (2004, republished 2011). His most recent book is *Redemption Ecology and Other Essays* (2012).

The one aspect that defines and directs Lane's work more than any other is a sense of place. The place-based work of poet Gary Snyder had a profound influence on Lane, and he continues in the tradition of Snyder by making an understanding of place the single most important element of his own writing. This sensibility pervades virtually all of Lane's work, whether that place is the community in which one lives, a forest, or a river on which one happens to be traveling.

It is perhaps Lane's 2007 book *Circling Home* that best exemplifies place as the fundamental subject of his work. In her preface to her 2008 interview with Lane, Julie Schwietert describes the provenance of the book: Lane put a saucer over the location of his home on a small-scale map, traced a circle around the saucer, and then set out to learn everything he could about everything within the limits of that traced circle. In that same interview, Lane admits to the possible limitations of writing a book in such a way, noting: "you risk writing a book that is only interesting to your immediate neighbors." Nonetheless, Schwietert accurately identifies the real advantage of writing such a book, claiming that "*Circling Home* is . . . a book about the very idea of place and our relationship with it."

In Lane's nature writing, place becomes the true protagonist and Lane, as narrator, is left to tell the reader the true story of the place by evoking a series of emotional responses arising from his own personal confrontation with the setting. This is perhaps understood best in one of Lane's more recent books, *Paddling to the Sea* (2004, 2011), which is also one of Lane's most critically well-received and most widely read publications. In his review, Hal Crimmel notes that "the book is by turns provoking, exhilarating, nerve-wracking, and soothing, providing the full quiver of emotions one experiences when descending a river." As a result, Lane provides for the reader what Crimmel describes as Lane's "ever-evolving relationship with the Piedmont region." The book is ostensibly the tale of Lane's journey from Lawson's Creek in his own backyard down a series of Carolina rivers to the ocean, but the setting or place described in the book—a river, with all of its hazards and joys—is the real focus. Nor is that relationship always a pleasure. *My Paddle to the Sea* describes the often ugly, forced intrusion of the modern world into the Carolina wilderness; but, as Crimmel deftly notes, the book "is a lesson in how to embrace the local," even when the local is at times marred by the creeping tentacles of modern society. *My Paddle to the Sea,* therefore, is overtly a tale about river conservation, but the real story is the love affair between the author and the natural world which he inhabits, and this is the relationship that inspires and guides Lane in all of his work. In 2014 he was inducted into the South Carolina Academy of Authors. ERIC R. CARLSON

Crimmel, Hal. "A Paddler's Journey down a Modern Southern Riverway." *Terrain.org: A Journal of the Built and Natural Environments* 29 (Spring/Summer 2012).
Schwietert, Julie. "Circling Home: An Interview with John Lane." *The Southern Nature Project* (February 2008).

Lathan, Robert (1881–1937). Editor, journalist, Pulitzer Prize winner. Lathan was born in York County, South Carolina, on May 5, 1881, the son of the Reverend Robert Lathan, a Presbyterian minister and educator, and Frances Eleanor Barron.

Lathan received his bachelor of arts from Erskine College and then taught English and journalism from 1898 until 1899. In 1900 Lathan joined the editorial staff of the *State* newspaper in Columbia, where he remained for three years. From 1903 to 1906 he worked as an official court reporter and studied law. After moving to Charleston in 1906, he became state news editor and city editor of the *News and Courier*. In 1910 he was promoted to chief editor, a position he held until 1927.

The political nature of Lathan's writing underwent substantial growth during this period, which was best represented in his editorial entitled "The Plight of the South," which appeared in the *News and Courier* on November 5, 1924. Something of a culmination of his political philosophy, "Plight of the South" focused on the South's lack of influence and leadership at the national level. "What political leaders has it [the South] who possess weight or authority beyond their own States? What constructive policies are its people ready to fight for with the brains and zeal that made them a power in the old days?" The essay offered no solution to the South's "plight" but rather presented its situation in bold terms in the hope that answers might soon be found. "Who is to speak for the South? How many of her citizens are prepared to help formulate her replies?" A highly respected and widely read piece of contemporary journalism, "Plight of the South" earned Lathan and the *News and Courier* the Pulitzer Prize for editorial writing in 1925.

An ardent Democrat, Lathan was also an active affiliate in many professional associations, including the Carnegie Endowment for International Peace and the advisory board to the University of South Carolina School of Journalism. In addition he served as president of the South Carolina Press Association (1925–1926) and was a life member of the Poetry Society of South Carolina. The Carnegie Endowment provided Lathan with opportunities to travel among several western and eastern European locations, where he learned the economic and political histories that surfaced in his later writing.

Lathan closely monitored both the South Carolina and the United States Supreme Courts. He was also concerned about all matters agricultural, as was most pronounced in a July 1926 address before the National Press Association calling for the "radical revision" of the South's agricultural system, in which he stated his belief that "every farmer (should be) a landowner." In the formative years of the Great Depression, Lathan wrote numerous editorials on farm foreclosures and described the rise in joblessness as a unique consequence of "Republican misrule."

Lathan also wrote on the traditional southern themes of states' rights and taxation, which he deemed as continual punishment from the North upon the South. He viewed state government as the "people's government" and was an ardent opponent of American entry into the League of Nations. He spent his last years as editor for the *Asheville (N.C.) Citizen*. He died in Asheville on September 26, 1937. He

was survived by his wife, Bessie Early of Darlington, whom he had married in 1904. They had no children. Lathan was buried in Grove Hill Cemetery in Darlington.
KRISTIN M. HARKEY

Brennan, Elizabeth A., and Elizabeth C. Clarage, eds. *Who's Who of Pulitzer Prize Winners.* Phoenix: Oryx, 1999.
Lathan, Robert. Papers. South Carolina Historical Society, Charleston.
————. Papers. South Caroliniana Library, University of South Carolina, Columbia.
Sloan, William David, and Laird B. Anderson, eds. *Pulitzer Prize Editorials: America's Best Editorial Writing, 1917–1993.* 2d ed. Ames: Iowa State University Press, 1994.

Legaré, James Mathewes (1823–1859). Poet, artist, inventor. Born in Charleston, South Carolina, in 1823, Legaré could trace his American ancestry on his father's side of the family through six generations. The son of John D. Legaré, founding editor of the farm journal *Southern Agriculturalist,* and Mary Doughty Mathewes, Legaré came from enterprising stock, and from an early age, he was expected to work hard and bring honor to the family name.

In 1841, as part of a twenty-member freshman class, he entered the College of Charleston where he matriculated for one year before transferring to St. Mary's College in Baltimore, perhaps to be closer to his influential cousin Hugh Swinton Legaré, who was then serving as U.S. Attorney General. Whatever benefit the family anticipated might accrue to the young Legaré from this connection came to naught when Hugh S. Legaré died suddenly while on a trip to Boston with other members of President Tyler's cabinet in 1843.

Despite the loss of his cousin's hoped-for patronage, Legaré returned to Charleston, empowered by his undergraduate experience in Baltimore, to take up the duties of law clerk. He also began showcasing his creative talent by exhibiting his paintings in local exhibitions and submitting poems to local periodicals. It was also during this period that a series of lung hemorrhages gave early indication that he had contracted pulmonary tuberculosis. In quest of a healthier climate and greater financial opportunity, his parents and he moved to Aiken, which then had a reputation as a therapeutic resort, especially for those suffering from consumption.

Once settled in a small cottage, which still stands at the bottom of Laurens Street, his father took up his duties as the local postmaster, and James Legaré tried his hand at a number of activities that he hoped would add to the family's coffers and also enhance his reputation as a man of intellectual promise. He set up a painting school for the young ladies of the area; apparently not only his teaching skills but also his dark good looks soon attracted the attention of a number of female admirers, among them was to be numbered his future wife, Anne Andrews of Augusta, Georgia.

Legaré also focused considerable time and energy on mechanical invention, including the development of a new type of encaustic tile, an inexpensive glazier's putty, and a material he called "lignine" or "plastic cotton" from which he fashioned shingles and furniture. Several of his furniture pieces ornamented with plastic cotton decorative elements, including a corner cupboard and a library screen, are in the permanent collection of the Charleston Museum.

Legaré also sought recognition for his poetry and fiction. In 1848, he published the slim volume of verse by which he is best known. Entitled *Orta-Undis,* roughly translated as "Sprung from the Waves"—a probable reference to the birth of Venus—the book, published by William Ticknor of Boston, attracted good reviews, including the endorsement of Henry Wadsworth Longfellow, who became a faithful correspondent. He also published seventeen stories in some of the most popular national periodicals of the day, including the *Knickerbocker Magazine* and both *Graham's* and *Putnam's Monthly Magazines.* Often he was the only southern contributor.

Despite his fragile health, Legaré had a head full of ambitious schemes, most of which remained untried when he died of consumption in 1859 at the age of thirty-five. He is buried in the churchyard of St. Thaddeus Episcopal Church in Aiken; the grave is marked by a memorial stone financed by local high school students in 1942.

Orta-Undis clearly establishes Legaré as a southern poet in the Romantic tradition. Therein are echoes of two versifiers that he especially admired and from whom he derived inspiration: Henry Wadsworth Longfellow, particularly in their shared tendency to moralize, and Edgar Allan Poe, especially in their shared devotion to the transforming power of the imagination. Of the poems published during his lifetime, most modern critics give highest marks to those that describe his engagement with the southern landscape, especially the native flora of his home state, like "Haw-Blossoms" and "To Jasmines in December." Some critical praise has also been lavished on the longest poem in his personal canon, "Ornithologoi" or "Bird Voices," which celebrates bird song and laments the practice of shooting birds for sport.

Legaré's verse certainly compares favorably to the compositions of other southern poets of his age, including Henry Timrod and Paul Hamilton Hayne. Had his life not been cut short by illness, he may have made a greater claim to literary celebrity. As it is, like the English poet Thomas Chatterton, whose early death and misunderstood genius made him a Romantic icon, Legaré stands as an exemplar of largely unfulfilled promise. TOM MACK

Davis, Curtis Carroll. *That Ambitious Mr. Legaré: The Life of James M. Legaré of South Carolina, Including a Collected Edition of His Verse.* Columbia: University of South Carolina Press, 1971.

Mack, Tom. *Hidden History of Aiken County.* Charleston: The History Press, 2012.

Lewisohn, Ludwig (1883–1955). Novelist, critic, activist. Born on May 30, 1883, in Berlin, Germany, Lewisohn immigrated to America in 1890 with his assimilated Jewish parents, Jacques Lewisohn and Minna Eloesser. The family stayed with relatives in St. Matthews, South Carolina, for two years before moving on to Charleston, where the young Lewisohn's stellar performance in high school and at the College of Charleston, from which he graduated with a bachelor of arts and master of arts, sustained the family. He was brilliant but did not fit in either intellectually or socially. His Semitic looks stamped him as an outsider and denied him access to a fraternity, even though he considered himself Methodist. Nevertheless, Charleston gentlemen helped pay for his schooling at Columbia University. The practice of denying professorships in English to Jews so dismayed him that he took no degree. In 1906 he married Mary Arnold Child Crocker, twenty years his senior.

Lewisohn's first novel, *The Broken Snare,* was published in 1908. Trumpeted by the naturalist writer Theodore Dreiser, it was condemned in Charleston for the author's advocacy of "free love." In 1910 he taught German at the University of Wisconsin followed by his service as a faculty member at the Ohio State University from 1911 to 1917. His promoting and translating of German literature at the outbreak of World War I stymied his advancement, which frustrated him greatly. From 1919 to 1924 he was drama critic for the *Nation,* and in 1922 his first important book, *Upstream,* a veiled autobiography in which he grappled with the issues of Puritanism, xenophobia, and the American dream, appeared. Although the term was not in vogue then, his book was a call for pluralism. This landmark work made Lewisohn a champion to intellectuals and immigrants.

In 1924, unable to get a divorce from Crocker, Lewisohn moved to Europe with the singer Thelma Spear. His novel *The Case of Mr. Crump,* set partially in Charleston and based on his disastrous marriage, was published in Paris in 1926. Hailed by Sigmund Freud and Thomas Mann, it is one of the finest naturalistic novels produced by an American in the 1920s. Lewisohn began to investigate his Jewish heritage and write novels and nonfiction on the subject. He was one of the first to see the looming horrors of Hitler. He became an elegant polemicist and propagandist for the Zionist cause, but his fiction suffered, and there was embarrassment to the cause from his personal entanglements. The tabloid press followed his non-married life with Spear, their breakup, the histrionic displays of his first wife, and then two subsequent marriages. Only with the death of Crocker and the relaxing of obscenity laws could an unexpurgated edition of *The Case of Mr. Crump* appear in the United States in 1947. By that time his critical work—on drama, American life, and literature—was largely forgotten, although he had published more than a dozen works on these topics.

In 1948 Lewisohn became a founding member of the Brandeis University faculty. He died in Miami on December 31, 1955. By then Lewisohn, who had been praised and vilified in his lifetime, merited almost no notice in the press. His great works include some of his literary criticism, *The Case of Mr. Crump, Upstream,* and *The Island Within,* one of his Jewish-themed novels that helped open up fiction writing to the many American Jewish novelists who followed him. HARLAN GREENE

Lainoff, Seymour. *Ludwig Lewisohn.* Boston: Twayne, 1982.
Melnick, Ralph. *The Life and Work of Ludwig Lewisohn.* 2 vols. Detroit: Wayne State University Press, 1998.

Lott, Bret (b. Robert Bretley Lott, 1958). Novelist, short story writer, memoirist, educator. Although Lott himself was born in Los Angeles, California, on October 8, 1948, his parents, William Sequoia Lott and Barbara Joan Holmes, were southerners by lineage. Lott earned a B.A. in English from California State University-Long Beach in 1981. His matriculation was interrupted, however, by a decision to enter the workforce in 1979–1980 as a salesman for RC Cola, a temporary experience that was to hold him in good stead when he wrote his first novel *The Man Who Owned Vermont* (1987), which recounts the tale of a route salesman for a soft drink company who comes to grips with his personal shortcomings in time to save his shattered marriage.

It was in his senior year as an undergraduate that Lott decided to become a writer, and initially he tried his hand at journalism, working for the *Commercial News* in Los Angeles (1980–1981). After graduation, however, he came east to pursue an M.F.A. in creative writing (1984) at the University of Massachusetts in Amherst, where he studied with the celebrated American novelist James Baldwin.

After a couple of years of teaching at the Ohio State University—it was during this period that he won an Ohio Arts Council Fellowship—he arrived in South Carolina to take up a position as both a writer-in-residence and professor at the College of Charleston, where he has remained to this date except for a three-year-period (2004–2007) when he was affiliated with Louisiana State University as editor of *The Southern Review.*

In addition to *The Man Who Owned Vermont,* his early works include three novels, *A Stranger's House* (1988), *Jewel* (1991), and *Reed's Beach* (1991), and two short story collections, *A Dream of Old Leaves* (1989) and *How to Get Home* (1996).

By 1999 these works had earned Lott an enviable reputation for empathetic characterization and lyrical prose, but his career reached a much higher plateau of critical attention and commercial success when television host Oprah Winfrey selected his novel *Jewel* for her incredibly influential on-air book club. The novel, first published in 1991, was hastily reprinted due to Winfrey's endorsement and became an overnight bestseller; in 2001, it was made into a television movie, directed by Paul Shapiro and starring Farrah Fawcett in the title role.

In this career-making novel, the protagonist and first-person narrator Jewel Hilburn decides to uproot her entire family in the 1940s to find the enlightened medical support that she needs for her youngest offspring, a daughter named Brenda Kay, who is diagnosed with Down Syndrome. The essential plot of the book is based loosely on the real-life story of the author's grandmother, who packed up her six children and moved from Mississippi to California in order to get for her youngest child the help that the "cracker doctors" of her native state could not provide.

Ultimately, Lott is a writer about families. In an interview with Robert Hall, he asserted, "Whether you are writing away from the family or trying to extract from the family or trying to get hold of the family, or the family's dying or being born, or you are meeting your soul mate or your lover or whatever; it's all about family."

Most often Lott's fictional families are in crisis, coping with the sadness resulting from some loss; in *Reed's Beach,* a couple must re-navigate their marriage after the death of their seven-year-old son; in *A Song I Knew by Heart* (2004), a widow, whose grief is compounded after her son is killed in a car accident, must offer a path forward for her equally devastated daughter-in-law.

A departure from his customary family-centered narratives are the two books to date featuring the character Huger Dillard, whom readers first meet as a fifteen-year-old boy in *The Hunt Club* (1998) and then as a twenty-seven-year-old college dropout in *Dead Low Tide* (2012). Although both works contain the author's distinctive attention to characterization and concrete setting—in this case, both the sharp class divisions of Charleston society and the lush landscape of the Carolina lowcountry—they are also mysteries during which the male protagonist solves a crime and simultaneously takes yet another step toward autonomous adulthood.

Because of their dramatic twists and turns, both books stand out from the rest of Lott's canon, which is composed chiefly of narratives focused on the ordinariness of most people's lives—the familiar everyday challenges that most individuals face, particularly in their relationships with others.

In addition to his fiction writing and editorial work, Lott has experimented with the genre of personal narrative. Three generations of Lott males provide the subject matter for *Fathers, Sons and Brothers* (2000), the first of three personal memoirs. The other two, *Before We Get Started: A Practical Memoir of the Writer's Life* (2005) and *Letters and Life: On Being a Writer, On Being a Christian* (2013), draw upon his years as both a professional writer and a teacher.

Among the various prizes that Lott has won over the years are three Syndicated Fiction Project Awards from PEN/NEA and a South Carolina Arts Commission Fellowship in Literature. He lives with his wife Melanie in Hanahan, South Carolina; they have two children. TOM MACK

"Lott, Bret." *Contemporary Southern Writers.* Edited by Robert Matuz. Detroit: St. James Press, 1999.

Marbura, Lily. "Interview with Bret Lott." *Center: A Journal of the Literary Arts* 8 (2009): 157–165.

Ludvigson, Susan (b. 1942). Poet. Born in Rice Lake, Wisconsin, on February 13, 1942, Ludvigson is the daughter of the entrepreneur Howard C. Ludvigson and Mabel Helgeland. In 1961 she married David Bartels with whom she had one son. Ludvigson entered the University of Wisconsin–River Falls, from which she earned a B.A., with honors, in English and psychology in 1965. For seven years she taught school in River Falls and in Ann Arbor, Michigan. She received an M.A. in English at the University of North Carolina at Charlotte in 1973 and then studied for two years with James Dickey at the University of South Carolina. She and Bartels divorced in 1974, and she married the novelist Scott Ely in October 1988. Both taught at Winthrop University in Rock Hill, spending part of each year in southern France. Since 1979 Ludvigson's work has earned many awards, including Guggenheim and Fulbright Fellowships. In 2009 she was inducted into the South Carolina Academy of Authors.

In a 1986 interview, Ludvigson recalled that she first wrote poems while in her teens. As an adult she became committed to poetry under the influence of colleagues and friends. Her first volume, *Step Carefully in Night Grass,* appeared in 1974. Her second, *Northern Lights* (1981), shows greater maturity and began her connection with Louisiana State University Press, which published the six collections that followed. Much of the material depicts memories in which horses, parents, and childhood anxieties are prominent. The middle section, based on nineteenth-century news articles, portrays thirteen troubled Wisconsin women.

In *The Swimmer* (1984), Ludvigson's third collection, poems such as "Trying to Come to Terms" (written in terza rima) express grief following the deaths of three friends. Through this collection, water in its various forms—snow, rain, lakes— becomes symbolic, sometimes suggesting grief, as in "A Day of Snow," sometimes freedom and renewal, as in the title poem. Several poems based on paintings anticipate the visual-arts influence prominent in her later work.

The Beautiful Noon of No Shadow (1986) draws on themes established in earlier collections, such as the power of dreams, and the elemental force of light and dark, of water and sky. "Waiting for Your Life" and "The Will to Believe" (an extended elegy for her father) are longer and more ambitious than previous poems.

Her fifth book, *To Find the Gold* (1990), begins with "The Gold She Finds," a widely praised, nineteen-part poem containing an imaginative reconstruction of the life of the sculptor Camille Claudel and her passionate but troubled relationship with Auguste Rodin. Other poems, such as "This Beginning" and "Paris Aubade," are autobiographical, often touching on life in France.

Everything Winged Must Be Dreaming (1993) contains long poems on marriage and extended relationships. Several, such as "Happiness: The Forbidden Subject," refer to her own marital contentment. As the title suggests, *Trinity* (1996) shows a greater concern with religious themes.

Sweet Confluence (2000) consists of selected poems from previous volumes, as well as twenty new poems, including "Where We Have Come," a kind of elegy for her mother. This volume, along with *Escaping the House of Certainty: Poems* (2006), demonstrates the versatility of form and subject and the maturity that earned Ludvigson her place as a prominent American poet. KEN AUTREY

Swanson, Gayle R., and William B. Thesing. *Conversations with South Carolina Poets.* Winston-Salem, N.C.: John F. Blair, 1986.

Whitehead, Gwendolyn. "Susan Ludvigson." In *Dictionary of Literary Biography.* Vol. 120. *American Poets since World War II, Third Series.* Edited by R. S. Gwynn. Detroit: Gale, 1992.

Lumpkin, Grace (ca. 1896–1980). Novelist, social activist. Lumpkin was born in Milledgeville, Georgia, the ninth of eleven children born to William Wallace Lumpkin and Annette Caroline Morris. Her year of birth is uncertain, but cemetery records suggest that she was born on March 3, 1896. Like many prominent southern families, the Lumpkins suffered a reversal of fortune after the Civil War. William, a Confederate army veteran and devout proponent of the "Lost Cause," moved his family to Columbia around 1900, installing them as parishioners at Trinity Episcopal Church. In 1910 the Lumpkins moved to a farm in Richland County. William Lumpkin died shortly afterward, leaving his large family to fend for itself.

Grace Lumpkin subsequently earned a teacher's certificate from Brenau College (1911) and then held various jobs in the Carolinas and in France as a teacher, home demonstration agent, and social worker. At home she conducted night classes for adult farm and mill workers and attended meetings of the nascent interracial cooperation movement. She harbored a desire to write, and in 1925 she moved to New York City, where she took a job with *The World Tomorrow,* a pacifist Quaker publication. Her coverage of the Communist-led textile strikes in Passaic, New Jersey, in 1926 struck a militant chord. Almost immediately Lumpkin went to work for a Soviet-affiliated trading company and joined a chapter of the John Reed Club for leftist writers. Her first published piece, "White Man, a Story," appeared in the September 1927 issue of *New Masses.* Five years later Lumpkin published her first novel, *To Make My Bread,* the material for which she had gathered as a witness to the Gastonia, North Carolina, textile strikes of 1929. The book, winner of the 1932

Maxim Gorky Prize, chronicles the farm-to-factory transformation of the McClure family; it has been excerpted, anthologized, republished in England, and adapted for the New York stage by Alfred Bein as *Let Freedom Ring.*

Lumpkin's second novel, *A Sign for Cain* (1935), appeared during a frenetic period of speech-making and investigative work in the South on behalf of the Communist Party (which she never officially joined). Her personal life was similarly complicated. She lived with (and perhaps married) Michael Intrator, a labor organizer who had been expelled from the Communist Party in 1929, and another married couple, Whittaker Chambers and Esther Shemitz, who became Communist spies. Lumpkin and Intrator broke up in the late 1930s, allegedly after an abortion that left her distraught. She subsequently took refuge with an ardently anti-Communist organization run by an Episcopal priest in New York, the Moral Re-Armament Movement.

In 1948 Whittaker Chambers, now an anti-Communist and an editor at *Time,* accused former State Department official Alger Hiss of spying for the Russians. Investigators interviewed Lumpkin, hoping that she might discredit Chambers's testimony. Instead, she took up her former housemate's defense in a New England speaking tour, lauding Chambers's role in her own renunciation of Communism. She testified before Senator Joseph McCarthy's Permanent Subcommittee on Investigations in 1953, telling the panel that she had written "the fundamental philosophy of communism" into *A Sign for Cain* after party functionaries threatened to "break" her literary career.

Lumpkin's final novel, *Full Circle,* which appeared in 1962, is a fictionalized account of her peculiar ideological and spiritual life journey, which she delineated as her Communist and "return to God" phases. She died in Columbia on March 23, 1980. Though her grave is unmarked, Lumpkin is buried in her family's plot at Elmwood Cemetery in Columbia. She was inducted posthumously into the South Carolina Academy of Authors in 1996. ELIZABETH ROBESON

Hall, Jacquelyn Dowd. "Women Writers, the 'Southern Front,' and the Dialectical Imagination." *Journal of Southern History* 69 (February 2003): 3–38.

Lumpkin, Grace. Papers. South Caroliniana Library, University of South Carolina, Columbia.

———. *To Make My Bread.* 1932. Reprint, Urbana: University of Illinois Press, 1995.

Mays, Benjamin Elijah (1894–1984). Memoirist, civil rights activist, college president. Mays was born on August 1, 1894, in rural South Carolina near Rambo in Edgefield County (now Epworth in Greenwood County). He was the youngest of eight children born to Hezekiah Mays and Louvenia Carter, former slaves turned tenant farmers. Growing up in the rural South at a time when African Americans were disfranchised by law, Mays experienced a climate of hate where lynchings and race riots were common. In fact, Mays's first memory was the 1898 Phoenix Riot, in which his cousin was murdered by whites.

Early in life Mays developed an "insatiable desire" for education, but racial inequality and prejudice had severely handicapped his educational aspirations. Struggling against his limited schooling, his family's poverty, and his father's insistence that he remain on the farm, Mays enrolled at the high school of the racially segregated South Carolina State College. Four years later, in 1916, Mays graduated at the top of his class and became engaged to fellow student Ellen Harvin.

Mays looked to continue his education at a northern college. Rejected because of his race from his top choice, Holderness School in New Hampshire, Mays enrolled at Bates College in Lewiston, Maine, where he graduated with honors in 1920. Following graduation, Mays briefly returned home to South Carolina to marry Harvin, who had been teaching home economics at Morris College in Sumter. The couple moved to Chicago, where Mays enrolled at the University of Chicago to study divinity. After three semesters at Chicago and as a result of a personal invitation from John Hope, president of Morehouse, Mays took a teaching position at Morehouse College in Atlanta, Georgia, where he taught algebra and mathematics from 1921 through 1924 and served for a year as acting dean. During his tenure at Morehouse, Mays, who was ordained in 1921, served as the pastor of the Shiloh Baptist Church, which allowed him to grow in his spiritual faith and deal with the loss of his wife Ellen, who died in 1923.

Following his wife's death, Mays left Morehouse to continue his graduate work at the University of Chicago, where he earned an M.A. in 1925. Although he considered pursuing his doctorate, Mays instead returned to South Carolina State to teach English. There he met Sadie Gray, who became his second wife in 1926. After marrying, the couple moved to Florida to work with the National Urban League to improve the housing, employment opportunities, and health conditions of African Americans. A few years later, in 1928, expecting to be fired for challenging segregation, they resigned from their jobs and moved to Atlanta, where Benjamin took a position with the national Young Men's Christian Association (YMCA) and worked to integrate that organization in the North and the South. In 1930 Mays left the YMCA to conduct a study of black churches with fellow minister Joseph W. Nicholson. That study, which focused on 609 urban congregations and 185 rural congregations, was published in 1933 as *The Negro's Church*. In 1931 Mays returned to the University of Chicago School of Religion to finish his Ph.D., which he received in 1935. In 1934, as Mays was completing his doctoral studies, he accepted appointment as dean of the School of Religion at Howard University in Washington, D.C. In this position Mays traveled overseas to visit world leaders, such as Mahatma Gandhi of India.

After six years at Howard, Mays accepted an offer in 1940 to become president of Morehouse College in Atlanta. For the next twenty-seven years Mays worked tirelessly at Morehouse, collecting $15 million in donations, overseeing the construction of eighteen buildings, and conducting well-attended Tuesday morning chapel talks with students. Mays unrelentingly preached engagement, responsibility, and stewardship to his Morehouse students. His inspiring leadership made Morehouse one of the most prestigious black universities in America, graduating a disproportionately high number of future Ph.D.s, college presidents, and community leaders. Several of his gifted students, including Julian Bond and Maynard Jackson, went on to become leading lights of the national civil rights movement of the 1950s and 1960s, prompting one writer to describe Mays as "Schoolmaster of the Movement." One student whom Mays particularly impressed was Martin Luther King, Jr., who often stayed late with Mays to discuss theology. King and Mays became lifelong friends. In 1968 Mays delivered the eulogy at King's funeral.

In 1967 Mays retired as president of Morehouse College and took the position of chairman of the school board in Atlanta, where he worked to correct racial inequalities in the public school system. In 1970 Mays finished his autobiography, *Born to Rebel*, which has stood as an invaluable contribution to the study of American race relations. The life of Benjamin E. Mays has been consistently celebrated. During his lifetime, he was awarded forty-nine honorary degrees and inducted into the South Carolina Hall of Fame. He died on March 28, 1984, in Atlanta; he was posthumously inducted into the South Carolina Academy of Authors in 1997.
ORVILLE VERNON BURTON AND MATTHEW CHENEY

Bennett, Lerone, Jr. "Benjamin Elijah Mays: The Last of the Great Schoolmasters." *Ebony* 33 (December 1977): 72–80.
Carter, Lawrence E., ed. *Walking Integrity: Benjamin Elijah Mays, Mentor to Martin Luther King, Jr.* Macon, Ga.: Mercer University Press, 1998.
Jones, Edward A. *A Candle in the Dark: A History of Morehouse College.* Valley Forge, Penn.: Judson, 1967.
Mays, Benjamin E. *Born to Rebel: An Autobiography.* 1971. Reprint, Athens: University of Georgia Press, 1987.
———. Papers. Moorland-Spingarn Research Center, Howard University, Washington, D.C.
Rovaris, Dereck J. *Mays and Morehouse: How Benjamin E. Mays Developed Morehouse College, 1940–1967.* Silver Spring, Md.: Beckham House, 1995.

McCants, Elliott Crayton (1865–1953). Novelist, short story writer, educator. Born near Ninety-Six, South Carolina, on September 2, 1865, Elliott Crayton McCants was a man of two callings: educator and novelist. McCants attended the Citadel, graduating in 1886; as a condition of his scholarship to that institution, McCants was required to teach for two years in Abbeville, South Carolina. After fulfilling this obligation, McCants then tried his hand at farming, but this venture was a miserable failure; after a year on the farm, McCants found himself broke, so he returned to the classroom, which is where he would remain for the remainder of his professional career. He died on October 23, 1953, in Anderson, South Carolina, at the age of 86.

While McCants was inducted posthumously into the South Carolina Academy of Authors in 1996, teaching was his professional calling. He spent 58 years as an educator, most of those years in Anderson, South Carolina, where he closed out his career as the superintendent of the city's public schools, retiring in 1945. He is remembered there as one of the most public-minded citizens of his day, and McCants Middle School is named after him. McCants was a vigorous and outspoken educator whose pastoral sensibilities found their way into the classroom in a significant way: he believed hard work to be the single most important aspect of a student's education. His writings on the topic continually stress the importance of education not solely for the talented students but as much or more for the average learners who make up the majority of any student body. McCants was a true believer in the role of education to create a better society; in the February, 1937 issue of *Forum* magazine, he writes, "Left to themselves, most people, whatever their need, will teach themselves nothing." Shortly thereafter he provides an effective synopsis of the role of the educator in society: "Even with all the aid which environment gives, self-made men are usually ill made." Effective education, McCants believed, would lead to a better society.

Yet teaching was only one side of McCants's life of letters; he was also a novelist of some note in his own time. McCants's literary output was never very prolific, undoubtedly due to his obligations as an educator. His publications fall into two distinct stages. In the first stage, the first decade of the twentieth century, McCants published the works for which he is perhaps best remembered: the postbellum novel *In the Red Hills: A Story of the South Carolina Country* (1904) and a volume of shorter pieces titled *One of the Gray Jackets* (1908). While he wrote and published hundreds of short stories in his career, McCants fell silent in terms of longer works for nearly two decades. Then, in the late 1920s and early 1930s, he published a spate of books including *Histories, Legends, and Stories of South Carolina* (1927); the novel *White Oak Farm* (1928), set in Reconstruction-era South Carolina; and the novel *Ninety-Six* (1930), a work also set in South Carolina, but this time during the Revolutionary War.

McCants's literary works consistently deal with pastoral and historical themes within the specific context of South Carolina and its people. In the preface to *Histories, Legends, and Stories of South Carolina*, McCants describes the book as "an attempt to present that which, for want of a better name, may be called the atmosphere of South Carolina history." His novels, likewise, explore the collective psyche of the state. Nowadays his tales might be seen as traditional and sentimental, but they were well-received in their day. The most dominant aspect of McCants's work, however, is the celebration of the independent spirit of South Carolina and its people. It is not difficult to see that McCants prided himself in his identity as a South Carolinian, and his fiction represents a continuing celebration of his native state. He wrote in the preface to *One of the Gray Jackets,* "Truly, we of Carolina have our troubles as others do, but God has been good to us. Because of all this, at the feet of his mother State the author places his humble offering."

Perhaps most telling is the novel *White Oak Farm.* In this novel McCants explores the reconfiguration of the status quo and the racial tensions that existed in agrarian South Carolina after the Civil War. The racial views of Pembroke Gautier, the novel's narrator and protagonist, may strike readers now as somewhat distasteful, crude, and ignorant. Yet McCants has his narrator present himself openly and honestly as a man whose views of race are at the same time both blameworthy and laudable—he may not believe that racial equality is possible, but at the same time he finds racial oppression to be morally repugnant. As a result, this character undoubtedly personifies McCants's own view of what it means to be a South Carolinian: proud and independent, at times to a fault, but willing to see that fault where it lies. At one point in the novel, Pembroke claims, "I am a South Carolinian, above all else. If this be a small and narrow patriotism peculiar to ignorance and the agrarian class, then grant me, I pray you, the license of the ignorant. Permit me to be myself. I believe that South Carolina had a right to secede from the Union; I also believe that she was exceedingly ill-advised in attempting to exercise that right. I feel that slavery was a moral wrong and an economic blunder."

In hindsight, through characters such as Pembroke Gautier, McCants presents us with all that is good and all that is regrettable about the state he loved so, and thus his works display the continuing social education of the state of South Carolina. McCants is willing to see the faults his state's citizens had embraced in the past, but he cannot allow himself to engage in wholesale condemnation—he loves his birthplace too much. ERIC R. CARLSON

Cauthen, Charles Edward. *South Carolina Goes to War, 1860–1865.* Columbia: University of South Carolina Press, 2005.
Epps, Edwin C. *Literary South Carolina.* Spartanburg, S.C.: Hub City Press, 2004.
Gordon, John W. *South Carolina and the American Revolution: A Battlefield History.* Columbia: University of South Carolina Press, 2007.

McKissick, James Rion (1884–1944). Journalist, educator, university president. McKissick was born in Union, South Carolina, on October 13, 1884, the son of Isaac Going McKissick and Sarah Foster. He graduated from South Carolina College in 1905 and attended Harvard Law School before turning to a career in journalism. At the *Richmond (Va.) Times-Dispatch,* McKissick rose from reporter to chief editorial writer. In 1914 he returned to South Carolina, where he was admitted to the bar and practiced law until joining the *Greenville News* in 1916 as editor. In 1919 McKissick became editor of another leading newspaper, the *Greenville Piedmont.*

McKissick was elected to the University of South Carolina's board of trustees in 1924 and then joined the faculty in 1927 as dean of the School of Journalism. He married Caroline Virginia Dick that same year. During his tenure as dean, he earned a master of arts in journalism from the University of Wisconsin. Although he never earned a doctorate, McKissick excelled as a teacher and mentor to his students, who affectionately dubbed him "the Colonel." In 1936 McKissick became one of the few Carolina alumni to become the university's president. He was devoted to the university, writing in 1942, "I would rather be president of the University than hold any other position in this state and country. . . . If I could live my life over, I would give much more of it to Carolina."

McKissick led the university through the tumultuous times of the Great Depression and World War II. With help through the New Deal, McKissick presided over the construction of a new library and five dormitories, as well as a general refurbishment of the campus. During World War II, McKissick guided the university into the war effort, establishing civilian pilot and laboratory technician training programs, adjusting the curriculum to include defense-oriented science and engineering courses, and establishing the nation's first Red Cross nurse's aide course.

McKissick's greatest accomplishments may have come in public relations for the university. He declared that the institution had long been the target of "unjustifiable criticism" and discrimination in state appropriations because of a century-long "whispering campaign" against the university by its political enemies. As a result of his successful efforts to dispel the insinuations that Carolina was an immoral and elitist institution, the university made great gains in popularity.

McKissick died suddenly of a heart attack on September 3, 1944. "The Colonel" was such a respected and beloved figure to students and faculty that they petitioned the university's board of trustees to allow McKissick to be buried on campus, the only person ever to receive such an honor. After the funeral service during which his body lay in state in the new library, McKissick was buried in front of the South Caroliniana Library, which he had helped to establish through the donation of his own personal collection of more than five thousand books, manuscripts, and papers. Several months after his death, the new university library (now a museum) was named for McKissick. ELIZABETH CASSIDY WEST

Lesesne, Henry H. *A History of the University of South Carolina, 1940–2000.* Columbia: University of South Carolina Press, 2001.

"McKissick Rites to Be Tomorrow." *Columbia Record,* September 4, 1944, 1, 2.

Miller, Kelly, Jr. (1863–1939). Essayist, editor, publisher, educator. Miller was born on July 18 or 23, 1863, in Winnsboro, South Carolina, to Kelly Miller, Sr., a free black man, and Elizabeth Roberts, a slave. His father was a Confederate army veteran. Miller's initial education was at a grammar school in Winnsboro. His considerable skill in mathematics drew the attention of Willard Richardson, a northern missionary. By 1878 Miller was attending Fairfield Institute, also in Winnsboro. Two years later he was awarded a scholarship to the preparatory department of Howard University in Washington, D.C.

After graduating from Howard in 1886, Miller studied sciences and mathematics with Captain Edgar Frisly, a British mathematician at the U.S. Naval Observatory. Through Frisly's influence, Miller became the first African American to attend Johns Hopkins University in Baltimore, but financial considerations forced him to withdraw during his junior year. In 1890 he was appointed to a mathematics professorship at Howard University. He remained there throughout his professional career. He received his M.A. (1901) and LL.D. (1903) from Howard. On July 17, 1894, he married Annie May Butler of Baltimore. Their marriage produced five children.

Early in his career Miller was a professor of both mathematics and sociology, but he eventually chose to concentrate primarily on sociology, believing it to be an effective means to study race relations in America. In 1907 Miller was appointed dean of Howard's College of Arts and Sciences. He remained an active teacher and administrator until his retirement in 1934. His influence on Howard University in the early twentieth century was such that the school was known to many as "Kelly Miller's University."

From his leadership at Howard and through his prolific writings, Miller became a national figure in the debate on race in America. Deemed by most to be a moderate and a harmonizer, he pursued a middle course between the accommodationist views of Booker T. Washington and the more radical stance of W. E. B. Du Bois. Miller agreed with Washington's contention that agriculture was vital to southern blacks, and he did not oppose Washington's emphasis on industrial education. Miller also supported Washington's call for African American clergymen to promote higher education. But, like Du Bois, Miller felt that a liberal arts curriculum was vital for students drawn from the growing urban black population and that such a foundation was absolutely necessary for the creation and expansion of a black professional class of physicians, lawyers, and teachers. By 1912 Miller was actively assisting Du Bois with editing *Crisis*, the official journal of the National Association for the Advancement of Colored People (NAACP). They became estranged in the 1930s, however, when Du Bois became closely associated with the American Communist Party. In contrast, Miller was an outspoken critic of Marxist ideology.

Throughout his career as an educator and spokesman for African Americans, Miller was a prolific author. He wrote numerous articles and pamphlets, many of which were open letters challenging the racial views of public figures. In 1913 he began his own journal, *Kelly Miller's Monographic Magazine*. His 1917 pamphlet "The Disgrace of Democracy: An Open Letter to President Woodrow Wilson" sold more than 250,000 copies. His major monographs were *Race Adjustment* (1908), *Out of the House of Bondage* (1914), and *The Everlasting Stain* (1924).

Miller died at his Washington, D.C., home on December 29, 1939. He was buried in Lincoln Memorial Cemetery in Washington. Miller was posthumously inducted into the South Carolina Academy of Authors in 1993. MILES S. RICHARDS

Eisenberg, Bernard. "Kelly Miller: The Negro Leader as a Marginal Man." *Journal of Negro History* 45 (July 1960): 182–97.

Meier, August. "The Racial and Educational Philosophy of Kelly Miller, 1895–1915." *Journal of Negro Education* 29 (Spring 1960): 121–27.

Wright, W. D. "The Thought and Leadership of Kelly Miller." *Phylon* 39 (June 1978): 180–92.

Moïse, Penina (1797–1880). Poet, hymn writer, educator, activist. Moïse was born on April 23, 1797, in Charleston, South Carolina, the youngest daughter of Abraham and Sarah Moïse. Her father was a trader who came to South Carolina after fleeing the Santo Domingo slave insurrection in 1791. He died when Penina was twelve, forcing her to leave school to take care of her ailing mother.

Despite ending her formal education at the age of twelve, Moïse continued to engage in intellectual efforts. From a young age she found solace in writing poetry. In 1819 Moïse published her first poem. Thereafter the prolific poet submitted her verse to the *Charleston Courier*, the *Boston Daily Times*, the *New Orleans Commercial Times*, the *Washington Union*, *Godey's Ladies Book*, the *Home Journal of New York Occident*, and the *American Jewish Advocate*. In 1833 Moïse published a volume of secular poems titled *Fancy's Sketch Book*. Demonstrating a cosmopolitan worldview, Moïse addressed the issues of anti-Semitism, politics, and history and also included personal insights on society. Her poems contained romantic, sentimental, and classical themes, as well as emotional and nondenominational religious topics.

An observant Jew, Moïse was an active member of Charleston's Kahal Kadosh Beth Elohim synagogue. In 1841 her brother Abraham and another prominent Jewish Charlestonian, Isaac Harby, spearheaded the effort to alter the synagogue service to a reformed service. Her brother and Harby commissioned Moïse to write the new hymnal. Consequently, Moïse composed the vast majority of the hymns included in the first American Reform Jewish hymnal. Dedicated to the celebration of Judaism and desiring to encourage communal and individual fidelity to Judaism, the poet divided the hymnal into nine sections. Separately and collectively the hymns were designed to promote a continued faith in and a tolerance for Judaism in the midst of a highly evangelical Protestant South. Moïse was also a superintendent of Charleston's first Jewish school.

During the Civil War, Moïse avidly supported the South in her writing and educational efforts. Seeking refuge in Sumter during the war, Moïse, now blind and ill, returned to Charleston when hostilities ceased. She was cared for by her sister and her niece; all three established a Sunday school in their home for Charleston's younger students. Curricula included classical and religious education. Moïse never married. She died on September 13, 1880, and is buried in the Coming Street Cemetery in Charleston. Penina Moïse was posthumously inducted into the South Carolina Academy of Authors in 1999. JENNIFER A. STOLLMAN

Hagy, James. *This Happy Land: The Jews of Colonial and Antebellum Charleston.* Tuscaloosa: University of Alabama Press, 1993.

Moïse, Penina. *Secular and Religious Works of Penina Moïse with a Brief Sketch of Her Life.* Charleston: Nicholas G. Duffy, 1911.

Reznikoff, Charles. *The Jews of Charleston: A History of an American Jewish Community.* Philadelphia: Jewish Publication Society of America, 1950.

Molloy, Robert (1906–1977). Novelist, short story writer, editor, critic. Son of R. William Molloy and Edyth Estelle Johnson, Robert Molloy was born on January 9, 1906, in Charleston, South Carolina, the place he would always remember and summon up vividly in his writing. Living first on Tradd Street and then near Colonial Lake, the boy was the next to youngest of five siblings in a comfortably middle-class Catholic family. His first artistic passion was for the piano, and later in life he would be an accomplished musician. At about the age of twelve, following financial reverses, he moved with his family first to Philadelphia and then to New York City. Molloy never spent any significant time in Charleston after that.

A good student, with a flair for languages (many of which he would teach himself later in life), Molloy had his plans for college dashed with his father's death. He supported himself with numerous jobs and married Marion Knapp Jones on June 29, 1929. They would have two sons, Brian and Thomas, both professional musicians. A job as a publisher's reader led him into writing book reviews; translating (with Madeleine Boyd) two of Lucien Pemjean's works from French (*Captain D'Artagnan* and *When D'Artagnan Was Young*); and translating Spanish-speaking authors, including Romulo Gallegos (*Dona Barbara*, 1931), Luis Spota, and Victor Alba. He also authored articles on European literature for the first edition of the *Columbia Encyclopedia* and contributed to the *Encyclopedia Americana* and *British Authors of the Nineteenth Century*.

By 1936 Molloy was working as book reviewer and copy editor for the *New York Sun*. In that capacity he befriended the British novelist William McFee. Molloy eventually became literary editor of the *Sun* from 1943 to 1945; and interested in writing, he took a course under the gifted writing instructor Sylvia Chatfield Bates. He first wrote short stories, seeing them published over the years in such magazines as *Good Housekeeping, Woman's Home Companion, Colliers,* and others. After Bates suggested he try novel writing, he dedicated his first, *Pride's Way* (1945), to her. In this engaging social comedy of a large Charleston Catholic family, Molloy summoned up the city of his youth, viewing his characters and his native city with affection, humor, and gentle irony. It was the May 1945 Literary Guild selection, a play version was staged in Charleston, and two novels in the same vein followed: *Pound Foolish* (1950) and *A Multitude of Sins* (1953). Two other works featured Charleston exclusively: the nonfiction *Charleston: A Gracious Heritage* (1947) and *An Afternoon in March* (1958), a fictional retelling of the 1888 Thomas McDow murder of *News and Courier* editor Francis W. Dawson. Molloy's New York City novels include *Uneasy Spring* (1946); *The Best of Intentions* (1949); *The Reunion* (1959), partially set in Charleston; and *The Other Side of the Hill* (1962). The latter two reflect a mature, sophisticated, and urbane worldview, reflective of Molloy himself. He died in Paramus, New Jersey, on January 27, 1977. HARLAN GREENE

Greene, Karen. "Writer Draws on Charleston Childhood." Charleston *News and Courier,* April 9, 1975, B2.

Jones, Katherine M., and Mary Verner Schlaefer. *South Carolina in the Short Story.* Columbia: University of South Carolina Press, 1952.

"Robert Molloy, Writer Is Dead." Charleston *News and Courier,* February 6, 1977, A17.

Yoken, Melvin B., ed. *The Letters (1971–1977) of Robert Molloy.* Lewiston, N.Y.: Edwin Mellen, 1989.

Monroe, Mary Alice (b. 1951). Novelist, environmental conservationist. Born on May 25, 1951, in Evanston, Illinois, Monroe is the daughter of Werner Monroe, a pediatrician, and his wife Elayne. Monroe grew up in the Chicago suburbs with four sisters and five brothers. She attended the Ted Liss Studio for Performing Arts in Chicago and studied journalism at Northwestern University in Evanston, Illinois. In 1972 she married Markus Kruesi, a child psychiatrist. Inspired by her honeymoon trip to Japan, she pursued a B.A. in Asian studies and Japanese from Seton Hall University in South Orange, New Jersey. Monroe went on to receive her M.A. in education from Seton Hall.

Prior to her career as an author, Monroe worked as an assistant to the general editor of the *Encyclopedia Britannica,* spent time as a teacher, and helped establish a program to teach English as a second language to southeast Asian refugees. In 1980 she co-wrote her first nonfiction work, *Crossroads to Literacy,* which served as a guide to help immigrants acclimate to life in the United States. Monroe's first foray into fiction occurred in 1995. Confined to bed rest during her third pregnancy,

Monroe was encouraged by her husband to take up the pen. The result was her first novel, *The Long Road Home.*

Monroe's early fiction, including *The Long Road Home* (1995), *The Girl in the Mirror* (1998), *The Book Club* (1999), and *The Four Seasons* (2001), evokes themes of strong women with personal struggles who overcome tragedy and develop healing interpersonal relationships.

In 1999 Markus Kruesi accepted a job at the Medical University of South Carolina in Charleston, and the family relocated to the Isle of Palms. During this time, Monroe's work evolved from formulaic women's fiction to more mature, textured narratives. Notably, Monroe's works also shifted to focus on environmental themes. Marking a considerable development in her evolution as a novelist, her writings began to blend both women's fiction with environmental messages and metaphors—thus tying together her life as a writer and conservationist. First seen in her southern fiction debut, *The Beach House* (2002), Monroe artfully blends the emotional dynamics of a mother-daughter relationship with a conservationist's efforts to protect endangered loggerhead sea turtles.

Embracing her adopted home, Monroe has set most of her novels since 1999 in the Carolinas. To add authenticity to her stories, Monroe conducts research by immersing herself in the real worlds of her novels. In preparation for her novel *Skyward* (2003), a romance set in a birds of prey rescue center, Monroe volunteered at the Center for Birds of Prey of the Avian Conservation Center in Awendaw, South Carolina. For her 2005 novel *Sweetgrass,* Monroe learned the craft of the lowcountry's African American sweetgrass basket makers. Expanding her knowledge regarding loggerhead sea turtles, Monroe volunteered at the South Carolina Aquarium's sea turtle rehabilitation program to research *Swimming Lessons* (2007), a volume that marked a return to the characters and Isle of Palms setting of *The Beach House.* For her *New York Times* bestseller, *Last Light over Carolina* (2009), Monroe embedded herself into the local shrimping culture.

In rare contrast to her now-customary Carolina lowcountry setting, Monroe's 2008 release *Time is a River* takes place near Asheville, North Carolina, and tells the story of a breast cancer survivor's retreat to a mountain cabin and subsequent discovery of an unsolved mystery. The protagonist sets about simultaneously unlocking the mystery and advancing her own journey to recovery. Monroe's *New York Times* bestseller, *The Butterfly's Daughter* (2011), follows four women along the migration path of the monarch butterfly between Wisconsin and Mexico. This coming-of-age story focuses on the spiritual journey of the main protagonist, Luz Avila, as she carries her grandmother's ashes to Mexico. Winner of the 2011 International Book Award in the category of "Fiction: Environmental/Green Fiction," this title was also selected as a Southern Independent Booksellers Alliance (SIBA) Book Award finalist.

With the 2012 release of *Beach House Memories,* Monroe completed a trilogy ten years in the making. Serving as the prequel to her novels *Beach House* and *Swimming Lessons, Beach House Memories,* set in 1974, examines the painful and passionate early life of the memorable character, Olivia "Lovie" Rutledge. *Beach House Memories* reached the *New York Times* bestseller list during its first week of release. Sullivan's Island is the setting for Monroe's latest book, *The Summer Girls* (2013), the tale of a savvy grandmother who contrives to use a summer sojourn to reunite her three granddaughters, all half sisters.

Writing under her married name Mary Alice Kruesi, Monroe published two romantic fantasy novels: *Second Star to the Right* (1999) and *One Summer's Night* (2000). Both titles weave fairy tale fantasy worlds with romantic story lines. Monroe also published a children's book, *Turtle Summer: A Journal for My Daughter* (2007) as a companion to her 2007 novel, *Swimming Lessons.* Teaching children about coastal conservation, this juvenile title eventually won several awards including the ASPCA Henry Bergh Award for 2007 and the Children's Book Council Award.

Monroe has received numerous honors for her work, including the South Carolina Center for the Book Award for Fiction. Multiple novels have appeared on both the *New York Times* and *USA Today* bestseller lists. While not originally from the Carolina coast, Monroe has been embraced by the community and given the title "Queen of Lowcountry Fiction." She is an active member of Charleston Volunteers for Literacy, sits on the board of the South Carolina Aquarium, and lives as a "turtle lady" on the Isle of Palms. DEBORAH TRITT

Epps, Edwin. *Literary South Carolina.* Spartanburg, S.C.: Hub City Writers Project, 2004.

"Mary Alice Monroe." *Contemporary Authors Online.* Detroit: Gale, 2012.

Naifeh, Steven Woodward (b. 1952). Writer, publisher, painter, Pulitzer Prize winner. Born in Tehran, Iran, in 1952, Steven Naifeh is the son of George Amel Naifeh, a U.S. diplomat and founder of the American-Arab Affairs Council, and Marion Lanphear Naifeh, an educator. Naifeh graduated summa cum laude from Princeton University before earning both a J.D. and M.A. from Harvard. It was while studying law at Harvard that he met his life partner Gregory White Smith.

Choosing not to pursue a career in law, Naifeh eventually turned to his primary area of interest—art. His first book, *Culture Making: Money, Success, and the New York Art World,* was published in 1976 while he was still pursuing graduate education. That same year he worked as a staff lecturer at the National Gallery of Art in Washington, DC.

When he and Smith decided to pool their talents and collaborate on book projects, one of their first joint efforts was a monograph on the painter Gene Davis (1981); this was followed by a volume entitled *The Bargain Hunter's Guide to Art*

Collecting (1982). During this period when they were turning out largely commercial titles—including some true crime sagas—in order to pay the rent, Naifeh and Smith were devoting most of their free time to research on the life and career of iconic American abstract expressionist painter Jackson Pollock.

After seven years of research, including interviewing 2,500 individuals and examining every authenticated piece of the artist's work that they could find, *Jackson Pollock: An American Saga* was published in 1989. It was nominated for the National Book Award in 1990 and won the Pulitzer Prize in 1991. Most of the critics were impressed by the book's exhaustive research into not only Pollock's life but also the milieu in which he worked, but some questioned the authors' psychological approach to the subject, including their posthumous probing into the nature of Pollock's sexual orientation and other aspects of his interior life. The book was subsequently used as the basis for the film *Pollock* (2000), directed by and starring Ed Harris. For her role as Pollock's wife Lee Krasner, Marcia Gay Harden won an Academy Award for Best Supporting Actress.

The publication of this monumental biography coincided with the authors' relocation from New York City to Aiken, South Carolina, where they purchased Joye Cottage, the sixty-room mansion built in 1897 by tycoon William C. Whitney. The book *On a Street Called Easy, In a Cottage Called Joye* is the often-humorous account of their frequently nonjoyous attempt to renovate and restore the estate, which takes up an entire block in the city's historic district. This impressive property both men have deeded to the Juilliard School in New York City to be used after their deaths as a retreat for performing artists.

Following the success of their first large-scale biography, Naifeh and Smith decided to tackle an individual whose life and work casts an even larger shadow over the world of modern art—Vincent Van Gogh. This time the research and writing took ten years, including unprecedented access to the archives at the Van Gogh Museum in Amsterdam.

The most controversial element of *Van Gogh: The Life* (2011) is the authors' contention that the artist did not commit suicide, which is the accepted version of how he died at the age of thirty-seven, but that he was the victim of an accidental shooting at the hands of careless adolescents. This theory melds two of Naifeh and Smith's greatest strengths as writers, relentless scholarship and a penchant for criminal investigation. For a fuller account of their three true-crime narratives, please refer to the entry for Gregory White Smith.

In addition to their writing careers, Naifeh and Smith have run a publishing firm from their home base. Using each of their middle names to make up the name of the company, they established Woodward/White, Inc., which has published the reference guide *The Best Lawyers in America* since 1982 and *The Best Doctors in America* since 1989.

Naifeh is an avid art collector; he is also a painter in his own right, having exhibited his work in solo shows in this country and abroad. In fact, in 2013, the Columbia Museum of Art hosted a large-scale one-man show entitled "Found in Translation: The Geometric Abstraction of Steven Naifeh," which curator Will Smith hailed as a "smart, vibrant way of encountering Middle Eastern ideas." TOM MACK

Mack, Tom. *Hidden History of Aiken County.* Charleston: The History Press, 2012.
Naifeh, Steven and Gregory White Smith. *On a Street Called Easy, In a Cottage Called Joye.* New York: Little, Brown, 1996.

Nelson, Annie Greene (1902–1993). Novelist, playwright. The first African American woman from South Carolina to publish a novel, Nelson was born in Darlington County on December 5, 1902. She was the eldest of fourteen children born to Sylvester and Nancy Greene; she received her early education at a school on the Parrots' Plantation. Nelson overcame an impoverished childhood and later attended Benedict College and earned a degree in both education and nursing from Voorhees College in 1923. At age eighty, she took courses in drama at the University of South Carolina. She taught school in Darlington and Richland Counties and worked as a nurse for several Columbia area hospitals for almost twenty years.

Nelson's public writing career began in 1925 when her poem "What Do You Think of Mother" was published in the *Palmetto Leader* newspaper. She later wrote three novels: *After the Storm* (1942), *The Dawn Appears* (1944), and *Don't Walk on My Dreams* (1961). All three were reprinted in 1976. *To Paw with Love* is an autobiographical account of her own upbringing. Nelson wrote two plays as well: *Weary Fireside Blues,* produced off-Broadway, and *The Parrots' Plantation.* In the early 1990s, just prior to her death, she worked on her manuscript *Eighty, So What?* This work is imbued with the characteristically optimistic tone for which her writing is known.

Set in her native South Carolina, Nelson's writing typically recounts what life was like for ordinary African Americans of her community. *After the Storm* shows the home lives and customs of black people and their fight for dignity in the midst of deep poverty. Her first novel's success led to *The Dawn Appears,* which, Nelson said, was "affectionately dedicated to the Pee Dee section of South Carolina." This second novel focuses more specifically on the dynamics of white landlords and black workers on a southern plantation. In her 1961 book, *Don't Walk on My Dreams,* Nelson again combines her own experience with that of others within her community whom she knew or about whom she had heard.

Late in her life, Nelson was still an active author, frequently traveling around the state to give readings. She received the Lucy Hampton Bostick Award, an annual recognition given by Friends of the Richland County Public Library. She was

also honored with the P. Scott Kennedy Award for her contributions to African American theater. What Nelson said about one of her novels perhaps explains her writing in general: "If a person is going to write, it must be a compulsion. A book, a story is something that must be written so people can feel it, see it as it unfolds. The plantation life was one of my most favorite subjects—the faith, the struggle, the perseverance. They never gave up—the strict morals—the hard work. That is why I wrote *After the Storm*." Nelson died in Columbia on December 23, 1993.
AMY L. WHITE

Potts, James. "'Letters to Paw' and African American 'Ecriture': The Autobiography of Annie Greene Nelson." *South Carolina Review* 33 (Fall 2000): 63–74.

Nickens, Carrie Allen McCray (1913–2008). Poet, memoirist. Nickens was born on October 4, 1913, in Lynchburg, Virginia, where she spent the first seven years of her life and where she attended the Virginia Seminary Primary School. Her father, William Patterson Allen, was a lawyer; her mother, Mary Rice Hayes Allen, was a college teacher. Nickens numbered as her siblings John, Minnie, Malinda, Gregory, Wilelbert, Hunter, Rosemary, and Dollie, as well as one stillborn child. As the ninth of ten children, Nickens recalled a Virginia childhood filled with the warmth of a close community. When she was seven, the writer's family moved to Montclair, New Jersey, where she attended Spaulding Elementary School, Hillside Junior High, and Montclair High School. She received her bachelor of arts degree from Talladega College in 1935 and her master's degree in social work from New York University in 1955. Nickens's 1940 marriage to Winfield Scott Young, which produced her son and only child, the second Winfield Scott Young, ended in divorce in 1945. Her second marriage, to John H McCray, lasted until his death in 1987. In November of 2007, she married long-time friend, John Nickens. She died on July 25, 2008 at the age of 94; a year later, she was posthumously inducted into the South Carolina Academy of Authors. Since 2009 the Academy has sponsored an annual poetry fellowship in her name.

Asked, in a 1999 interview, what she remembered as the best of her childhood, she pointed to the following: "My seven years in Lynchburg . . . the school there and running down the road to visit our playmates who lived in an old, run-down house, but the warmth within was enveloping. We would sit around an old pot-belly stove eating turnip greens and cornbread and their mama would sing with us and play games. Cracks were stuffed with paper in the sides of the house to keep wind out, but the love there kept us warm." By contrast, she recalled the family's move to New Jersey as edged with unhappiness and fear: "When we moved to Montclair, New Jersey—the threats to put us out of the white neighborhood. I was seven then and my father was receiving frightening calls and was warned about a possible cross-burning."

Despite the early difficulties of the Allen family's life in New Jersey, the parents created a happy home for their children in Montclair. At the same time, they maintained a high level of civic and community involvement on behalf of their immediate family and the larger African American community. Thus, McCray Nickens's childhood became a splendid mix of the eminent and the down-to-earth. James Weldon Johnson and Langston Hughes, among others, were guests in the Allen home.

The tensions of race that had defined the writer's early life continued into her adult years. She is explicit about an experience that occurred in the 1960s, when she travelled to the South with a friend from India to visit the friend's cousin, a student at Auburn University: "While there, he took us to a restaurant he thought I would be accepted in. It turned out to be a frightening experience. They served everyone except me, and when we left, a truckload of men with rifles followed the car. We were saved because a train came. We got through. They didn't."

McCray Nickens was very much aware of the complex demands made upon women in general and upon African American women in particular as she negotiated the demands of motherhood, higher education, and her career in the context of two marriages. Later, she would become aware of similar tensions in her role as a writer and community worker. In 1999 she stated: "As a woman [I've found that] sometimes men still don't listen to us. I found this in a community development organization I belonged to: I mean in meetings, etc. There's still a little hangover of the male superiority. As an African American [I find] there are still some obstacles, although certainly things are much better. I had a wonderful experience with Algonquin Books; however, I've heard many stories from African American writers who have had trouble because publishers want to put us all in one mold—more sex, more drugs, more crime—even when there was none."

Like many women of her generation, Carrie Allen McCray Nickens came to writing relatively late in life, after the obligations of family and career had been met. Nevertheless, her list of publications is substantial, including "Ajös Means Goodbye," published in John A. Williams's *Beyond the Angry Black* (Cooper Square, 1966) where her work is anthologized with that of James Baldwin, Richard Wright, Gwendolyn Brooks, and others. The story was also used in a theater production by Luna Theater, Montclair, New Jersey, and reprinted in an anthology for classroom use published by McDougal, Littel in 1989. Other published works are an article, "The Black Woman and Family Roles" published in *The Black Woman* (Sage Publications, 1980) and the poetry chapbook *Piece of Time* (Chicory Blue Press). Her poems have also appeared in *Ms. Magazine, The River Styx,* Gloria Steinem's book *Moving Beyond Words, The Crimson Edge: Older Women Writing* (Chicory Blue Press), *The South Carolina Collection, Point, Cave Canem I,* and *The Squaw Review.* Her first-person memoir *Freedom's Child: The Life of a Confederate General's Black*

Daughter, devoted to reconstructing her mother's life, was published by Algonquin Books of Chapel Hill in 1998, and her last book, *Ota Benga Under My Mother's Roof,* is a rendering in powerfully moving poetry of the experience of Ota Benga, a Congolese Pygmy once exhibited in the Museum of Natural History in New York and then in the Bronx Zoo, who was taken in by the Allen family in 1910. Her early poems about Ota Benga were featured in performance at the Columbia Museum of Art in 2007.

Always generous to beginning writers, Carrie Allen McCray Nickens consistently urged others, "Write for the joy of writing. Don't be anxious about publishing. It will come. Accept constructive criticism from seasoned authors. It helped me to develop my writing. Don't let anyone discourage you." Ever quick to credit the friendship and influence of other writers, she acknowledged, in particular, contemporary poets Galway Kinnell, Sharon Olds, Lucille Clifton, Susan Ludvigson, Sonia Sanchez, Toi Derricotte, and many of the writers of the Harlem Renaissance. PHEBE DAVIDSON

McCray, Carrie Allen. *Freedom's Child: The Life of a Confederate General's Black Daughter.* Chapel Hill: Algonquin Books, 1998.

———. *Ota Benga Under My Mother's Roof.* Columbia: University of South Carolina Press, 2012.

McCray, Carrie Allen. Personal Interview. 17 May 1999.

Obituary. Columbia *State,* July 28, 2008.

Parish, Margaret Cecile (1927–1988). Children's author. "Peggy" Parish was born in Manning, South Carolina, on July 14, 1927, the daughter of Herman Stanley Parish and Cecile Rogers. She attended Manning public schools and graduated from the University of South Carolina with a degree in English in 1948. Parish also completed graduate work at Peabody College of Vanderbilt University in 1950. She lived briefly in Oklahoma and Kentucky before moving to New York to teach reading and to serve as director of second and third grades at the Dalton School in New York City. While teaching at Dalton, Parish began writing books for children. Her first book, *My Golden Book of Manners,* was published by Golden Pleasure Books in 1962. A second book, *Let's Be Indians,* published in 1963, remained a popular children's book for decades.

International fame for Parish, however, followed the creation and publication of *Amelia Bedelia* in 1964. The title character is a maid who interprets everything literally, leading her to use real sponges to make a sponge cake and to "dress" a turkey in stylish clothes, much to the delight of children all over the world. *Thank You, Amelia Bedelia* (1965) and *Amelia Bedelia and the Surprise Show* (1967) followed. Ultimately, Parish wrote a series of eleven books about Amelia Bedelia and her comic antics, as well as more than thirty other children's books. Her books have sold more than seven million copies and have been translated into many different languages.

In 1972 Parish returned to her hometown, where she continued her writing until her untimely death in 1988. She won a Palmetto State Award, a Garden State Children's Book Award, and a School Library Journal award for *Dinosaur Time* in 1977. Parish also received the Milner Award from the city of Atlanta in 1984 and the Keystone State Children's Book Award from the Commonwealth of Pennsylvania in 1986 for *Teach Us, Amelia Bedelia*. In addition to continuing her writing after returning to Manning, Parish became the children's book reviewer for the *Carolina Today* television show on WIS-TV in Columbia. She also participated in teacher workshops and taught creative writing techniques to elementary school children.

In 1988, to celebrate Amelia Bedelia's twenty-fifth birthday, the publishers Harper and Row and Greenwillow and Avon sponsored celebrations across the nation, encouraging students to send thousands of cards and letters to special mailboxes installed in libraries and bookstores. In August 1988 Parish published *Amelia's Family Album*. Three months later, on November 19, 1988, she died of a ruptured abdominal aneurysm in a Manning hospital. A bronze statue of Amelia Bedelia, commissioned by the citizens of Manning in 1999, stands in front of the Clarendon County Library. Since 1995 the author's nephew Herman Parish has augmented his aunt's legacy by publishing additional adventures featuring her popular character. BARBARA OWENS GOGGANS

Obituary. Columbia *State*, November 20, 1988, D6.

Peterkin, Julia Mood (1880–1961). Novelist, short story writer, Pulitzer Prize winner. Peterkin was born on October 31, 1880, in Laurens County, South Carolina, the youngest daughter of Julius Mood, a schoolteacher, and his wife, Alma Archer. Julius Mood went on to become a doctor and to practice medicine in Sumter. Alma Mood died of tuberculosis when Peterkin was eighteen months old, and Julius Mood soon remarried. Peterkin was sent to live with her paternal grandparents, while her older sisters stayed with their father and his new wife. The loss of her mother and the sense that she had been "given away" would later become a haunting refrain in Peterkin's fiction.

Peterkin graduated from Converse College in 1896 and went on to earn a master's degree from Converse a year later. She taught in a one-room school in Fort Motte; married the cotton planter William George Peterkin on June 3, 1903; and moved to Lang Syne Plantation near St. Matthews, where she would live for the rest of her life. Peterkin had one son, William George Peterkin, Jr., and spent the first twenty years of her marriage trying to fill the archaic role of plantation mistress.

Peterkin did not begin to write until she was forty years old. She began by telling tales of plantation life to her piano teacher, Henry Bellamann, a poet with literary leanings who encouraged her to write them down. Ambition soon led her to approach famous writers and critics, notably Joel Spingarn, Carl Sandburg, and H. L. Mencken, even while secretly taking a correspondence course on magazine writing. Her stories found a home in Emily Clark's new magazine the *Reviewer* and in Mencken's more widely read *Smart Set.* Within two years Peterkin had contracted to publish a book with Alfred A. Knopf, then just beginning to establish a distinguished reputation. The result was *Green Thursday* (1924), a collection of linked short stories about a black farm laborer named Killdee; his wife, Rose; and their foster daughter, Missie. Peterkin drew on what she knew about the lives of real people at Lang Syne, rendering some of them so acutely that the portraits are recognizable to their descendants. Yet the emotional force of many of the tales comes from her own life experience, especially the trauma of losing her mother and growing up apart from her father.

Peterkin's stark, poignant stories about black country folk were among the first flowerings in the movement toward ironic, realistic regional fiction later known as the Southern Renaissance. In 1929 she became the first southern writer to win the Pulitzer Prize for fiction, for the novel *Scarlet Sister Mary* (1928). Two of her books, *Black April* (1927) and *Scarlet Sister Mary,* became bestsellers, and her last, *Roll, Jordan, Roll* (1933), with photographs by her friend Doris Ulmann, was one of the groundbreaking documentaries of the 1930s.

White southerners found Peterkin's early stories offensive and considered her a traitor to her race, though their animosity faded as her celebrity grew. Her mature work gained international fame and was unlike anything that had come before it. Peterkin had the gift of luring mainstream white audiences into what was to them a strange new world: the community of black farm workers who lived by traditions that were largely African in origin. Whites seldom appear in her work, except in trivial roles. Peterkin had a great ear for language and eventually worked out a literary rendering of the difficult Gullah dialect that was true to the cadences and flavor of the original but understandable to ordinary Americans. Her novels were considered racy and subversive, partly for their frank celebration of sex but also because they dared to reveal hard truths about how blacks were forced to live in the Jim Crow South. Taken together, *Green Thursday, Black April, Scarlet Sister Mary,* and *Bright Skin* (1932) chronicle the decline of the plantation economy and the wrenching personal and social forces that drove African Americans to leave the rural South.

Peterkin's stories won high praise from black writers and scholars associated with the Harlem Renaissance, including W. E. B. Du Bois, Walter White, Alain Locke, and Countee Cullen. African American novelists who emerged soon after, including Zora Neale Hurston, show clear signs of Peterkin's influence. During the Depression, Peterkin's fiction fell out of fashion, and it was largely ignored during the 1970s and 1980s, when the works of many other women writers were resurrected and appreciated. Yet her best work has the timeless quality of great literature and seems as fresh and vibrant in the twenty-first century as it did in the 1920s.

Peterkin died in Orangeburg on August 10, 1961, of congestive heart failure. She was buried in the family plot across the street from the Episcopal Church near Fort Motte. In 1988, Peterkin was posthumously inducted into the South Carolina Academy of Authors. SUSAN MILLAR WILLIAMS

Perry, Carolyn, and Mary Louise Weaks, eds. *The History of Southern Women's Literature*. Baton Rouge: Louisiana State University Press, 2002.

Williams, Susan Millar. *A Devil and a Good Woman, Too: The Lives of Julia Peterkin*. Athens: University of Georgia Press, 1997.

Phifer, Mary Hardy (1879–1962). Journalist. Phifer was born in Spartanburg, South Carolina, on August 25, 1879, the daughter of Washington Hardy and Rebecca Carson. Both parents died when she was a toddler, so she was raised by her grandmother, an aunt, and an uncle. She attended Converse College, graduating in 1898. After teaching school for a year, she married the Spartanburg hardware store owner Moulton Phifer in July 1899. The couple had seven children. Phifer was an active member of Spartanburg's Episcopal Church of the Advent.

Once all her children were enrolled in school, Phifer became a journalist. She began as society editor for the Spartanburg *Herald,* a position she held for nearly twenty years. She continued to write a weekly column for the paper well into the 1950s. She also worked as a freelance journalist, interviewing literary figures for *Holland's Magazine* and writing gardening articles for various other magazines, including *House Beautiful.*

In the 1930s the Phifers moved to a farm in a rural section of southern Spartanburg County, where Mary Phifer developed a large garden. Eventually she opened a cannery to produce her own peach sauce, which was marketed at specialty stores in New York City and around the country. The business closed during World War II due to a shortage of labor and sugar.

During World War II, a Spartan Mills executive asked her to edit its new employee newsletter, entitled the *Beaumont E.* She also produced a series of radio programs during the war. "Miss Mary" became famous among the Beaumont mill operatives for her lively interviews with workers and her "Phiferisms," the morale-boosting aphorisms she published in the newsletter. Among them was one that described her own philosophy: "I am an old lady who has looked at life a long time, and has learned that happiness dwells most securely with those who work. Taking it by and large working people are the happiest people in the world."

Phifer retired at the end of the war and devoted her time to gardening, canning, weaving, and her family. In 1951 Converse College awarded her its Mary Mildred

Sullivan Award for her service to the community. Throughout her retirement Phifer continued to write and to speak to community groups. She published her own memoir and a biography of South Carolina bishop Kirkman George Finley. She was also elected an honorary member of Delta Kappa Gamma, an organization of women educators. Phifer died at her home near Clifton on February 20, 1962, and was buried at Greenlawn Memorial Gardens. MELISSA WALKER

Dodge, Susan. "Mary Hardy Phifer." In *The Lives They Lived: A Look at Women in the History of Spartanburg County*. Edited by Linda Powers Bilanchone. Spartanburg, S.C.: Spartanburg Sesquicentennial Focus on Women Committee, 1981.

Pinckney, Josephine (1895–1957). Poet, novelist, civic leader. Josephine Pinckney was born on January 25, 1895, in Charleston, South Carolina, into a family long prominent in the state's history. She was a direct descendant of Eliza Lucas Pinckney and Governor Thomas Pinckney. Her parents were Thomas Pinckney, one of South Carolina's last great rice planters, and Camilla Scott of Virginia. In 1912 she graduated from Ashley Hall School, where she helped establish a literary magazine, and later attended the College of Charleston, Radcliffe College, and Columbia University. She received an honorary degree from the College of Charleston in 1935 and was named an honorary member of the William and Mary Chapter of Phi Beta Kappa in 1934. She received numerous honors for her writing, including the Southern Authors Award in 1946.

Pinckney played a key role in the literary revival that swept through the South after World War I. She worked closely with DuBose Heyward, Hervey Allen, and John Bennett in founding the Poetry Society of South Carolina in 1920. During the following decade, Pinckney emerged as a poet of national reputation when her work, often evocative eulogies to a vanishing way of southern life, appeared in influential journals such as the *Saturday Review of Literature* and *Poetry*, as well as in numerous anthologies. Her only book of poems, *Sea-Drinking Cities* (1927), received praise from Donald Davidson for "a luxuriance of phrase, a quiet humor controlling deep emotion."

Pinckney participated in other aspects of the Charleston Renaissance through her dedicated involvement in local cultural institutions, such as the Carolina Art Association, the Charleston Museum, and Dock Street Theatre. Active in the Society for the Preservation of Spirituals from its inception in 1922, Pinckney helped with the transcriptions and musical annotations for the African American songs included in *The Carolina Lowcountry* (1931). She also worked quietly behind the scenes of the historic preservation movement in Charleston and was posthumously honored by the American Scenic and Historic Preservation Society for the manner in which she "tactfully and persuasively, firmly and wisely" helped to restore the city's neighborhoods and notable buildings.

During the 1930s Pinckney embraced a modernist sensibility and turned her writing talents to prose. The *Virginia Quarterly Review* published her two short stories "They Shall Return as Strangers" (1934) and "The Marchant of London and the Treacherous Don" (1936). Her essay "Bulwarks against Change," which appeared in *Culture in the South,* edited by W. T. Couch (1934), remains an insightful commentary on the evolving South. In 1941 Pinckney published her first novel, *Hilton Head,* followed by the bestselling social comedy *Three O'Clock Dinner* (1945), which made her one of America's best-known women fiction writers. Her third novel, *Great Mischief* (1948), a Book-of-the-Month Club selection, was followed by *My Son and Foe* (1952) and *Splendid in Ashes* (1958). Her editor at Viking Press remembered Pinckney "more warmly" than any other of his distinguished writers of the day for the "charm and grace of her character, the intelligence of her insights into people, the delights of her Charleston ambiance tempered by her cosmopolitan ways and her irony."

Although Pinckney traveled widely, she maintained a home in Charleston and her family plantation on the Santee River, El Dorado. Josephine Pinckney died on October 4, 1957, and was buried in Magnolia Cemetery, Charleston. In 1988, she was posthumously inducted into the South Carolina Academy of Authors. BARBARA L. BELLOWS

Kibler, James E., Jr. "Josephine Pinckney." In *Dictionary of Literary Biography.* Vol. 6. *American Novelists since World War II, Second Series.* Edited by James E. Kibler, Jr. Detroit: Gale, 1980.

Pinckney, Josephine. Papers. South Carolina Historical Society, Charleston.

———. *Three O'Clock Dinner.* 1945. Reprint, Columbia: University of South Carolina Press, 2001.

Shippey, Herbert P. "Josephine Pinckney." In *South Carolina Women Writers.* Edited by James B. Meriwether. Spartanburg, S.C.: Reprint Company, 1979.

Powell, Padgett (b. 1952). Novelist, educator. Padgett Powell was born on April 25, 1952, in Gainesville, Florida, the son of Betty Palmer Powell and John Padgett Powell. When he was a child, he moved with his family to South Carolina. Powell earned a degree in chemistry from the College of Charleston and a master of fine arts degree from the University of Houston, where he studied with the noted American writer Donald Barthelme. He also attended the University of Tennessee as a graduate student in chemistry.

His debut novel, *Edisto* (1984), was nominated for a National Book Award and was excerpted in the *New Yorker.* In the same year he joined the English department of the University of Florida as a professor of creative writing, a position he continues to hold. *Edisto* is a coming-of-age novel set on the coast of South

Carolina. Walker Percy praised *Edisto* as "a truly remarkable first novel, both as a narrative and in its extraordinary use of language. It reminds one of *Catcher in the Rye*, but it's better—sharper, funnier, more poignant." Later in his career, Powell returned to the coast of South Carolina for the setting of *Edisto Revisited* (1996), which continues the protagonist's story into adulthood.

Since 1984, Powell has written eight novels and collections of short stories. His early fiction is set in the newly urbanized South and peopled with recognizable southern characters. In these works, the New South is seen to be largely dehumanizing, sterile, and banal, burdened with meaningless traditions and lacking clear directions for the future. Powell's second novel, *A Woman Named Drown* (1986), follows the career of a man, a failed graduate student, who discovers the emptiness of what could be called the middle class life. His crisis is mirrored in the lives of unanchored people who share his condition.

Beginning with *Typical* (1991), a story collection, and continuing into his most recent publications, Powell's writing has veered away from traditional literary models and grows increasingly experimental. As is true of many contemporary southern writers, Powell wants to avoid the label of "regional" writer by experimenting with new modes of setting, character exposition, and thematic arrangement. His book entitled *Interrogative Mood: A Novel?* (2009) is composed of sets of questions, questions that add up to what is definitely not a traditional novel. Novelist Josh Emmons characterized this volume as "a remarkable collection of philosophical inquiries, stimulating either/ors and good faith attempts to measure who we are as a species and where we belong."

Powell's 2011 book, *You and Me*, a dramatic dialogue, owes its form to *Waiting for Godot*. He introduces the book with this description: "Two worldly agreeable dudes are on a porch in a not upscale neighborhood, apparently within walking distance of a liquor store, talking a lot." The two men discuss aging, marriage, children, holidays, drinking, the general human condition in the world, and a host of philosophical questions. Their language is distinctly American, often distinctly southern, but no place or time is identified. *You and Me* received the James Tait Black Memorial Prize in 2011.

Powell's short fiction has been widely published. His short stories have appeared in the *New Yorker*, the *Paris Review*, *Harper's*, *Grand Street*, *Oxford American*, and in other literary journals and magazines. The beginnings of his experimental fiction first appeared in his short stories. For his work, Powell has received the Whiting Writers' Award and the Rome Fellowship in Literature from the American Academy of Arts and Letters. CHARLES ISRAEL

Abernathy, Jeff. *To Hell and Back: Race and Betrayal in the Southern Novel.* Athens: University of Georgia Press, 2003.

O'Gorman, Farrell. "Language of Mystery: Walker Percy's Legacy in Contemporary Southern Fiction." *Southern Literary Journal.* Spring, 2002.

Vice, Brad. "Padgett Powell." *Dictionary of Literary Biography.* Vol. 234. *American Short Story Writers Since World War II, Third Series.* Detroit: Gale, 2001.

Ward, Alex. "A Better Class of Fools: Interview with Padgett Powell." *New York Times Magazine.* 7 June 1987.

Pringle, Elizabeth Allston (1845–1921). Nonfiction author, rice planter. Pringle was born on May 29, 1845, on Pawleys Island, South Carolina, at her family's summer home at Canaan Seashore. Her parents were Robert Francis Withers Allston and Adele Petigru. Her father, a state legislator and governor, owned 630 slaves and more than fourteen hundred acres planted in rice or covered by timber. The Allstons' home, Chicora Wood, was situated by the Pee Dee River near Georgetown. A governess tutored Pringle until she was nine, when she was sent to Madame Acelie Togno's Charleston boarding school.

The Civil War disrupted Pringle's education. She sought shelter in various places. After her father died in 1864, Pringle endured economic hardships because he had mortgaged most of his possessions. She taught in a Charleston boarding school her mother established until her dower's rights to Chicora Wood were legally recognized and the Allston family members were reinstated in their home. She married her neighbor John Julius Pringle on April 26, 1870, and they lived at nearby White House. The couple's only son died as an infant, and in 1876 Pringle's husband succumbed to malaria.

By 1880 Pringle was able to buy her home and fields from her husband's family, and she later acquired Chicora Wood after her mother's death in 1896. Pringle relied on the premise that her land would yield profitable rice crops in order to pay her mortgages and taxes. She wanted her family to regain its prestige and affluence lost during the Civil War, and she persevered to overcome obstacles in a largely patriarchal society. Her brother and other men questioned Pringle's ability because she lacked agricultural experience. With minimal assistance from family and friends, Pringle oversaw both farms, utilized scientific agricultural methods, and decided to plant fruits such as peaches and to rent property to hunters to supplement her income. She refused to sell her land.

Desperate because rice production in the lowcountry faced decreased profits, Pringle convinced the *New York Sun* editor to buy weekly articles she wrote about being a female rice-plantation owner. Under the pseudonym "Patience Pennington," Pringle's essays were printed from 1904 to 1907. In 1913 her articles were collected in a single volume, *A Woman Rice Planter.* Pringle edited her previous pieces to resemble a diary, with vignettes that describe plantation life from a sentimental, aristocratic point of view that is often patronizing and racist. She included insightful details about African American folk life, white-black relationships, and racial attitudes. As the book's narrator, Pringle subtly criticizes contemporary popular opinion that southern women should be passive.

Pringle's bestselling book eased her financial worries. By 1920 she began writing another book to tell about her childhood and how women fared during the Civil War and Reconstruction. She died on December 5, 1921, at her family home and was buried in Magnolia Cemetery. Her manuscript was published posthumously the next year. Like her first book, *Chronicles of Chicora Wood* depicts an aristocratic view, which gives the impression that white southerners heroically endured traumatic social changes and, incorrectly, assumes that slaves enjoyed their servitude. In 1994 Pringle was posthumously inducted into the South Carolina Academy of Authors. ELIZABETH D. SCHAFER

Blythe, Anne Montague. "Elizabeth Allston Pringle's 'The Woman Rice Planter': The New York Sun Letters, 1903–1912." Ph.D. diss., University of South Carolina, 1987.
Pringle, Elizabeth Allston. *Chronicles of Chicora Wood.* New York: Scribner's, 1922.
———. *A Woman Rice Planter.* 1913. Reprint, Columbia: University of South Carolina Press, 1992.

Quillen, Robert (1887–1948). Newspaper publisher, editor, columnist. Hailed as "the Sage of Fountain Inn" by the highly influential critic Alexander Woolcott, Quillen used the files of the *Fountain Inn Tribune* to take his anecdotes and opinions of daily life in small-town, upstate South Carolina to an international audience. The Mark Twain or Garrison Keillor of his day, Quillen developed a widely accepted reputation as an authentic voice of village life, and his words were reprinted in *Collier's*, the *Saturday Evening Post*, the *Literary Digest*, and many similar publications. At the height of its syndication, Quillen material could be found in more than four hundred newspapers published in North America and Europe with a combined circulation of more than twelve million.

Born in Syracuse, Kansas, Verni Robert Quillen grew up in Overbrook (population 273), a village near Topeka where his printer father, J.D. Quillen, was publisher of the *Overbrook Citizen*. Quillen, one of four children, attended local schools and in January 1914 produced the first issue of *Vox Populi*, an ambitious semi-monthly magazine filled with articles, drawings, and cryptic sayings that would become his trademark: "diplomat: a liar who draws a salary for it"; "physician: a scientific guesser"; and "crank: a person who persists in telling the truth."

Then, two months later, shortly before his seventeenth birthday, this budding writer raised his right hand before a U.S. Army recruiting officer in Omaha, Nebraska, swore he was twenty-one years of age, and signed the name of "William Stewart" to documents placed before him. Although he sometimes referred casually to his military career—apparently sparked by an affair of the heart gone sour—Quillen never produced a full explanation and obviously was somewhat embarrassed by this incident. After a few months in the Philippines, his superiors realized—perhaps because of protests lodged by his father—that an error had been made. By January 1905 his real name appeared on military records, and six months later he was a civilian once more.

Released from the army in the northeastern United States, Quillen spent the next few months working on various newspapers in that region. Then, early in 1906, he answered an advertisement seeking an editor for a weekly newspaper that a Belton, South Carolina publisher planned to launch in Fountain Inn, seventeen miles south of Greenville. This rural market town, equidistant from Greenville and Laurens and named for a small inn near a spring that once catered to weary stage coach travelers, then harbored misplaced hopes of becoming the capital of a new county.

Quillen's initial association with the community that eventually would become his home lasted only ninety days, just long enough for him to win the heart of a local girl, Donnie Cox, a milliner in her mid-twenties, whose father's shop adjoined the newspaper office. Dissatisfied with his new job, Quillen moved to a printing house in Americus, Georgia, where the young couple was united in wedlock. Two months later, he published his first issue of the *Americus Christian*, an eight-page monthly that he shepherded into print until moving with his bride to Washington state where the rest of his family was busy producing weeklies in the Puget Sound area. With Quillen's arrival, a new monthly entitled *Love One Another* was added to the list along with a Swedish dialect column "The Observations of Knute Olafson."

Meanwhile, back in Fountain Inn, Donnie's brother, Ford Todd Cox, had become co-owner of *News and Notions*, a local weekly. An opportunity to buy this paper outright, coupled with bleak prospects in the Northwest, led to a fateful decision. In December 1910, Robert Quillen, having dispensed with his first name and borrowed two hundred dollars, headed east where he proceeded to transform *News and Notions* into the *Fountain Inn Tribune*. Two years later, while urging subscribers to settle their accounts, Quillen said that he had gone "busted" in the West, was still in debt, and needed their help.

Transformation soon ensued. *News and Notions* gave way in February 1911 to a well-organized publication overflowing with news of the local community. An editorial on small-town life published three months later caught the attention of *Collier's*, which eventually led to a national column, "Small Town Stuff."

During these years, Quillen's personal life was a roller coaster of highs and lows. Unable to have children of their own, he and his wife adopted "Louise," who would be immortalized in numerous columns. Then Donnie Quillen suddenly died following a routine operation, and in December 1922, Robert married yet another local girl, Marcelle Babb. Although syndicate work continued, he sold the *Tribune* and turned his attention to two novels published by Macmillan, neither of which sold well.

In the spring of 1925, aware that he really needed his work on the *Tribune* as fodder for his syndicate work, Quillen bought back the weekly and eventually established firm ties with a publishing group based in Chicago. Except for 1929, files of the *Tribune* are complete from 1928 to the time of his death in 1948.

Quillen eventually realized that he needed Fountain Inn, but this did not keep him from dreaming of expanding his sphere of influence. Despite his failure as a novelist and magazine publisher, he kept his sense of humor and somehow came to grips with the cards that life had dealt him. After all, being known as the best "paragrapher" of his day was no mean accolade. In 2014 Quillen was posthumously inducted into the South Carolina Academy of Authors. JOHN HAMMOND MOORE

Moore, John Hammond. *The Voice of Small-Town America: The Selected Writings of Robert Quillen, 1920–1948*. Columbia: University of South Carolina Press, 2008.

Rash, Ron (b. 1953). Poet, novelist. Rash was born in Chester, South Carolina, on September 23, 1953, the son of James Hubert Rash and Sue Holder. He earned a B.A. in English at Gardner-Webb College in North Carolina and then received his M.A. in English from Clemson University. He has taught writing and literature at Tri-County Technical College in Pendleton and in the master of fine arts program at Queens University in Charlotte, North Carolina. In 2003 he was named John A. Parris, Jr. and Dorothy Luxton Parris Distinguished Professor in Appalachian Cultural Studies at Western Carolina University in Cullowhee, North Carolina.

Rash's family has lived in the southern Appalachian Mountains and in the Piedmont of the Carolinas since the mid-1700s. He uses the agrarian life in the mountains as a main theme in much of his poetry and fiction, showing the humor and tragedy of farm people struggling against the vagaries of weather and unstable farm prices on isolated, hardscrabble patches of land. Rash's third book of poems, *Raising the Dead* (2002), and his novel, *One Foot in Eden* (2002), take as their central theme the plight of mountain people who are about to be displaced from their family lands by the waters of a lake built by an electric power company. Generations of people tied to ancestral soil undergo the anxieties of removal into the textile mill towns of the Piedmont.

These mill towns serve as the locales for three of Rash's books: his first book of stories, *The Night the New Jesus Fell to Earth and Other Stories from Cliffside, North Carolina* (1994); his book of stories *Casualties* (2000); and his book of poems *Eureka Mill* (1998). These poems and stories center on the lives of those who have left their mountain homes in search of stable wages and security in the mills. All too often they find hardship and poverty instead.

His novels *Saints at the River* (2004) and *The World Made Straight* (2006) are set in contemporary Appalachia. His fourth novel, *Serena* (2008), returns to the Appalachia of the first decades of the twentieth century. Serena and her husband are the rapacious and murderous owners of a lumber company. They are determined to deforest the mountains before the U.S. Congress can establish the Smoky Mountains National Park. *Serena* is now being made into a movie. Rash's fifth novel, *The Cove* (2011), is set in the mountains at the time of World War I.

Rash considers himself an Appalachian writer, and his published work typically uses the mountains as a setting. However, his major literary themes and concerns are universal: the nature of evil in human beings, the incessant struggle for certitude despite the chaos of existence, and the tragedy of unfulfilled lives. In an interview, Rash has pointed to a central feature of his fiction and poetry: themes of the topical and temporary (creation of manmade lakes, the deforestation of mountains) are contrasted to the themes of the permanence of nature, as in "a blade of grass or a waterfall" that have universal and timeless appeal. Also central to his work is a vast array of literary influences: Shakespeare, Sophocles, ancient Welsh poetry, Faulkner, Chaucer, and James Dickey, to name a few.

Ron Rash has received the Academy of American Poets Prize, the South Carolina Academy of Authors Poetry Award, the National Endowment for the Arts Poetry Fellowship, the Sherwood Anderson Award, the O'Henry Prize, the Southern Book Critics Award, and the Frank O'Connor International Short Story Award, among others. In 2010 he was inducted into the South Carolina Academy of Authors.
CHARLES ISRAEL

Bjerre, Thomas. "Ron Rash's *One Foot in Eden.*" *Still in Print: The Southern Novel Today.* Ed. Jan Nordby Gretlund. Columbia: University of South Carolina Press, 2010.
Lane, John. "The Girl in the River: The Wild and Scenic Chattooga, Ron Rash's *Saints at the River,* and the Drowning of Rachel Trois." *South Carolina Review* 41 (Fall 2008): 162.
Lang, John, ed. Ron Rash issue. *Iron Mountain Review* 20 (Spring 2004).

Ravenel, Beatrice Witte (1870–1956). Poet, journalist. Born in Charleston, South Carolina, on August 24, 1870, Beatrice Ravenel was one of six daughters of Charlotte Sophia Reeves of Charleston and Charles Otto Witte of Hanover, Germany. She and her sisters, who married into many elite lowcountry families, grew up in the mansion which was subsequently turned into the private girls' school Ashley Hall. Finishing her education at Miss Kelly's School in Charleston, Ravenel entered the Harvard Annex (later Radcliffe College) as a special student in 1889. She studied for three years, left, and then returned in 1895 for two more years. During that period, she published a few short stories and poems and was considered a bright intellect, equal to many of the men at Harvard.

Forsaking the promise of an independent life in the North, Beatrice Witte returned to Charleston and in 1900 married Francis Gualdo Ravenel, son of Mrs. St. Julien Ravenel, author of the classic *Charleston: The Place and the People* (1906). Francis Ravenel invested much of his wife's inheritance, lost it, and died in 1920, leaving her to care for their daughter, also named Beatrice (later the author of *Architects of Charleston*). Turning to writing to support herself, Beatrice Ravenel produced poetry, some of it splendid, and short stories, mostly derivative and plot-heavy, although one, "The High Cost of Conscience," was published in the first volume of the *O. Henry Memorial Short Stories.*

Ravenel is possibly the best example of the influence of the Poetry Society of South Carolina on local writers; its founding in the year of her husband's death brought her into a poetry-conscious environment. Here she met the poet Amy Lowell when the latter lectured in Charleston in 1922. Lowell and the Imagist school were strong influences on Ravenel, prompting great changes in her work, which Lowell encouraged and championed. The poetry that Ravenel wrote in the 1920s reveals a broad intellectual outlook and a warm sensual glow. She wrote of outsiders and the dispossessed, such as the Yamassee Indians who lost their land to the whites, and a young actress, soon to die, musing on her young son. The latter, "Poe's Mother," was her most reprinted work and shows her difference from other Charleston poets, who often celebrated local lore, while Ravenel examined subtle subconscious states and philosophic points. This was perhaps due to her having been a student of William James, George Santayana, George Baker, and others.

In 1919 Ravenel also began to write editorials, mostly on foreign affairs, and reviews for her brother-in-law William Watts Ball, editor of the Columbia *State.* Her one volume of poems, *The Arrow of Lightning,* came out in 1925, with Ravenel paying part of the cost. She married Samuel Prioleau Ravenel, a distant cousin of her first husband, in 1926 and, no longer needing to support herself, slowed her production. She traveled widely and still wrote arresting and sensual lyrics, which were not published in her lifetime. Ravenel died on March 15, 1956, and was buried in Charleston's Magnolia Cemetery, all but forgotten. In 1969 a book of her poems, edited by the Charlestonian Louis Rubin, was published, and in the ensuing years scholars and critics began to claim her as the best poet of the Charleston Literary Renaissance and the author of some excellent individual works. In 1995, Ravenel was posthumously inducted into the South Carolina Academy of Authors. HARLAN GREENE

Heyward, DuBose. "Beatrice Ravenel." In *The Library of Southern Literature,* supplement 1, edited by Edwin Anderson Alderman and Charles Alphonso Smith. Atlanta, Ga.: Martin and Hoyt, 1923.

"Mrs. S. Prioleau Ravenel, Author and Poet, Dies." *Charleston Evening Post,* March 15, 1956, A2.

Rubin, Louis. *The Yemassee Lands: Poems of Beatrice Ravenel.* Chapel Hill: University of North Carolina Press, 1969.

Ravenel, Harriott Horry Rutledge (1832–1912). Novelist, biographer, historian. Ravenel was born on August 12, 1832, in Charleston, South Carolina, the daughter of Edward Cotesworth Rutledge and Rebecca Motte Lowndes. In her youth, she received private tutoring at her home in Charleston and attended Madame Talvande's prestigious female academy. On March 20, 1851, she married a prominent physician, St. Julien Ravenel, with whom she would have nine children. During the Civil War her husband oversaw a Confederate hospital and medical laboratory, and she accompanied him to Columbia. While her husband was away on Confederate business, Ravenel resisted Sherman's soldiers and protected her home from fire, prompting Mary Chesnut to write in her diary, "Mrs. St. Julien . . . actually awed the Yankees into civil behavior." Ravenel's brief memoir, "When Columbia Burned," was presented as a speech to the Daughters of the Confederacy and appeared several years later in *South Carolina Women in the Confederacy.*

Though she wrote poetry, brief essays, and stories on other subjects, Ravenel's major works focused on southern history and manners. Her most successful piece of fiction, *Ashurst; or "The Days That Are Not,"* fondly depicted antebellum lifestyles and landscapes. The novelette was featured as the prize story in the Charleston *Weekly News* under the pen name Mrs. H. Hilton Broom before being published in book form in 1879. Ravenel's other major works were born of her interest in preserving state and family history. A descendant of the statesmen John Rutledge and politician William Lowndes and a relative of the famed Charles Cotesworth Pinckney, Ravenel drew on her "intimate knowledge of family history and traditions" as well as letters, journals, and archives to shape her writings.

In 1896, as part of a national series entitled "Women of Colonial and Revolutionary Times," Ravenel published a brief biography, *Eliza Pinckney,* to preserve the achievements of her great-great-grandmother. Five years later she published *Life and Times of William Lowndes of South Carolina, 1782–1822* as a tribute to her maternal grandfather, who served in Congress with John Calhoun and Langdon Cheves. Her final work, *Charleston: The Place and the People,* appeared in 1906, tracing the history of her native city from its lively colonial past to the Civil War era. While Ravenel's works received many favorable contemporary reviews, her books were also noted for reflecting a "sympathetic interest" and "uncritical" perspective. Ravenel observed the difficulty of writing history that held such deeply personal meaning for the author. In her recollection of Columbia's burning, for example, she humbly offered her vantage point as one of many that sought to contribute "a real and correct picture in true and perfect proportions." Characterized as "a great lady of the Old South," Ravenel worked devotedly on her last publication even while in feeble health. She died in Charleston on July 2, 1912, and was buried in Magnolia Cemetery. SANDRA BARRETT MOORE

Ravenel, Harriott Horry. *Ashurst; or, "The Days That Are Not": The Prize Story from the Charleston Weekly News.* Charleston: News and Courier Book Presses, 1879.

———. *Charleston: The Place and the People.* New York: Macmillan, 1906.

———. Papers. South Carolina Historical Society, Charleston.

———. "When Columbia Burned." In *South Carolina Women in the Confederacy.* Edited by Mrs. Thomas Taylor. Vol. 1. Columbia: State Company, 1903.

Rees, Ennis (1925–2009). Poet, literary critic, translator, children's author. Ennis Samuel Rees, Jr. was born on March 17, 1925, in Newport, Virginia, to Ennis Samuel and Dorothy Drumwright Rees. He received his A.B. from the College of William and Mary in 1946, where he was a member of Phi Beta Kappa and Omicron Delta Kappa and where he received the Botetourt Medal for distinguished scholarship. The same year he married Marion Ensor Lott. Also in 1946, near the end of World War II, Rees served his country in the U.S. Army. By 1948 he received his M.A. and in 1951 his Ph.D. in comparative literature, both from Harvard. From 1949 until 1952, Rees was an English instructor at Duke University, and he taught at Princeton from 1952 until 1954. For the next thirty-four years Rees served as a professor of English at the University of South Carolina in Columbia where he raised his three children and retired in 1988. In 1984 Rees was nominated the Poet Laureate of South Carolina.

In 1954 Rees's book-length analysis, *The Tragedies of George Chapman: Renaissance Ethics in Action,* was published. The collected essays draw critical attention to George Chapman's tragic plays. In the introduction, Rees suggests that Chapman divided his tragic heroes into either active or contemplative characters to emphasize and complicate his moral and aesthetic beliefs. Rees ultimately suggests that Chapman's plays are underappreciated works of literature with strong moralistic and philosophical intentions.

Rees published his lyrical translation of *The Odyssey of Homer* in 1960 to critical acclaim, and three years later his translation of *The Iliad of Homer* was published. Although in the introduction of *The Odyssey* he acknowledges multiple thematic aspects of the poem that might be brought out in translation, Rees also expresses his dedication to creating readable stories that use natural diction, syntax, and a loose iambic pentameter.

In 1964 Rees saw the publication of *Riddles, Riddles Everywhere,* a book of popular riddles based on stories in American and English folklore that Rees places in rhyming verse quatrains characterized by wordplay and a sense of humor. That same year Rees published another children's book in free verse, *The Song of Paul Bunyan and Tony Beaver*, which transforms into verse the exploits of the fabled northern logger, Paul Bunyan, and his southern counterpart, logger Tony Beaver. In a 1986 interview Rees labeled the story as "comic heroic, not mock heroic."

Also in 1964, Rees's first collection of original poems was published by the University of South Carolina Press. Entitled simply *Poems*, the book contains verse that reveals an overall optimistic outlook on life, celebrating the everyday, and also experiments with formal concerns such as meter and rhyme.

Rees published *Pun Fun* in 1965, a book of rhymes adapted from English and American folklore, and the next year he published a verse translation of *Fables from Aesop*, illustrated by J.J. Granville. Over the next several years, Rees saw the publication of numerous children's books, including *Windwagon Smith* (1966), *Tiny Tall Tales* (1967), *Teeny Tiny Duck and the Pretty Money* (1967). *Brer Rabbit and His Tricks* (1967), *The Little Greek Alphabet Book* (1968), *Gillygaloos and Gollywhoppers* (1969), and *Potato Talk* (1969). These books are all characterized by a lyrical sense of whimsy, a fascination with southern folk stories, and strong moral lessons. In 1971 he published a follow-up to *Fables of Aesop* entitled *Lions and Lobsters and Foxes and Frogs: Fables from Aesop*, written in rhyming verse and illustrated by playfully macabre artist Edward Gorey. Many of Rees's children's books have become classics of the genre and are among his bestselling works.

In 1973 the University of South Carolina Press released his *Selected Poems*, which contains most of the pieces from his first collection along with newer works that exhibit a looseness of form and embrace the absurdity of the human condition. The collection also includes large excerpts from his translations of *The Odyssey* and *Aesop's Fables* and two long dream-based poems, "Daze" and "Snakes and Butterflies," which attempt to touch on archetypal concerns and avoid the stylistic conventions of contemporary poetry. In regards to his own verse, Rees once said, "All my poems have South Carolina settings, even if they are not specifically mentioned." Due to an economic downturn in publishing in the late 1970s, Rees continued writing but had trouble finding publishers for his work until Boyd Mills Press published *Fast Freddie Frog and Other Tongue Twister Rhymes* in 1993.

In 1999 Ennis Rees was awarded recognition for his literary contributions by being inducted into the South Carolina Academy of Authors. He counted his influences as Homer, Chaucer, Emerson, and Whitman. All of his writing—his children's books, his various translations, and his own poetry—is notable for its uncomplicated diction, sense of optimism, humor, and wordplay. ROY SEEGER

"Ennis (Samuel) Rees, (Jr.)." *Contemporary Authors Online.* Detroit: Gale, 2001.

Swanson, Gayle R. and William B. Thesing. *Conversations with South Carolina Poets.* Winston-Salem, N.C.: John F. Blair, Publishing. 1986. 73–98.

Rice, John Andrew, Jr. (1888–1968). Memoirist, short story writer, educator. A prominent figure in higher education in the United States, Rice was born at Tanglewood Plantation in Lynchburg in Lee County, South Carolina, on February 1, 1888. He was the eldest son of John Andrew Rice, a Methodist minister, and Anna Bell Smith, the sister of U.S. Senator Ellison D. "Cotton Ed" Smith.

During Rice's early childhood, his family lived in several South Carolina towns as his father moved from one Methodist congregation to another, finally securing the presidency of Columbia Female College in 1894. After his mother died in 1899, Rice lived with relatives near Varnville in Colleton County. He left South Carolina in 1905, when his stepmother, Launa Darnell Rice, urged him to attend the Webb School, a highly regarded preparatory academy in Bell Buckle, Tennessee.

After graduating with a B.A. from Tulane University in 1911, Rice won a Rhodes Scholarship to study abroad. He graduated from Oxford University with first honors in jurisprudence in 1914 and in the same year married Nell Aydelotte. They had two children. He later attended the University of Chicago but left before completing his Ph.D. in classical Greek and Latin philosophy and language. During a succession of faculty appointments, Rice developed a reputation as an expert classics scholar and brilliant Socratic teacher. He also became known as critical and candid, railing openly at the administration of his own institutions and others. In widely published articles, he chastised American higher education for teaching unconnected course subjects with pedagogy that still emphasized lecture and response.

In 1933 Rice first gained nationwide attention when the demand for his resignation from Rollins College sparked a highly publicized investigation by the American Association of University Professors (AAUP). Although the AAUP exonerated Rice and censured Rollins, Rice had already made plans to start Black Mountain College, near Asheville, North Carolina. Black Mountain became a renowned site of experimental and progressive education, especially known for Rice's commitment to experiential learning, artistic expression in support of learning in any discipline, democratic governance among faculty and students, and the absence of outside trustees. As founder and first rector of the college, Rice recruited faculty talent that included Josef and Anni Albers, Buckminster Fuller, and Dante Fiorello. Other visitors who frequented the classrooms included John Dewey, Thornton Wilder, Aldous Huxley, Henry Miller, and Marcel Breuer.

Rice, ever unable to check his stinging candor, left Black Mountain College in 1940 at the insistence of his colleagues. He divorced and returned to South Carolina and began a second career in writing with his memoir, *I Came Out of the Eighteenth Century* (1942). With his second wife, Dikka Moen, and their two children, he lived in the Charleston area from 1945 to 1948, writing short stories for the *New Yorker, Collier's*, the *Saturday Evening Post,* and other periodicals, largely on themes about life and race relations in the South. These appeared in anthologies and were collected as *Local Color* (1955). Later, Rice and his family moved to Maryland, where he died on November 17, 1968. KATHERINE REYNOLDS CHADDOCK

Duberman, Martin. *Black Mountain: An Exploration in Community*. New York: Dutton, 1972.

Reynolds, Katherine C. *Visions and Vanities: John Andrew Rice of Black Mountain College*. Baton Rouge: Louisiana State University Press, 1998.

Rice, John Andrew. *I Came Out of the Eighteenth Century*. New York: Harper and Brothers, 1942.

Richardson, Eudora Ramsay (1891–1973). Feminist author and lecturer, educator. Born in Versailles, Kentucky, on August 13, 1891, Richardson was the daughter of the Reverend David Marshall Ramsay and Mary Woolfolk. She grew up in Charleston, South Carolina, and Richmond, Virginia, where her father held pastorates at leading Baptist churches. She received bachelor's degrees from Hollins College and the University of Richmond (1911) and an M.A. degree from Columbia University (1914).

From 1912 to 1914 Richardson headed the English department at the Greenville Female College (renamed the Greenville Woman's College in 1914), a South Carolina institution for which her father served as president from 1911 to 1930. Popular as a teacher, Richardson named the literary societies that played a significant part of campus life. She also became noted for her promotion of women's suffrage, with her stated goal at the Greenville Woman's College being to educate "girls who are staunch advocates of women's rights." Such a view was perhaps shocking to some but was accepted with good grace at the conservative Baptist institution, which would merge with the all-male Furman University during the Great Depression.

Leaving the Greenville Woman's College in 1914, Richardson embarked on a three-year speaking career as field director of the National American Woman Suffrage Association. She worked closely with the suffragist Carrie Chapman Catt. She met her future husband, Fitzhugh Briggs Richardson of Richmond, while campaigning for votes for women. The couple married on December 13, 1917. The union produced one daughter, Eudora (Dolly).

During much of her married life, Richardson devoted herself to lecturing and writing. In the 1920s she spoke frequently at the Greenville Woman's College, became affiliated with the Southern Women's Educational Alliance, and served as president of the Richmond branch of the American Association of University Women. She published *Little Aleck; A Life of Alexander H. Stephens* (1932), *The Woman Speaker; A Handbook and Study Course on Public Speaking* (1936), and *The Influence of Men—Incurable* (1936). In much of her speaking and writing, Richardson's goal was to further her feminist agenda and to have women taken seriously as political leaders, community activists, and employees. She opposed protective legislation, seeing it as an attempt to take away from women the legal equality they had fought so long and hard to achieve.

In 1938 Richardson was selected to serve as director of the Federal Writers' Project in Virginia and the state supervisor of the Virginia Writers' Project. Her efforts led to a variety of publications, including *Virginia; A Guide to the Old Dominion* (1940) and *The Negro in Virginia* (1940). When her agency was abolished in 1943, Richardson found employment as a writer for the Quartermaster Technical Training Service at Camp Lee, Virginia. She retired in 1950 with a meritorious service commendation.

After retirement, Richardson continued to write and remained dedicated to her feminist views. Critical of the "women's lib" movement of the early 1970s, she stated in an interview, "Not too much has changed since we got the vote. . . . We were effective but they're not accomplishing anything much now." She died in Richmond, Virginia, on October 6, 1973, and was buried in Hollywood Cemetery.
MARIAN ELIZABETH STROBEL

Garner, Anita M. "Richmond's Own Eudora." *Richmond Quarterly* 7 (Winter 1984): 15–19.
Martin-Perdue, Nancy J., and Charles L. Perdue. *Talk about Trouble: A New Deal Portrait of Virginians in the Great Depression*. Chapel Hill: University of North Carolina Press, 1996.
Richardson, Eudora Ramsay. Papers. Special Collections Department, Alderman Memorial Library, University of Virginia, Charlottesville.
"What Happened to . . . Eudora R. Richardson." *Richmond Times-Dispatch*, July 12, 1971.

Rigney, James Oliver, Jr. (1948–2007). Novelist, critic. Rigney was born in Charleston, South Carolina, on 17 October 1948, the second of three sons to James Oliver and Eva May Rigney (nee Grooms). His father, a World War II veteran, worked for a time as a policeman before he became a hand and then supervisor at the Charleston Naval Shipyard. He consistently worked odd jobs on the side to provide for his blue-collar, Baptist family. When he was four years old, James Oliver Rigney, Jr. taught himself to read with the incidental aid of a twelve-years-older brother who failed to finish a book that he was reading to his younger sibling. By the time he was five, Rigney was tackling Mark Twain and Jules Verne on his own. He remained an avid reader for the rest of his life—his library held over 14,000 books when he died.

Recruited to play football at Clemson, Rigney attended the university for a year before he volunteered for enlistment in the U.S. Army. From 1968 to 1970 he served two tours in Vietnam with the 68th Assault Helicopter Company, aka the Top Tigers, of the 145th Combat Aviation Battalion, 12th Aviation Group, 1st Aviation Brigade. Originally assigned to a clerical role in Vietnam due to his intellect, Rigney managed to use his position to get himself posted as a helicopter door gunner. He would leave Vietnam with a Distinguished Flying Cross with Oak Leaf Cluster, a Bronze Star with "V," and two Vietnamese Crosses of Gallantry with Palm.

Returning to the United States, Rigney studied at the Citadel under the veteran's program, graduating in 1974 with a degree in physics. He then joined the U.S. Navy (civil service) as a nuclear engineer, writing test procedures for the overhaul of nuclear submarines. In 1977 an accidental fall from a submarine at the Charleston Naval Yard shattered his leg and knee. Postsurgical difficulties nearly killed him, and he would use a cane for much of the rest of his life. Rigney turned to writing as a way of passing his lengthy recovery time, and he composed his first (and still unpublished) fantasy novel, *Warriors of the Altaii,* in thirteen days.

A year later, still recovering, Rigney told a Charleston bookshop owner that he was writing a "bodice-ripper" novel, and the owner passed this information to poet Harriet McDougal (nee Popham), an experienced editor for New York publisher Tor/Forge who was starting her own imprint. She left her card with the bookshop owner, who ultimately gave it to Rigney; on her encouragement he wrote a novel of historical fiction, *The Fallon Blood,* which was edited by McDougal and published by her Popham Press in 1980 under the pseudonym Reagan O'Neal. Rigney began dating McDougal soon afterward, and the two were married in March of 1981, around the same time that his second novel, *The Fallon Pride* was published by Tor/Forge. A third installment (*The Fallon Legacy*) followed in 1982, which also saw him publish the novel *Cheyenne Raiders,* this time under the name Jackson O'Reilly. McDougal continued to serve as his editor, as she would for the rest of his career. They lived in Charleston in a house built around 1797 that was praised by the writer H.P. Lovecraft in his published walking tour of the city.

Rigney returned to writing fantasy novels, now publishing under the name Robert Jordan. From 1982 to 1984 he completed seven novels reinvigorating the classic character of Conan the Barbarian: *Conan the Invincible* (1982), *Conan the Defender* (1982), *Conan the Unconquered* (1983), *Conan the Triumphant* (1983), *Conan the Magnificent* (1984), *Conan the Destroyer* (1984), and *Conan the Victorious* (1984). During this same period, he also wrote dance and theater criticism under the name Chang Lung, for a variety of publications including *Library Journal, Fantasy Review,* and *Science Fiction Review.*

Already a popular author, Rigney became an international bestselling phenomenon with his next fantasy series, The Wheel of Time, which began with the publication of *The Eye of the World* in 1990 (as Robert Jordan), the first of a planned six books. Subsequent volumes in this series (and works related to it) appeared with regularity over the next fifteen years, outstripping the original six-book vision as the scope of the project grew: *The Great Hunt* (1990), *The Dragon Reborn* (1991), *The Shadow Rising* (1992), *The Fires of Heaven* (1993), *Lord of Chaos* (1994, a Locus Award Nominee), *A Crown of Swords* (1996), *The World of Robert Jordan's The Wheel of Time* (1997, with Teresa Patterson), *The Path of Daggers* (1998), *A New Spring* (1998, a novella), *Winter's Heart* (2000), *Crossroads of Twilight* (2003), *A New Spring* (2004), and *Knife of Dreams* (2005). For his accumulated publication successes and his lifetime of service, he was awarded an honorary doctorate of literature from the Citadel in 1999.

In March of 2006, Rigney announced in a letter to *Locus* that he had been diagnosed with amyloidosis. That fall the Citadel established the James O. Rigney, Jr. Award for Creative Writing to be given annually in his honor. A far greater honor came when it was announced that he had earned a place in the South Carolina Academy of Authors.

Rigney lost his battle to amyloidosis on September 16, 2007. He was posthumously inducted into the South Carolina Academy of Authors in 2008. After his death, his wife and editor selected the author Brandon Sanderson to complete the still-unfinished Wheel of Time series, for which Rigney had left copious instructions and materials, including plot outlines, drafted chapters, and the completed ending. The final three volumes thus appeared as works of co-authorship: *The Gathering Storm* (2009), *Towers of Midnight* (2010), and *A Memory of Light* (2013).

Rigney's work has been favorably compared to that of J.R.R. Tolkien. Edward Rothstein, reviewing one of his novels for the *New York Times,* opined that he "has come to dominate the world Tolkien began to reveal." At his death he had sold more than thirty million books, and they had been translated into more than twenty languages. Rigney's greatest success is undoubtedly the monumental Wheel of Time series, which is known for its multi-dimensional characters, intricately realized plotting, grandly epic scale, and complex usage of mythological and historical sources. MICHAEL LIVINGSTON

Fox, Margalit. "James O. Rigney, Jr., Who Wrote as Robert Jordan, Dies at 58." *New York Times* 18 Sept. 2007.

Lilley, Ernest. "SFRevu Interview: Robert Jordan." *SFRevu* (Jan. 2003).

Rothstein, Edward. "Flaming Swords and Wizards' Orbs." *The New York Times,* December 8, 1996.

Ripley, Alexandra Braid (1934–2004). Novelist. Ripley was born in Charleston, South Carolina, on January 8, 1934, the daughter of Alexander and Elizabeth Braid. After graduating from Ashley Hall, she attended Vassar College on a United Daughters of the Confederacy scholarship. After earning a B.A. in Russian in 1955, Ripley worked a succession of jobs, living in New York City, Washington, D.C., and Florence, Italy. In 1963 she returned to Charleston, where she held various positions from travel agent to tour guide to ghost writer. She returned to New York and began working in publishing and then moved to Virginia in the early 1970s to pursue a writing career. Ripley published her first historical novel, *Charleston,* in 1981 while working at a bookstore. She followed with a sequel, *On Leaving Charleston* (1984), and then two more works of historical fiction, *The Time Returns* (1985) and *New Orleans Legacy* (1987), the latter of which became a Literary Guild alternative and a Reader's Digest Condensed Book selection.

In 1986 Ripley was chosen to write a sequel to Margaret Mitchell's Pulitzer Prize–winning classic, *Gone With the Wind* (1936), by Mitchell's estate. In 1988 Warner Books successfully bid $4,940,000 for the publishing rights. On September 25, 1991, *Scarlett: The Sequel to Margaret Mitchell's Gone With the Wind* appeared in bookstores. It spent sixteen weeks on the *New York Times* bestseller list, selling two million copies by the end of the year. The book follows Scarlett O'Hara Hamilton Kennedy Butler as she makes her way from Charleston to Savannah, Georgia, and finally to Ireland, where she restores her ancestral estate, raises her daughter, joins an insurrectionist movement, and marries an English earl before finally reuniting with Rhett Butler. Despite the heady sales figures and intense, if brief, popularity of *Scarlett,* reviewers uniformly panned the book. Ripley shrugged off the criticism, however, and continued to write after the hoopla over *Scarlett* subsided. She published two more historical novels, *From Fields of Gold* (1994) and *A Love Divine* (1996), which were both well received.

Ripley was married to Leonard Ripley from 1958 until their divorce in 1963. In 1981 she married John Graham, a rhetoric professor at the University of Virginia. Ripley had two daughters from her first marriage. She died at her home in Richmond, Virginia, on January 10, 2004. R. F. STALVEY

Ripley, Clements (1892–1954), and **Katharine Ball** (1898–1955). Novelists, short story and nonfiction writers. "Believe it or not, the Ripleys—Clements and Katharine —are Charleston's most prolific and best known national authors," asserted the *Charleston Evening Post* on September 5, 1949. Between 1923 and 1953 the couple published ten books—including novels and memoirs—and dozens of short stories and nonfiction pieces. Furthermore, they became successful collaborative screenwriters during the 1930s and 1940s, traveling between Charleston and Hollywood to fulfill contract obligations under Clements's name. In a letter of February 17, 1940, Ripley wrote Louis F. Edelman, his contact man at Warner Brothers Pictures: "You must realize that anybody who deals with me is getting the services of two trained writers—my wife and myself."

Born on August 26, 1892, in Tacoma, Washington, Clements "Clem" Ripley was the son of the offspring of two old Vermont families, Thomas Emerson Ripley and Charlotte Howard Clement. Katharine "Kattie" Ball Ripley, the daughter of the legendary newspaperman William Watts Ball and Fay Witte, was born in Charleston, South Carolina, on March 20, 1898. Clem was educated at the Taft School at

Watertown, Connecticut, and graduated from Yale in 1916. Kattie attended Chatham Episcopal Institute (Virginia), where in 1914 she saw her work published in the school's student literary journal. They met while Clem was stationed as an army officer during World War I at Camp Jackson, near Columbia. They were married in 1919. Their son, William Y. "Warren" Ripley, was born in 1921.

In the early 1920s Clem resigned his commission and, with a $30,000 advance on his inheritance, invested in a hundred acres in the sandhills of North Carolina, where for seven years he and Kattie tried their hands at peach farming (the subject of her first book, *Sand in My Shoes,* 1931). In order to augment the farm income, Clem also tried his hand at writing, selling a story for $110 in 1922. By 1927, when they decided to give up the farm, Clem had sold his novel *Dust and Sun* to *Adventure* for $3,000. From 1924 to 1953 his adventure yarns and action tales—as either serialized novels, novelettes, or short stories—appeared in magazines and newspapers across the nation. In addition to *Dust and Sun* (1929), Clem published six other novels: *Devil Drums* (1930), *Black Moon* (1933), *Murder Walks Alone* (1935), *Gold Is Where You Find It* (1936), *Clear for Action* (1940), and *Mississippi Belle* (1942).

In 1932 the *Atlantic Monthly* published three of Kattie's stories. Her second book, *Sand Dollars* (1933), was a memoir written out of the experience of the stock market crash. In 1936 Doubleday Doran published her novel of modern Charleston manners, *Crowded House.* DuBose Heyward, remarking on its universality, wrote: "There is such a family in every community inviting at once our contempt and our sympathy. It is a tribute to Mrs. Ripley's sure characterizations that we think of them with an anger that has become positively a pleasure."

During his Hollywood years, Clem worked as a contract writer, producing scenarios of his own writings or adapting the works of others for the screen. His story "Voodoo Moon," released in 1934 under the title *Black Moon,* starred Jack Holt and Fay Wray. *Gold Is Where You Find It,* a vehicle for George Brent and Olivia de Havilland, was released by Warner Brothers in 1938. *Love, Honor, and Behave,* based on writing by Stephen Vincent Benet, appeared in 1936, and *Buffalo Bill,* an adaptation of a story by Frank Winch, in 1944. Clem also received top billing for the screen adaptation of Owen Davis's play *Jezebel* (1938), for which Bette Davis won an Academy Award.

Clements Ripley died in Charleston on July 22, 1954, and Katharine Ball Ripley died on July 24, 1955. Both are buried in Magnolia Cemetery. In 1990 Warren Ripley published a paperback selection of his parents' short fiction entitled *Cities of Fear and Other Adventure Stories.* Five years later Down Home Press published a paperback edition of Kattie's first nonfiction book, *Sand in My Shoes,* as one in its Carolina Classics series; she was posthumously inducted into the South Carolina Academy of Authors in 1998. THOMAS L. JOHNSON

Ripley, Clements, and Katharine Ball Ripley. Papers. South Caroliniana Library, University of South Carolina, Columbia.

Robertson, Benjamin Franklin, Jr. (1903–1943). Journalist, memoirist. Ben Robertson was born on June 22, 1903, in Clemson, South Carolina. His father, a member of the first graduating class of Clemson College, was a chemist for the Agricultural Extension Service. His mother, Mary Bowen, died when he was ten years old, and his stepmother, Hattie Boggs, died in the 1918 influenza pandemic. Robertson was a respected and well-traveled journalist and war correspondent and the author of three books, including a memoir of his youth in the South Carolina upcountry.

After graduating in 1923 from Clemson, where he edited the student newspaper, Robertson attended the School of Journalism at the University of Missouri and, after a year with the Charleston *News and Courier,* took his second bachelor's degree in 1926. That same year he landed a job with the *Honolulu Star-Bulletin,* leaving soon afterward to write for the *News* in Adelaide, Australia. After a few months with the U.S. Consulate in Java, he returned home to South Carolina by way of India and Europe.

In 1929 Robertson became a reporter for the *New York Herald-Tribune.* He moved to Washington, D.C., in 1934 to cover the New Deal for the Associated Press but resigned after two years. He then returned to Pickens County to write a novel. *Travelers' Rest,* published privately in 1938, was neither a critical nor a popular success, and Robertson went back to journalism, covering South Carolina politics for the *Anderson Independent.* In 1940 he was hired by *PM,* an innovative left-liberal newspaper published by the former *Fortune* editor Ralph Ingersoll, as its London correspondent during the Battle of Britain. During a two-month furlough in early 1941, he wrote *I Saw England,* a well-received account of British resolve in the face of constant bombardment by the German Luftwaffe that reached a wide audience after being condensed by *Reader's Digest.*

After another stint in London, Robertson returned to Clemson in August 1941 and began work on *Red Hills and Cotton: An Upcountry Memory,* which he finished in January 1942. A celebration of Scots-Irish folkways and the agrarian lifestyle, *Red Hills and Cotton* evokes a simpler time in rural South Carolina through a nostalgic portrayal of several generations of Robertson kin. While proudly asserting his heritage—"Honor is at the base of our personal attitude toward life"—he also looks to the future: "The South is our South and it must progress." An outspoken, if idiosyncratic, liberal during the 1930s, Robertson, who once said, "What we need is a man with the heart and mind of Jefferson and the tactics of Huey Long," may have softened his politics in *Red Hills and Cotton* in anticipation of a run for public office.

Over the course of 1942 Robertson covered World War II from Libya, the Soviet Union, and India for *PM*. In January 1943 he was hired again by the *New York Herald-Tribune*, this time to run its London Bureau. He never made it back to England. On February 22, 1943, the flying boat *Yankee Clipper* crashed into the Tagus River on its approach to Lisbon, Portugal, killing Robertson at the age of thirty-nine. His remains were returned to South Carolina and buried in the family burial plot near Liberty in Pickens County. The Liberty Ship SS *Ben Robertson* was launched in Savannah, Georgia, in January 1944 and supported the invasion of Normandy later that year. Robertson was posthumously inducted into the South Carolina Academy of Authors in 1992. HUGH DAVIS

Ford, Lacy K., Jr. "The Affable Journalist as Social Critic: Ben Robertson and the Early Twentieth-Century South." *Southern Cultures* 2 (Winter 1996): 353–73.

Robertson, Ben. *Red Hills and Cotton: An Upcountry Memory.* 1942. Reprint, Columbia: University of South Carolina Press, 1991.

Robinson, Eugene (b. 1955). Author, journalist, columnist, Pulitzer Prize winner. The son of Louisa Smith Robinson, a librarian at Claflin College, and Harold I. Robinson, an attorney and occasional professor of political science, Robinson was born in Orangeburg, South Carolina. He grew up in a two-story clapboard house built by his great grandfather, Major John Hammond Fordham. He attended Trinity Methodist Church and studied at Felton Training School (later Felton Laboratory School) on the campus of South Carolina State University. In 1967 Robinson began the tenth grade at Orangeburg High School, becoming one of a handful of black students enrolled in the school only a few years after desegregation.

Several months into Robinson's first year at Orangeburg High School, black students from Claflin College and South Carolina State were refused entrance into All-Star Lanes, a whites-only bowling alley. The event sparked protests. Governor Robert McNair blamed "outside agitators," and police focused attention on Cleveland Sellers, a Denmark, South Carolina native and organizer for the Student Nonviolent Coordinating Committee (SNCC), who was staying a few houses down the street from the Robinson home. Robinson looked on as a dozen police cars parked outside of his home, the officers' rifles aimed at the house down the street.

Robinson has called that moment "the first time [he] felt vulnerable" and "an awakening"; he has claimed that he no longer could think of "race as something [he] could just ignore.... The question was how to deal with it: how to cut it down to size, how to keep it in perspective, how to keep from being crushed by it. How to live with it." Three days later, police opened fire on a group of protesting students, killing three, in an event that would later be dubbed "The Orangeburg Massacre."

Robinson attended the University of Michigan in Ann Arbor, planning to study architecture. During his first architecture course, however, he recognized that he was "easily the most incompetent" student in the class. In the meantime, he won a student literary competition with an essay about the killings in Orangeburg. Predictably, he changed his academic focus to journalism. He wrote for the student newspaper, *The Michigan Daily*, all fours years of college, eventually becoming the first black student to be coeditor-in-chief.

Robinson began his journalism career at the *San Francisco Chronicle* where he covered the trial of newspaper heiress Patty Hearst. While living in the Haight-Ashbury District of San Francisco, he met his future wife, Avis, originally from Silver Spring, Maryland, who was in San Francisco completing postgraduate work.

In 1980 Robinson moved to Arlington, Virginia, to begin work at the *Washington Post* as a reporter covering city hall. He was named assistant city editor in 1981 and city editor in 1984. From 1988 to 1992, he was the *Washington Post*'s South American correspondent, based in Buenos Aires, Argentina. He was named the London bureau chief from 1992 to 1994 before returning to Washington to become the newspaper's foreign editor. He was promoted to assistant managing editor in 1999 and managed the "Style" section of the newspaper. He became a regular columnist in 2005, eventually writing a twice-a-week column that reflects on the relationships between politics and culture. He also hosts a weekly online chat session.

During his tenure in Buenos Aires, Robinson spent time in Brazil—time that eventually led to the material for his first book, *Coal to Cream: A Black Man's Journey beyond Color to an Affirmation of Race*, published in 1999. The *New York Times* described the book as a model for discussions of race. Simultaneously a memoir and a manifesto, *Coal to Cream* reflects on Brazilians' fascination with the broad spectrum of skin color in the context of Robinson's own experience in a world of two distinct races, both in the United States and elsewhere. In 2004 Robinson penned *Last Dance in Havana: The Final Days of Fidel Castro and the Start of the New Cuban Revolution*, in which the author anticipates a post-Castro Cuba and notes the embedded role that music and dance play in Cuban culture and politics.

Throughout the 2008 Democratic presidential primaries and, later, the presidential campaign, Robinson focused many of his newspaper columns on the rise of Barack Obama. Drawing on historical context and personal reflection, Robinson's coverage of the Obama campaign provided a fresh perspective on race and politics while steadfastly avoiding the politics of identity. The columns earned Robinson a 2009 Pulitzer Prize for commentary.

Several of the columns cited for the 2009 Pulitzer Prize may have laid the foundation for Robinson's 2010 book, *Disintegration: The Splintering of Black America*. In *Disintegration*, Robinson frames his discussion of contemporary black America by first identifying four discrete groups of black Americans: the Transcendent, the Mainstream, the Emergent, and the Abandoned. Robinson argues that the different interests and claims of each group must be acknowledged in order to respond with any success to the rapidly deteriorating plight of the Abandoned. The *New York Times* commented on the book's ability to "tell us something familiar . . . in such a creative and clear-eyed way and with such force that we begin to see things differently."

Robinson is a regular guest on television shows that focus on political commentary, including *The Rachel Maddow Show, Hardball with Chris Matthews, Morning Joe,* and *Meet the Press.* He was inducted into the South Carolina Academy of Authors in 2013. Eugene Robinson and his wife Avis are the parents of two sons: Aaron and Lowell. They live in Arlington, Virginia. KARL FORNES

Arsenault, Raymond. "The Great Unravelling." *New York Times.* December 29, 2010.

Bass, Jack. "Documenting the Orangeburg Massacre." Nieman Reports. The Nieman Foundation, February, 2003.

Robinson, Eugene. *Coal to Cream: A Black Man's Journey Beyond Color to an Affirmation of Race.* New York: Simon & Schuster, 1999.

———. *Disintegration: The Splintering of Black America.* New York: Anchor Books, 2011.

———. *Last Dance in Havana.* New York: Simon & Schuster, 2004.

Walton, Anthony. "Another Country." *New York Times,* September 12, 1999.

Rogers, George Calvin, Jr. (1922–1997). Historian, editor, educator. Rogers was born on June 15, 1922, in Charleston, South Carolina, the son of George Calvin Rogers, a school administrator, and Helen Bean. He attended the Craft School and the High School of Charleston. After receiving an A.B. degree from the College of Charleston in 1943, Rogers enlisted in the army and served during World War II as a meteorologist. His tour of duty in Great Britain nurtured his interest in the study of history. After his discharge, Rogers enrolled in the University of Chicago to study American and British history. He earned an M.A. degree in 1948 and a doctorate in history in 1953. His interest in and affection for English culture influenced his choice of research topics throughout his life.

Rogers began teaching at the University of Pennsylvania in 1953. In 1958 he joined the history department of the University of South Carolina (USC), where he remained for the rest of his career. Rogers's first book, *Evolution of a Federalist: William Loughton Smith of Charleston (1758–1812),* published in 1962, was a biography of a prominent South Carolina planter-politician. This study demonstrated Rogers's knowledge of political biography, elite culture, and the politics of the new American nation, subjects that informed his life's work. In 1965 he joined a documentary editing project, the *Papers of Henry Laurens,* which was sponsored by the South Carolina Historical Society and housed at the USC history department. From 1971 to 1981 Rogers was chief editor, and the project published nine volumes of Laurens's letters, business papers, and political records. In addition to the Laurens volumes, Rogers published *Charleston in the Age of the Pinckneys* in 1969.

His *History of Georgetown County, South Carolina* (1970) was the first modern history of a South Carolina county. It received an award for merit from the American Association of State and Local History and has been a model for other county histories. In addition to these and other books, Rogers published more than forty articles, essays, and introductions. The *South Carolina Historical Magazine* was his main vehicle of scholarly publication. He published twelve articles in the magazine and was its editor from 1965 to 1970. One of his articles, "Names Not Numbers," published in a 1988 issue of the *William and Mary Quarterly,* voiced his lifelong scholarly interest in personalities and events and admonished historians not to neglect the human and idiosyncratic elements of their subjects in favor of statistics and thesis-driven studies.

Rogers was a distinguished teacher and administrator. He was chair of the USC history department from 1983 to 1986 and served on the boards of the South Carolina Tricentennial Commission, the South Carolina Archives and History Commission, and the South Carolina Historical Society. Rogers retired from USC in 1986 and continued to write and publish on South Carolina history for another decade. He was awarded an honorary doctor of letters from the College of Charleston, was a member of the American Antiquarian Society, and in 1997 was inducted into the South Carolina Academy of Authors. He died on October 7, 1997, and was buried in Charleston's Magnolia Cemetery, the resting place of the South Carolina historians William Gilmore Simms, William James Rivers, Yates Snowden, and Anna Wells Rutledge. ALEXANDER MOORE

Chesnutt, David R., and Clyde N. Wilson, Jr., eds. *The Meaning of South Carolina History: Essays in Honor of George C. Rogers, Jr.* Columbia: University of South Carolina Press, 1991.

Obituary. Charleston *Post and Courier,* October 9, 1997, B1, B6.

————. *Journal of Southern History* 64 (February 1998): 187–88.

Rubin, Louis D., Jr. (b. 1923). Novelist, nonfiction writer, editor, publisher, educator. Rubin was born in Charleston, South Carolina, on November 19, 1923, the son of Louis D. Rubin, an electrical contractor, and his wife, Janet Weinstein. He was a third-generation Charlestonian, his grandfather Hyman having immigrated to the city from Russia in 1886. Rubin would live his first nineteen years in Charleston, attending the College of Charleston from 1940 to 1942. He never resided permanently in the city after 1942; but he would return to it for setting and inspiration in his novels *The Golden Weather* (1961), *Surfaces of a Diamond* (1981), and *The Heat of the Sun* (1995), and in evocative nonfictional works such as *Small Craft Advisory* (1991), *Seaports of the South* (1998), and *My Father's People* (2002).

After serving in the United States Army during World War II, Rubin received his B.A. in history from the University of Richmond in 1946, and he went on to earn a Ph.D. in the aesthetics of literature from Johns Hopkins in 1954. He was an instructor in English and editor of the *Hopkins Review* from 1950 to 1954 and assistant professor of American civilization at the University of Pennsylvania from 1954 to 1956. During the years Rubin pursued his graduate studies, he also worked in newspapers as an editor and staff writer, and from 1956 to 1957 he served as associate editor of the Richmond, Virginia, *News-Leader.* Years later he would publish a vivid account of these work experiences in *An Honorable Estate: My Time in the Working Press* (2001).

In 1957 Rubin turned permanently to teaching. For ten years he served on the faculty of Hollins College in Virginia. At Hollins he chaired the English department, taught the future writers Annie Dillard and Lee Smith, and continued his impressive scholarship and editing with works such as *Southern Renascence* (1953) and *Thomas Wolfe: The Weather of His Youth* (1955). In 1967 he joined the English faculty at the University of North Carolina at Chapel Hill. He taught at North Carolina for twenty-two years, guiding students and future teachers of southern literature and culture; mentoring noted southern writers such as Clyde Edgerton, Jill McCorkle, and Kaye Gibbons; and continuing an impressive academic career that would result in his authoring or editing more than fifty books. He retired from teaching in 1989 and continued to live in Chapel Hill with his wife, Eva Redfield Rubin, whom he married on June 2, 1951.

Rubin left teaching in order to concentrate all of his energies on Algonquin Books of Chapel Hill, a press that he had founded in 1983 to encourage talented young writers. By any measure, Rubin's publishing house has been an impressive success, launching the careers of McCorkle and Edgerton as well as Larry Brown, Dori Sanders, and many other authors.

Rubin's distinguished career as teacher, scholar, editor, and novelist has brought him numerous awards and honors, including honorary degrees from the University of Richmond, the College of Charleston, and Clemson University. He was named to the South Carolina Academy of Authors in 1987 and received the North Carolina Award for Literature and the R. Hunt Parker Memorial Award for his lifetime contributions to the literary heritage of North Carolina. These distinctions are appropriate for a man who during the course of a long and extraordinarily productive career has acquired, in the words of the critic Leonard Rogoff, "a cultural mantle . . . as Dean of Southern Literature." RITCHIE DEVON WATSON

Weaver, Teresa K. "Southern Fiction's Father Figure." *Atlanta Journal-Constitution*, December 29, 2002, M1–M3.

Rutledge, Archibald (1883–1973). Poet, memoirist. Rutledge was born in McClellanville, South Carolina, on October 23, 1883, the son of Henry Middleton Rutledge III, an army officer, and Margaret Hamilton. Descended from a lineage of notable South Carolinians, Rutledge included among his ancestors John Rutledge,

Edward Rutledge, Arthur Middleton, Charles Cotesworth Pinckney, and Thomas Pinckney.

Rutledge grew up in Georgetown County at Hampton Plantation, built in 1730 on a two-thousand-acre tract secured by his Huguenot ancestor Daniel Horry in 1686. Rutledge claimed that had it not been for his parents' insistence that he obtain an education, he might never have left the Santee River delta. In 1900 he graduated as salutatorian from Porter Military Academy in Charleston and was subsequently packed off to Union College in Schenectady, New York, where he earned both bachelor's (1904) and master's (1907) degrees. For nearly thirty-two years Rutledge headed the English department at Mercersburg Academy, a college preparatory school in south-central Pennsylvania. On December 19, 1907, he married Florence Hart, who died in 1934. She was the mother of his three sons. In 1936 Rutledge married Alice Lucas.

Rutledge began publishing poetry in 1907, but he did not earn recognition until 1918, when his memoir of youth, *Tom and I on the Old Plantation,* was published. While teaching, Rutledge published many books, poems, and articles in national magazines, including the *Saturday Evening Post* and *Good Housekeeping.* In 1934 the South Carolina General Assembly named Rutledge the state's first poet laureate, an honor he held for the remainder of his life.

As the title of his 1918 memoir suggests, Rutledge took life at Hampton as his literary subject, but to his national audience he spoke as the ambassador for an increasingly anachronistic Deep South. When treating the abundant natural beauty and wildlife of the Santee River delta, Rutledge crafted lyrical, engaging prose, but his homespun depictions of "my black henchmen" and their "happy blending with the plantation landscape" reflected what one colleague described as his "unreconstructed views on white supremacy." Rutledge wore the mantle of planter paternalism, a habit of mind mirrored in his alternate reverence and ridicule of the black men and women he "inherited" at Hampton. *Home by the River* (1941) and *God's Children* (1947) are particularly noteworthy for this tendency, which Rutledge discussed under the rubric of "dusky dilemmas."

Rutledge retired from Mercersburg Academy in 1937 and returned to Hampton, which he had inherited from his father in 1923. With the help of the plantation's black laborers, he lovingly restored the house and grounds, which once had played host to Francis Marion and George Washington. Rutledge died on September 15, 1973, at Little Hampton, his home in McClellanville. He is buried with his sons Archibald Jr. and Henry Middleton at Hampton Plantation, which he bequeathed to the state of South Carolina. Located sixteen miles south of Georgetown on U.S. Highway 17, it is open to the public as Hampton Plantation State Historic Site. In 1999, Rutledge was posthumously inducted into the South Carolina Academy of Authors. ELIZABETH ROBESON

Casada, Jim. *Hunting and Home in the Southern Heartland: The Best of Archibald Rutledge.* Columbia: University of South Carolina Press, 1992.

Rutledge, Archibald. *Home by the River.* Indianapolis: Bobbs-Merrill, 1941.

Wheeler, Mary B., and Genon H. Neblett. *Hidden Glory: The Life and Times of Hampton Plantation, Legend of the South Santee.* Nashville: Rutledge Hill, 1983.

Sanders, Dori (b. Dorinda (Sua) Watsee, 1934). Novelist, farmer. Dori Sanders was born in Filbert, York County, South Carolina, on June 8, 1934, the eighth of ten children born to Marion Sylvester Sanders, a rural elementary school principal and landowner, and his wife, Cazetta Sylvia Patton. The novelist's middle name reflects the Native American heritage of her paternal grandmother. During her childhood Sanders saw herself as an underachiever in the family but also as its most popular storyteller. Her family's more than two-hundred-acre farm, where fourteen varieties of peaches are grown, is one of the oldest African American-owned farms in York County.

Sanders attended Fairview Elementary School in Filbert and Roosevelt High School in Clover, South Carolina. For about a year in the early 1950s, she attended community colleges in Prince George's and Montgomery Counties in Maryland. She married in 1956; the marriage did not end officially until 1989. During the winter months she worked, especially when crops had failed, as an associate banquet manager in Camp Springs, near Andrews Air Force Base, and did some of her early writing there. During the growing season she was still helping farm the family land in the early twenty-first century, and in the summer she often helped staff Sanders' Peach Shed, an open-air produce stand on U.S. Highway 321.

After years of farming, Sanders tried writing, but her first literary effort, a Gothic romance about sharecroppers, was considered too melodramatic by Louis D. Rubin, Jr., her later publisher, and was not accepted for publication. Her first published novel, *Clover* (1990), gave a child's-eye view of racial differences in a fictional South Carolina town in the 1980s. When her father dies only hours after his interracial wedding, Clover is left with a white stepmother. The novel shows how stepmother and child are met with resentment by both races, but it also suggests that people can overcome the racial barriers of the rural and small-town South. The perceptive ten-year-old black girl resolves cultural and racial crises in the lives of several people. The lyrical and insightful novel drew rave reviews, stayed on the *Washington Post* bestseller list for ten weeks, and won the coveted Lillian Smith Book Award. Sanders's second novel, *Her Own Place* (1993), has an indomitable African American heroine who is abandoned by her husband, learns about life as a single mother of five children, works her own South Carolina farm, and copes with things as they come. Sanders's direct approach to the changing racial and gender situation did not disappoint. *Her Own Place: A Novel* was reprinted in

2013 by USC Press in the Southern Revival Series, with a new introduction by the author.

Sanders also published *Dori Sanders' Country Cooking: Recipes and Stories from the Family Stand* (1995), a cookbook and storybook. On Interstate 85 southwest of Charlotte, North Carolina, this book was advertised on a fourteen-foot, hand-painted roadside billboard showing her likeness marketing "Fine Produce and Books." On September 10, 1997, Sanders was awarded the Order of the Palmetto for her creative writing by Governor David Beasley. On the same date a movie version of *Clover* by USA Pictures TV was first aired. Sanders was inducted into the South Carolina Academy of Authors in 2000. JAN NORDBY GRETLUND

Odlum, Kalisha. "Sanders, Dori." *Literature, The New Encyclopedia of Southern Culture*, Vol. 9. Edited by M Thomas Inge. Chapel Hill: University of North Carolina Press, 2008. 409–10.

Powell, Dannye Romine. *Parting the Curtains: Interviews with Southern Writers*. Winston-Salem, N.C.: John F. Blair, 1994.

Sanders, Dori. "'After Freedom'—Blacks and Whites in the 1990s: The Facts and the Fiction." In *The Southern State of Mind*. Edited by Jan Nordby Gretlund. Columbia: University of South Carolina Press, 1999.

Tate, Linda. *A Southern Weave of Women: Fiction of the Contemporary South*. Athens: University of Georgia Press, 1994.

Sass, Herbert Ravenel (1884–1958). Journalist, novelist, nonfiction writer, naturalist. Sass was born in Charleston, South Carolina, on November 2, 1884, the son of the poet George Herbert Sass and Anna Ravenel, daughter of Dr. and Mrs. St. Julien Ravenel. His grandfather was the creator of submarines for the Confederacy, and his grandmother was the author of the classic *Charleston: The Place and the People*. Taking his inheritance seriously and rarely leaving the city, Sass graduated from the College of Charleston with a B.A. in 1905, an M.A. in 1906, and an honorary Litt.D. in 1922. Accepting a position at the *News and Courier* in 1908, he used his love of the lowcountry as the basis of his long-running column, "Woods and Waters." The nature artist and writer Charles Livingston Bull convinced him to send similar work to the *Saturday Evening Post,* which, along with other national magazines, published his nature stories. National publication enabled Sass to give up newspaper work in 1924, having served as both city editor and assistant editor.

Sass's collections of nature stories, showing his lush use of language and intimate knowledge of bird and animal life, include *The Way of the Wild* (1925), *Adventures in Green Places* (1926; enlarged, 1935), *Gray Eagle* (1927), and *On the Wings of a Bird* (1929). His fascination with lowcountry and Native American history is displayed in his historical novels *War Drums* (1928), *Hear Me, My Chiefs*

(1940), *Emperor Brims* (1941), and most especially in his best work, *Look Back to Glory* (1933), a tale of the Civil War. A chapter was published in *Fort Sumter* (1938) with a chapter from DuBose Heyward's novel *Peter Ashley.* In Heyward's novel the title character debated between his head and heart in throwing in his lot with the South; but Sass and his characters supported secession and the South wholeheartedly. The author saw no reason to doubt the rightness of the "lost cause" and argued passionately for the political principles of John C. Calhoun, in both his fiction and his magazine pieces. Believing that history should be colored with romance, he used his lyric talents to celebrate the lowcountry and a past he saw as fabled and tragic. This also showed in his nonfiction works: *A Carolina Rice Plantation of the Fifties,* with Alice R. H. Smith watercolors (1936); *Outspoken: 150 Years of the News and Courier* (1953), whose conservative racial views he championed (most especially in his 1956 *Atlantic Monthly* article "Mixed Schools and Mixed Blood"); and *The Story of the Carolina Lowcountry* (1956), in which he argued that the role of the lowcountry and that of the South in shaping the country had not been adequately acknowledged by historians. He was so adamant about this premise in his magazine pieces that the historian Bernard De Voto answered him in the pages of the *Saturday Evening Post.*

Shy, redheaded, tall, lean, and gracious, Sass was nicknamed "Hobo" for his wandering ways in the lowcountry and his hobbling together of income to support his wife, Marion Hutson, and three children. At least two of his short stories became the basis of films; *The Raid* came from his "Affair at St. Albans," and *Anne of the Indies* was drawn from his story of the same name. He died on February 18, 1958, and was buried in Charleston's St. Philip's Episcopal Cemetery. While all could not agree with him politically, none could deny his love or loyalty for the Carolina lowcountry. HARLAN GREENE

"Charleston Author Tells of Wild Life in Woods and of His Native Heath." Charleston *News and Courier,* December 4, 1938, 9–iii.

Coit, Margaret. "Myth, Says Devoto of Sass' Charges." Charleston *News and Courier,* January 12, 1954, A10.

———. "H. R. Sass Dies after Long Illness." Charleston *News and Courier,* February 19, 1958, A1, A11.

———. "Tribute to Herbert R. Sass." Charleston *News and Courier,* March 2, 1958, A12.

Sayers, Valerie (b. 1952). Novelist. Sayers was born on August 8, 1952, in Beaufort, South Carolina, the daughter of Paul Sayers and Janet Hogan. She grew up in Beaufort and was educated in local schools. One of her teachers was Pat Conroy. She eventually earned a B.A. degree from Fordham University and an M.F.A. in creative writing from Columbia University. She has taught creative writing at the

City University of New York and at the Low Country Technical College in Beaufort. In 1993 she joined the English department at the University of Notre Dame, where she became director of the master of fine arts program in creative writing.

Sayers is the author of six novels and several short stories. Her first novel, *Due East* (1987), serves as an anchor work for her subsequent four novels. Due East is the name Sayers gives to the thinly disguised Beaufort of her youth and adolescence. She has said, "I was raised in a little coastal town—Beaufort, South Carolina— suspiciously like Due East. I moved to New York at seventeen, but evidently have a compunction to return to that particular southern landscape." In part, her return to Beaufort is an imaginative return to her past life and to the past life of her large family. Her first book is a coming-of-age novel about the anxieties, cultural and otherwise, of a young Catholic girl located in the midst of a small-town Protestant culture.

Her second novel, *How I Got Him Back* (1989), and her third novel, *Who Do You Love* (1991), are also set in Due East, with the recurrence of many characters from her first novel. She has written, "Every time I write about Due East—which is mostly every time I write—I am trying to come to terms with South Carolina, with how that place has seeped into my being." In some ways, her first three novels form a trilogy, and they have clear elements of autobiography, though Sayers has created an overlay of shifts in time and shifts in narrative voice that discourages strictly autobiographical reading.

In her fourth novel, *The Distance Between Us* (1994), Sayers moves the action away from the South and into New York. Her fifth novel, *Brain Fever* (1996), continues the story of the lives of several characters that have appeared in earlier works. *Brain Fever* tells the story of a middle-aged man who is coping with emotional and family crises. Her latest book, *The Powers* (2013), recreates an America on the verge of war, right before Pearl Harbor in 1941, with a host of real and imagined characters, including the New York Yankees star Joe DiMaggio, whom the author endows with psychic powers.

Most of Sayers's fiction centers on the family and its discontents. Daughters are alienated from fathers, husbands are alienated from wives, and children struggle to find clear paths out of the maze of family struggles. A central theme of her fiction is romantic entanglements between men and women, conflicts that often remain unresolved. Sayers's characters sometimes feel isolated and disappointed, and frequently they are forced to settle for small victories of reconciliation and affection.

Sayers's fiction is wholeheartedly unsentimental. Its narrative force is carried by the author's strong display of comic irony. Several critics have suggested that Sayers's ironic stance is tempered by her self-declared Catholic religious faith, placing her in a way in the southern tradition of Flannery O'Connor and Walker Percy.

Valerie Sayers was the 1992 National Endowment for the Arts literature fellow, and she has served on the fellowship panel for the National Endowment for the Arts and on the fellowship panel for the South Carolina Arts Commission. She is a frequent book reviewer for the *New York Times* and the *Washington Post*. CHARLES ISRAEL

McCord, Charline R. "Interview with Valerie Sayers." *Southern Quarterly* (Winter 2000): 135–52.
Zubizarreta, John. "Valerie Sayers." *Catholic Women Writers.* Edited by Mary R. Reichmdt. New York: Greenwood Press, 2001. 345–50.

Simms, William Gilmore (1806–1870). Poet, historian, novelist, editor. Simms was born on April 17, 1806, in Charleston, South Carolina, the son of the Irish immigrant William Gilmore Simms and Harriet Ann Singleton. His mother died when Simms was an infant. His distraught father moved west, leaving his son to be reared by a grandmother who told him stories of Charleston during the Revolutionary War and the exploits of his ancestors. In 1818 Simms's father sent a representative to Charleston to bring his son west. The twelve-year-old boy refused his father's entreaties and chose to remain in Charleston.

Lacking much formal education, Simms was a voracious reader and an acute observer. From his reading and his travel he absorbed history as well as local legends and acquired material for the volumes he would later write. In 1825 he took up the study of law in Charleston. Literature, however, remained his passion, and in that same year he helped found and edit *The Album,* which characterized itself as "a weekly literary miscellany." He married Anna Malcolm Giles on October 19, 1826. That same year he was admitted to the bar. The birth of his daughter Anna added to the young family's joy even as it stretched their meager finances and reduced the time available for literary pursuits. In 1829 Simms became editor of the *City Gazette,* a Charleston newspaper through which he railed against nullification and John C. Calhoun's doctrine of state interposition.

In the early 1830s Simms experienced a series of devastating personal setbacks. In 1830 both his father and his grandmother died. His house in Summerville burned to the ground. In February, 1832, his wife succumbed to a lingering illness. Alone but for his four-year-old daughter, Simms resigned his editorship and went north to explore new opportunities. In New York he met James Lawson, a young Scots businessman and occasional poet. Through Lawson, Simms was introduced to a group of young writers and critics and their publishers. For the rest of his life he would engage in a lively correspondence with these new friends, and he would make almost annual visits to New York to renew and deepen their friendships.

Buoyed by the success of his trip, Simms returned to Charleston determined to make a living as a professional writer. During the next three years he published *Martin Faber* (1833), a ghost story and his first work of fiction; *Guy Rivers* (1834), the first of his "border tales" set in the Georgia frontier; *The Yemassee* (1835), a colonial romance based on an Indian uprising in 1715; and *The Partisan* (1835), the first of his Revolutionary War romances. Published by Harper and Brothers of New York, these works were widely and warmly reviewed and established Simms as one of his country's leading literary lights.

In 1836 Simms's life took another propitious turn with his marriage to Chevillette Roach, the nineteen-year-old daughter of a wealthy planter. The newlyweds made their home at Woodlands, one of the Roach plantations on the Edisto River near Orangeburg. Simms savored life at Woodlands and the setting it provided for his literary endeavors. Though he spent his summers in Charleston, Woodlands would be his home for the remainder of his life.

Despite the delights of plantation living, Simms felt himself a "man marked for the scourge." Of the fourteen children borne by Chevillette, only five would live to adulthood. His father-in-law's poor management of the plantation kept the family's financial situation precarious and forced on Simms a pace of composition that occasionally affected his health and morale.

Simms believed that "to be national in literature, one must needs be sectional." Indeed, he continued, "he who shall depict one *section* faithfully, has made his proper and sufficient contribution to the great work of *national* illustration." Though occasionally annoyed by an inaccurately perceived sense of neglect in his home state and prompted at times to consider removing to what he hoped might be a more hospitable literary climate in New York, Simms remained a South Carolinian and devoted his professional life to telling the Palmetto State's story. His efforts varied widely. He edited numerous literary journals, engaged in a rich and voluminous correspondence, and lectured widely. He wrote stories about the southern frontier, essays on literary and social topics, and reviews of newly published works.

But Simms's principal contributions to a broader understanding of South Carolina may be found in his poetry, his history, his biographies, and perhaps most notably, his fiction. Simms's best poetry, such as "Maid of Congaree" and "Dark-Eyed Maid of Edisto," conveyed the beauty and mystery of South Carolina. After the Civil War he collected and published *War Poetry of the South*, a valuable document of the Confederate experience. A committed historian, Simms possessed one of the finest private libraries of historical materials in the South. He published a history of South Carolina in 1840 (versions revised by his granddaughter Mary Simms Oliphant would become a staple for schoolchildren in the twentieth century), followed by biographies of Francis Marion and Nathanael Greene. His beloved Woodlands was put to the torch by Union troops in 1865 (though later rebuilt), and his entire library was destroyed. Simms retreated inland, where he witnessed the burning and devastation there, which he later described in *Sack and Destruction of the City of Columbia, S.C.*

In his fiction Simms was a master of the "romance," which he likened more to epic poetry. He covered the entire sweep of Carolina history, from the earliest years of French and Spanish settlement (*The Lily and the Totem* and *Vasconselos*), through the period of English colonization (*The Yemassee*), through the Revolution (a "cycle" of seven romances, most notably *The Partisan* and *Woodcraft*), up to Simms's own time, where a distinctive American character began to emerge (*Guy Rivers*).

Keeping nation and section in balance became increasingly difficult for Simms during the 1850s. Some critics have read *Woodcraft*, with its view of a coherent, hierarchical plantation society, as a rebuttal to *Uncle Tom's Cabin*. More certain was Simms's growing sense of alienation from the North, which came to a climax during a lecture tour in New York in 1856. Speaking on "South Carolina in the Revolution," he asserted his native state's contributions to the country's history and attacked the antislavery movement for its "defamation" of South Carolina. So negative were the reviews of his first lecture that Simms cancelled the remainder of his engagements and returned home. From that point on he became an advocate of southern secession.

Broken by the war and enfeebled by illness, Simms attempted in 1865 to revive his literary career, but the result was undistinguished. He died in Charleston on June 11, 1870, and was buried in Magnolia Cemetery. Simms was posthumously inducted into the South Carolina Academy of Authors in 1986. JOHN M. MCCARDELL, JR.

Guilds, John C. *Simms: A Literary Life.* Fayetteville: University of Arkansas Press, 1992.

McCardell, John. "William Gilmore Simms and Antebellum Southern Literature." In *The Oxford Encyclopedia of American Literature.* Vol. 4. Edited by Jay Parini. New York: Oxford University Press, 2004.

Oliphant, Mary C. Simms, Alfred Taylor Odell, and T. C. Duncan Eaves, eds. *The Letters of William Gilmore Simms.* 6 vols. Columbia: University of South Carolina Press, 1952–1982.

Simons, Katherine Drayton Mayrant (1890–1969). Poet, novelist, playwright, historian. Simons was born on January 21, 1890, in Charleston, South Carolina, the daughter of Sedgewick Lewis Simons and Katherine Drayton Mayrant. She spent her early years in and around Summerville in Dorchester County. She was educated at local schools and at Converse College in Spartanburg, where she earned a bachelor of letters degree in 1909. Converse awarded her an honorary doctor of literature degree in 1952 for "brilliant contributions" to the literary traditions of her state and nation.

Interested in literary pursuits since girlhood, Simons began writing seriously while in college. Her primary love was poetry, with a focus on lyrical verse, sonnets, and nature poems. The first of her three books of poetry, *Shadow Songs,* appeared in 1912 under the pen name "Kadra Maysi" (created from the first few letters of each unit of her full name). A decade later she became a charter member of the Poetry Society of South Carolina. She would go on to win every award given by the Poetry Society, and at the time of her death she was the only woman ever to have been elected its president. Her other books of poetry were *The Patteran* (1925) and *White Horse Leaping,* which the University of South Carolina Press published in 1951.

Simons later created a national reputation for herself in the field of fiction. Her serious interests in travel, the equestrian arts, and South Carolina history are reflected in the eight historical (sometimes labeled "romantic" or "dramatic") novels she published under the pseudonym "Drayton Mayrant" between 1948 and 1960: *A Sword from Galway* (1948), *The Running Thread* (1949), *First the Blade* (1950), *Courage Is Not Given* (1952), *The Red Doe* (1953), *Always a River* (1956), *Lamp in Jerusalem* (1957), and *The Land beyond the Tempest* (1960). Seven of these were chosen as book club selections. Critics alluded to her "genius for description" and described her work as "superlatively well written" and "warmly imaginative." "Perhaps because she was first a poet," one reviewer wrote, Simons "created sentences and paragraphs one returns to again and again for their beauty."

The author of numerous short stories, Simons also wrote or co-wrote five plays and a sketch for the ballet *The Lost Atlantis,* which was presented by the Charleston Civic Ballet Company in 1964. Furthermore, she wrote many articles or essays for newspapers and magazines. Between 1955 and 1967 she contributed regularly to the popular onomastic journal *Names in South Carolina.* Two small nonfiction books attest to her love for Charleston and the Summerville area: *Roads of Romance and Historic Spots near Summerville* (1925) and *Stories of Charleston Harbor* (1930).

Simons died on March 31, 1969, and was buried in Magnolia Cemetery in Charleston. In 1997 she was posthumously inducted into the South Carolina Academy of Authors. THOMAS L. JOHNSON

LaBorde, Rene. "In Memoriam: Katherine Drayton Mayrant Simons (1890–1969)." *Names in South Carolina* 16 (winter 1969): 4.

Pinckney, Elise. "A Huguenot Writer." Columbia *State Magazine*, September 28, 1952, 10.

Simons, Katherine Drayton Mayrant. Papers. South Caroliniana Library, University of South Carolina, Columbia.

Telfair, Nancy. "Katherine Drayton Mayrant Simons." *South Carolina Magazine* 12 (November 1949): 8, 34.

Sinclair, Bennie Lee (1939–2000). Novelist, poet. Sinclair was born on April 15, 1939, in Greenville, South Carolina, to Graham Sinclair and Bennie Ward. While she was in the first grade, her first published poem appeared in a teachers' magazine. Overwhelmed by the attention she received, she stopped writing poetry and returned to it only after the deaths of her father and her brother. A 1956 graduate of Greenville High School, Sinclair entered Furman University, where she received her B.A. in English and later received the Distinguished Alumni Award in 1996. In 1957 she married Thomas Donald Lewis.

Governor Richard Riley appointed Sinclair as poet laureate of South Carolina in 1986. The state's fifth poet laureate and the third woman to serve in the role, she held the position for the remainder of her life. She taught writing at Furman University and gave workshops at the University of Notre Dame, Western Carolina University, and Brevard College. Her commitment to teaching poetry included a twenty-eight-year connection with the South Carolina Arts Commission through its Artists-in-the-Schools program. Additionally, she taught poetry at the Governor's School for the Arts and Humanities. Sinclair promoted public appreciation for poetry via educational radio programs during National Poetry Month each April. She composed Coastal Carolina University's alma mater in 1994 and wrote poems for formal state functions, most notably one for Governor Jim Hodges's inauguration in 1999, a poem that also celebrated the end of the millennium.

In addition to four books of poetry, Sinclair published short stories as well as a novel, *The Lynching* (1992), which was based on the state's last lynching in 1947. She composed poems in her mind before writing them down and amazed everyone with her capacity for memorization. Sinclair died of a heart attack at her home, Wildernesse, near Cleveland, South Carolina, on May 22, 2000. REBECCA TOLLEY-STOKES

Singleton, George (b.1958). Short story writer, novelist, educator. Born in Anaheim, California, on May 13, 1958, and raised in Greenwood, South Carolina, Singleton graduated from Furman University in 1980 with a degree in philosophy. He earned an M.F.A. degree from the University of North Carolina at Greensboro in 1986. Singleton taught fiction writing and editing at the South Carolina Governor's School for the Arts and Humanities for thirteen years. He currently lives in Spartanburg, South Carolina, with the clay artist Glenda Guion and teaches at Wofford College where he holds the John C. Cobb Endowed Chair. Singleton was awarded a Guggenheim Fellowship in 2009 and in 2011 received the Hillsdale Award for Fiction from the Fellowship of Southern Writers. He has published more than a hundred short stories, many of them appearing in major literary and commercial magazines such as the *Georgia Review* and *Atlantic Monthly;* his work has been anthologized in multiple editions of *New Stories from the South.*

In a 2006 interview Singleton recalled his beginnings as a writer in the late 1970s, his decision in the 1980s to focus primarily on the short story form, and his slow but sure path to national prominence as a southern writer: "I plowed on until I found a voice, and understood that I would try to write about how the saddest moments can be the funniest." Certainly that distinctive voice is a key element in Singleton's first published collection of short stories, *These People Are Us: Stories* (River City Press, 2001). These fourteen works of short fiction, all written in first person and set in the South, strike a unique balance between things tragic and things comic as the two intertwine in the lives of Singleton's singularly southern characters.

With *The Half-Mammals of Dixie* (Algonquin Books of Chapel Hill, 2002), Singleton introduces readers to the fictional town of Forty-Five, South Carolina. This collection of fifteen tales, most written in first person and all linked by setting and theme, firmly establishes Singleton as a master of the tragicomic short story. In addition to the town of Forty-Five, it is in *The Half-Mammals of Dixie* that the character of Mendal Dawes makes his first appearance in the masterful "Show and Tell." The story, which first appeared in the *Atlantic Monthly* and was later anthologized in *New Stories from the South,* is narrated by nine-year-old Mendal, who gets caught up in his "widower" father's efforts to seduce his third-grade teacher.

Why Dogs Chase Cars: Tales of a Beleaguered Boyhood (Algonquin Books, 2004: reissued with a new introduction by USC Press, 2013) is a tightly knit short story cycle comprised of fourteen interconnected tales with a shared first-person narrator. The story cycle chronicles the life of Mendal Dawes, the narrator of "Show and Tell" in *The Half-Mammals of Dixie,* who wants most of all to get out of Forty-Five, South Carolina. This collection is particularly interesting not only because of the close connections among the stories that make it up but also because of its linkages of setting and character and theme with Singleton's previous book.

Novel (Harcourt, 2005) marks Singleton's debut with the novel form. Set in the fictional town of Gruel, South Carolina, *Novel* tells the uproariously funny story of a professional snake-handler named Novel (his brother and sister are named James and Joyce) who sets out to write his autobiography. While struggling to capture—and to come to terms with—his own story, Novel uncovers a dangerous and disturbing secret about the town of Gruel.

In the nineteen stories in *Drowning in Gruel* (Harcourt, 2006), Singleton returns to the fictional setting of Gruel, South Carolina. As was the case with *The Half-Mammals of Dixie* and *Why Dogs Chase Cars,* both *Novel* and *Drowning in Gruel* are directly linked through shared setting and characters and themes. The publication of *Drowning in Gruel* makes it clear that Singleton, in the tradition of Faulkner and Balzac, is creating a fictional world of his own.

The picaresque and hilarious *Work Shirts for Madmen* (Harcourt, 2007) marks Singleton's second foray into the novel form. The plot follows the struggles of the protagonist, Harp Spillman, to give up drinking and rehabilitate his career as an avant-garde metal sculptor by welding twelve angels out of hex nuts with the help of the Elbow Boys and his devoted wife Raylou.

With *Pep Talks, Warnings, and Screeds: Indispensable Wisdom and Cautionary Advice for Writers* (Writers Digest Books, 2008), Singleton tackles the genre of nonfiction. These practical lessons on writing take the form of aphorisms, pep talks, and a few rants, with color illustrations by novelist Daniel Wallace.

Stray Decorum (Dzanc Books, 2012) is Singleton's latest book. With these eleven stories that share settings and characters and revolve around a theme of "strays," the author returns to the short story cycle form. Although not as tightly linked as the fictional pieces in *Why Dogs Chase Cars,* the interconnected narratives in *Stray Decorum* further expand the hilarious, heartbreaking, and absolutely original fictional world created by George Singleton, and once again show why he has become one of the premier short story writers of his generation. ANDREW GEYER

Giraldi, William. "A Holy Impropriety: The Stories of George Singleton." *Georgia Review* 64.4 (2010): 619–627.

Kiem, Elizabeth. "A Novelist in Spite of Himself: A Profile of George Singleton." *Poets & Writers Magazine* 33.4 (2005): 42–47.

Smith, Gregory White (b. 1951). Writer, publisher, and Pulitzer Prize winner. Born in Ithaca, New York, in 1951, to William R. Smith, a hotel administrator, and Kathryn White, Gregory White Smith graduated from Colby College with an A. B. in English in 1973. He met his life partner Steven Naifeh when the two of them were studying law at Harvard University; each of them earned J.D. degrees in 1977, but neither of them decided to become practicing attorneys. Instead, both men opted to try their hand at writing books. What followed was a series of commercial titles, including such lifestyle guides as *Moving Up in Style: The Successful Man's Guide to Impeccable Taste* (1980), *What Every Client Needs to Know about Using a Lawyer* (1982), and *Why Can't Men Open Up?: Overcoming Men's Fear of Intimacy* (1984). It was, however, a series of true-crime narratives that brought the writing duo their first serious critical attention. The first of three such books, *The Mormon Murders* (1988), chronicled a forgery plot that turned deadly. Critics praised the bestselling volume for its meticulous research, which became the hallmark of Naifeh and Smith's compositional strategy.

In 1989 both men moved to Aiken, South Carolina, purchasing Joye Cottage, the former home of the wealthy Whitney family and one of the signature residences of the city's heyday as a glamorous winter resort. The challenges that they faced in rehabilitating the mansion, which had been empty for almost a decade, are recounted in the book *On a Street Called Easy, In a Cottage Called Joye: A Restoration Comedy*

(1996). That same year marked the publication of their monumental biography of American artist Jackson Pollock, which subsequently won the Pulitzer Prize. For more information on that book, please consult the entry on Steven Naifeh.

The Aiken years have been marked by a pattern of alternating subject matter: true crime narratives and artist biographies. In the former category are *Final Justice* (1993), which, as the subtitle indicates, focuses on the courtroom strategies employed by the legal team hired to defend "the richest man ever tried for murder," and *A Stranger in the Family* (1995), wherein the authors try to get inside the brain of a serial rapist-killer, Danny Starrett, who targeted young women along the Georgia-South Carolina border.

The same careful research and psychological insight that Naifeh and Smith applied to these true crime narratives also informs the biggest, most time-consuming project that the two men have tackled to date: the 953-page *Van Gogh: The Life* (2011). Just as they combed the prison journals of Danny Starrett to gain insight into his disturbed mind, they scoured the archives at the Van Gogh Museum in Amsterdam, perusing hundreds of unpublished Van Gogh family letters, to try to understand the exact nature of the artist's troubled genius.

To date, however, Smith's most personal book—and the one for which he gets top billing on the title page—is *Making Miracles Happen* (1997), which tells the story of his diagnosis, ten years earlier, of an inoperable brain tumor and his successful attempt to find a treatment to prolong his life and prove his physicians' dire prognosis wrong.

In addition to writing their own books, Naifeh and Smith started their own publishing firm, Woodward-White, Inc., which has published the directory *The Best Lawyers in America* since 1982 and the medical information service *The Best Doctors in America* since 1989. TOM MACK

Naifeh, Steven and Gregory White Smith. *On a Street Called Easy, In a Cottage Called Joye.* Boston: Little, Brown, 1996.

Smith, Gregory White and Steven Naifeh. *Making Miracles Happen.* Boston: Little, Brown, 1997.

Spears, Monroe K. (1916–1998). Editor, scholar, educator. Monroe Kirklyndorf Spears was born in Darlington, South Carolina, and educated at the University of South Carolina, where he earned his B.A. and M.A. degrees, and Princeton University, where he earned his Ph.D.. He taught at the University of Wisconsin (1940–1946), Vanderbilt University (1946–1952), University of the South (1952–1964), and Rice University (1964–1986). He is remembered for his "distinguished and humane career" at the latter. Like Robert Penn Warren and John Crowe Ransom before him, Spears was a leading proponent of and gatekeeper for southern literature.

Just like those hallowed literary figures, Spears wrote poetry and published several books of fiction and verse throughout his lifetime. Unlike the classic "Agrarians" before him, however, Spears expanded the range of his scholarly footprint by being an expert on British writers, especially Matthew Prior and W. H. Auden. Indeed, his work on the latter, *The Disenchanted Island,* is still regarded as one of the essential formalist critiques of Auden. This attention to Auden opened the door in his scholarship to other important modernists and their writings. In fact, Spears eventually argued that modern American literature reflects this country's "ambition to break with the past and with the Europe that embodies it." By concentrating on American writers like James Dickey and Hart Crane, Spears himself certainly was able to wedge this break from Europe as his career grew.

His biggest contribution to American letters, nevertheless, rests with his unprecedented legacy in southern literature. Not since H. L. Mencken, it can be argued, has one man been so influential in shaping this literary canon. In 1952 Spears became the editor of the *Sewanee Review.* Among southern scholars, poets, teachers, and students, this publication was the leading voice of intellectual and artistic expression during the second half of the twentieth century. Spears's high profile position immediately lifted him to a preeminent place throughout the mid-twentieth century Southern Renaissance. Like a dapper Moses, Spears built a promised land for little-known poets, enabling some of them to become household names.

He remained associated with this journal from the time of his editorship, which officially ended in 1961, until he died. Remarking on the centennial of the *Sewanee Review* in 1992, Spears wrote: "I should argue that the maintenance of [the] relation between criticism and creative writing is especially important at present, when there are strong pressures in the universities to separate them. The model of a critical quarterly, the review achieved the proper balance between the two: criticism informed by an awareness of the problems of the contemporary poet or fiction writer, and poetry and fiction informed by an awareness of the perspectives and standards of the best criticism."

To the general public, Spears is probably remembered most for his regular contributions to the *New York Review of Books.* Just as he did with his role at the *Sewanee Review,* Spears used these articles to define the American literary canon. Because of his many contributions to American letters, Monroe K. Spears was inducted into the South Carolina Academy of Authors in 1993. In addition, Rice University decided to fund an annual Monroe K. Spears Award in his honor. The award's webpage provides a fine assessment of this man: "Because everything Professor Spears wrote is marked by clarity, economy, and felicity of expression and by elegant and discerning interpretation, the award recognizes the essay published

in each volume of *SEL: Studies of English Literature 1500–1900* that most nearly achieves these qualities and that has given the editors the greatest pleasure to read."
MATTHEW L. MILLER

Prunty, Wyatt. "In Memoriam Monroe K. Spears." *Sewanee Review* 106.3 (1998): 533.

Spears, Monroe K. *American Ambitions: Selected Essays on Literary and Cultural Themes.* Baltimore: Johns Hopkins University Press, 1987.

———. *Countries of the Mind: Literary Explorations.* Columbia: University of Missouri Press, 1992.

———. *The Poetry of W. H. Auden: The Disenchanted Island.* New York: Oxford University Press, 1963.

———. "Reflections on the Centennial of the *Sewanee Review.*" *Sewanee Review* 100.4 (1992): 657–61.

Spillane, Mickey (b. Frank Morrison Spillane, 1918–2006). Novelist, short story writer. Nicknamed "Mickey" by his Irish Catholic father, Spillane was born in Brooklyn, New York, on March 9, 1918, the only child of John Joseph Spillane and his wife, Catherine Anne. After graduating from Brooklyn's Erasmus High School in 1935, he attended Kansas State College in 1939, intending to study law, although he dropped out that year. In 1940 he began work as a scripter and assistant editor for Funnies, Inc., a Manhattan producer of comic books. He joined the U.S. Army Air Force in December 1941, spending four years as a cadet flight instructor in Mississippi and Florida.

Spillane married Mary Anne Pearce in Greenwood, Mississippi, in 1945. Discharged from service as a captain, he returned to New York and the comic-book business. Needing money for a house, he turned out his first novel, *I, the Jury* (1947), in three weeks. The protagonist, Mike Hammer, a hard-drinking private investigator fond of buxom women and vigilante justice, became a household name by 1953, with five more Hammer novels selling millions of paperbacks. His hard-boiled plots and characters inspired the "Girl Hunt" production number with Fred Astaire and Cyd Charisse in the MGM musical *The Band Wagon* (1953).

Spillane became interested in the Grand Strand after judging the Myrtle Beach Sun-Fun Festival beauty contest, and in 1953 he moved his wife and four children to Murrells Inlet, where he lived the rest of his life. The already twice-divorced Spillane married the actress Sherri Malinou in 1965 and then the former Miss South Carolina Jane Rodgers Johnson in 1983.

The Mike Hammer character was developed for radio, movies, and TV, including a 1980s series starring Stacy Keach. Spillane portrayed the character in the 1963 movie *The Girl Hunters* and starred as himself in *Ring of Fear* (1954). His TV credits include *The Milton Berle Show* and a 1974 episode of *Columbo*. During the 1970s and 1980s he was also featured in commercials for Miller Lite Beer.

The author created other successful characters, including espionage agent Tiger Mann, introduced in *Day of the Guns* (1964), and Mako Hooker, a former U.S. government operative working as a fishing boat captain in *Something's Down There* (2003), a thriller set in the Caribbean. Spillane's many magazine short stories have been collected in multiple volumes, and one of his children's books, *The Day the Sea Rolled Back* (1979), earned a Junior Literary Guild award.

As of the early twenty-first century, Spillane's books had sold more than 140 million copies. He received the Grand Master Award of the Mystery Writers of America in 1995. Although his books proved to be a pervasive guilty pleasure during the first two decades of his career, they were almost universally panned by mainstream critics for their then-graphic depictions of sex and violence, as well as Hammer's "eye for an eye" sense of justice. Nevertheless, Spillane has accrued the respect attendant to his authorial longevity and the ongoing popularity of Mike Hammer, with the *New York Times* stating, "There's a kind of power about Mickey Spillane that no other writer can imitate."

Following his death in 2006, Spillane's widow, Jane, has continued to champion his work. To date, she has assigned seven of his uncompleted Mike Hammer manuscripts to writer Max Allan Collins, who worked with Spillane on the science fiction comic-book series in the 1990s based on his character Mike Danger. Most recently, Collins penned introductions to omnibus editions of Spillane's earlier Hammer novels.

Besides this active posthumous publication record, Spillane has been the subject of a number of belated honors in his adopted state. In 2011 a stretch of Highway 17 through Murrell's Inlet was renamed the Mickey Spillane Waterfront Highway, and he was inducted into the South Carolina Academy of Authors in 2012. DAVID MARSHALL JAMES

Spielman, David G., and William W. Starr. *Southern Writers.* Columbia: University of South Carolina Press, 1997.

Spillane, Mickey. *The Hammer Strikes Again.* New York: Avenel, 1989.

Springs, Elliott White (1896–1959). Short story writer, memoirist, businessman, aviator. Springs was born in Lancaster, South Carolina, on July 31, 1896, the son of Leroy Springs, a wealthy textile manufacturer, and Grace Allison White. He graduated from Culver Military Academy in Indiana in 1913 and received an A.B. from Princeton University in 1917. On October 4, 1922, he married Frances Hubbard Ley of Massachusetts. They had one daughter, Anne Kingsley Springs, who married H. William Close, and one son, Leroy "Sonny" Springs II, who was killed in an airplane crash in 1946.

Elliott Springs was one of the most daring pilots of World War I. Following his enlistment, Springs was sent to England for training with the Royal Flying Corps.

Selected for the prestigious British 85th Squadron, Springs racked up four kills before he was wounded after crash-landing on June 26, 1918. Upon his recovery, he was promoted to captain and transferred to the 148th Squadron of the U.S. Army. He became an "ace" (five kills) on August 3. By the end of the war, Springs had shot down eleven planes (other likely "kills" were not confirmed) and was the fifth-ranking American ace of World War I. He was awarded the British Distinguished Flying Cross and the American Distinguished Service Cross. He would return to military service in 1941 during World War II and retired as a lieutenant colonel.

After World War I, Springs briefly worked as a test pilot for the LWF Engineering Company of New York. He then went back to South Carolina to work in the family's textile business. His demanding father assigned him a variety of jobs to learn the family business, but the work did not suit Springs. To relieve the tedium, Springs took to writing accounts of his war-time experiences. He began by publishing short stories and then wrote *War Birds: The Diary of an Unknown Aviator,* a thinly disguised account of his time in England and France during World War I. Published in 1926, the book was an instant critical and commercial success. From 1927 to 1931 Springs published dozens of short stories and seven more books, mostly about his flying experiences. Although his later works fell far short of the acclaim garnered by *War Birds,* Springs nevertheless earned $250,000 from his writings.

After his father died in 1931, Springs defied predictions that he would quickly run through the estate (supposedly valued at $5 million) and took over his father's textile company. At the time, Springs Cotton Mills consisted of six aging plants in Chester, Lancaster, and York Counties. Springs mastered technical details as well as business principles, working on a loom in his basement to test the proposals of his workers and supervisors. He found that "for a man who loves machines, a cotton mill beats an airplane." He learned to tell by sound whether a machine was running properly.

During the 1930s and 1940s Springs consolidated his mills into one company, built a finishing plant, established a sales arm, and modernized the business. By 1958, the last full year he managed the company, he had built assets to $138.5 million, compared to $13 million when he became president. Sales were $163 million, more than nineteen times greater than in 1933. Springs was the seventh-largest textile company in the nation but led the industry in profitability. The company had become the world's largest producer of sheets and pillowcases. In particular, Springs won acclaim (as well as criticism) for his humorous and risqué advertisements promoting his company's "Springmaid" sheets. He was also known for special benefits he provided employees, including medical care, profit sharing, and recreational facilities.

Springs died on October 15, 1959, in New York City. His remains were cremated and returned to Fort Mill for interment in the White family plot of the Presbyterian cemetery. He was named to the South Carolina Business Hall of Fame in 1985 and inducted into the South Carolina Academy of Authors in 2000. ROBERT A. PIERCE

Davis, Burke. *War Bird: The Life and Times of Elliott White Springs*. Chapel Hill: University of North Carolina Press, 1987.

Springs, Elliott White. *Clothes Make the Man or How to Put the Broad in Broadcloth*. New York: Empyrean Press, 1958.

———. *Letters from a War Bird: The World War I Correspondence of Elliott White Springs*. Edited by David Vaughan. Columbia: University of South Carolina Press, 2012.

Steadman, Mark (b. 1930). Novelist, short story writer, educator. Steadman was born in Statesboro, Georgia, on July 2, 1930, the son of Mark Sidney Steadman, Sr., an engineer with the highway department, and Marie Hopkins. The family lived in Decatur from 1940 until 1947. After his father died, Steadman moved with his family to Savannah, where they had kin. He attended Armstrong Junior College (A.A., 1949) and Emory University (B.A. in English, 1951). He married Joan Anderson, a school librarian, on March 29, 1952. They have three sons: Clayton, Todd, and Wade.

Steadman served in the U.S. Navy as a naval air cadet from 1951 to 1953. From June 1953 he worked as a copywriter for the publishing company W. R. C. Smith in Atlanta. He then went back to school, at Florida State University (M.A. in English, 1956). In July 1957 he took a job as an instructor at Clemson College, and since then his life has been centered in rural Pickens County. He received his Ph.D. from Florida State University in 1963 for a thesis on "Modern American Humor." The subject reflects his permanent preoccupation.

Steadman taught humor and the American novel at Clemson for forty years. From 1980 until 1997 he was also writer in residence there. In 1968 he took a year's leave of absence and accepted a position as visiting professor at the American University in Cairo, Egypt, where he "found his voice" as a writer of fiction. By the time he left Cairo in June 1969, he had written six stories, and back in South Carolina he added seven more. They were published in 1971 as *McAfee County: A Chronicle*. It is set in an imaginary coastal county with a population of 6,254, fifty-eight percent of whom are African American. The county serves as a microcosm of a southern coastal city around 1960. With a Gothic sense of the comic and with much compassion, Steadman shows the grotesqueness in most lives. The book did well and was brought out in British, French, and German editions.

In 1976 *A Lion's Share* was published. The novel is about the greatest southern high school football player of all time. But we see more than his triumph; we also witness the hero's tragic failure in college, in his job, and in his marriage. As William Koon put it, Steadman "moves from comedy to genuine tragedy" in this novel. The book was not a public or critical success, and Steadman came to regret that he had not made the football part of it a separate novel. So fourteen years later he rewrote the funny and nostalgic part and published it as *Bang-Up Season*.

In 1983 Steadman was Fulbright lecturer at Leningrad State University and began work on his third novel, which became *Angel Child* (1987). It is a hilarious story about Langston James's "misformative years," but it is also about a grotesque-looking young southerner's dreams and troubled longing. In 1991 Steadman wrote the entry on "Humor" in the *Encyclopedia of Southern Culture*. Since leaving Clemson in 1997, he has been working on some "autobiographical fiction" and enjoying his retirement in Pickens County. He was inducted into the South Carolina Academy of Authors in 2002. JAN NORDBY GRETLUND

Boyd, Molly. "Rural Identity in the Southern Gothic Novels of Mark Steadman." *Studies in the Literary Imagination* 27 (1994): 41–54.

Greiner, Donald J. "The Southern Fiction of Mark Steadman." *South Carolina Review* 9 (November 1976): 5–11.

Koon, William. "Mark Steadman." In *Dictionary of Literary Biography*. Vol. 6. *American Novelists since World War II, Second Series*. Edited by James E. Kibler. Detroit: Gale, 1980.

Nuwer, Hank. "Mark Steadman's Comedy of Ethos: An Interview." *Rendezvous: Journal of Arts and Letters* 21 (1985): 92–99.

Steele, Max (b. Henry Maxwell Steele, 1922–2005). Short story writer, novelist, educator. Max Steele was born in Greenville, South Carolina, on March 30, 1922, the son of John M. Steele and Minnie Russell. He attended Furman University for two years and Vanderbilt University while serving in the U.S. Air Force. He received a B.A. degree from the University of North Carolina at Chapel Hill in 1946. He did further study at the Académie Julian and the Sorbonne in Paris. On December 31, 1960, Steele married Dianna Whittinghill. They had two sons.

Steele's first published story, "Grandfather and Chow Dog: A Story," appeared in *Harper's* in 1944. His novel *Debby* was published in 1950, when it won the Harper prize of the year. It also received the Eugene F. Saxon Memorial Award and the Mayflower Cup for best book by a North Carolinian in 1950. *Debby* was reprinted by Perennial Library in 1960 as *The Goblins Must Go Barefoot* and by Louisiana State University Press in 1997 with its original title.

Steele is best known for his short stories, which have appeared in *Harper's* and other magazines including *Atlantic Monthly, New Yorker, Cosmopolitan, Esquire, Mademoiselle,* and *Quarterly Review of Literature*. Several stories have been included in anthologies used by teachers in middle- and high-school English classes, and Funk and Wagnall's selected "The Cat and the Coffee Drinkers" for its *Great Short*

Stories of the World textbook. Three volumes of Steele's stories have been published: *Where She Brushed Her Hair and Other Short Stories* (1968); *The Cat and the Coffee Drinkers* (1969); and *The Hat of My Mother: Stories* (1988).

Steele began teaching in 1956 at the University of North Carolina at Chapel Hill, where he later served as writer in residence, professor, and director of the creative writing program. Under his leadership, the writing program produced some of the nation's most promising young writers, including Jill McCorkle and Randall Kenan. He retired from UNC in 1988 as professor emeritus. He also taught at the University of California at San Francisco, Bennington College, South Carolina Governor's School for the Arts, Bread Loaf Writers' Conference, and Squaw Valley Writers' Conference. He was an advisory editor of the *Paris Review* from 1952 to 1954 and subsequently an editor of *Story* magazine starting in 1988. He received two O. Henry prizes, two National Endowment for the Arts and Humanities grants, the Standard Oil Award for Excellence in Undergraduate Teaching, and honorary degrees from Belmont Abby and Furman University.

In 1992 Steele was inducted into the South Carolina Academy of Authors. In his acceptance speech he said, "All of my work was written away from home but with an unbreakable tie to it." After his eightieth birthday he concentrated solely on writing short-short stories, published in *Harper's* and the *Washington Post*. In 2005, he died in Chapel Hill. MARGUERITE HAYS

Nostrandt, Jeanne R. "Max Steele." In *Contemporary Southern Writers*. Edited by Roger Mautz. Detroit: St. James, 1999.

Stevenson, Ferdinan Nancy Backer (1928–2001). Journalist, novelist, lieutenant governor, civic leader. "Nancy" Stevenson was born on June 8, 1928, in New Rochelle, New York, the daughter of William Bryant Backer and Fernanda Legaré. Upon the death of her husband, Fernanda, who was descended from several prominent Charleston families, returned in 1932 to her Charleston home with Nancy and her brother. Nancy attended Ashley Hall School and was awarded a bachelor of arts degree from Smith College in 1949. From 1950 to 1954 she was married to Olav Moltke-Hansen, a Norwegian diplomat, and lived in Norway and New York City with their two sons. From 1952 to 1954 she worked for the *New York Herald Tribune*, writing book reviews and doing overseas reporting. After a divorce, she returned to Charleston with her sons and taught junior high school. From 1956 to 1980 she was married to Norman Williams Stevenson of Charleston, an attorney and state legislator. They had three children. She continued her interest in writing and, using a pseudonym, co-wrote three mystery novels.

Stevenson was an active civic leader during the 1960s and 1970s, with a special interest in drama and historic preservation. Between 1965 and 1978 she was a trustee of the Historic Charleston Foundation, co-chair of the Save Charleston

Foundation, trustee and secretary of the College of Charleston Foundation, president of Footlight Players, and vice president of the South Carolina Historical Society. Frustrated by the lack of support for historic preservation from the General Assembly, she decided to run for office in 1974 and won Charleston's House District 110 seat. She was reelected in 1976. Her two major legislative interests were the Fiscal Accountability Act, which mandated a more uniform fiscal reporting system, and the Water Reporting Act, designed to report water usage and allocate water in times of drought.

In 1978 Stevenson successfully ran for lieutenant governor, becoming the first woman to serve in a statewide office in South Carolina. As lieutenant governor, she worked with Governor Richard Riley to pass significant legislation designed to improve South Carolina schools. Colleagues described her as an effective leader of the senate and an active participant in the governor's policy discussions. She instituted the Lieutenant Governor's Writing Awards Program, which presented awards to fifth-graders and eighth-graders for creative writing, and the Public Assistance Line (PAL), a toll-free line designed to help citizens find out which agency or organization to call for assistance with personal and public problems.

Although not an active member of women's organizations, Stevenson demonstrated that women could be effective political leaders and work well with men. She set up the public hearings in the senate devoted to the ultimately unsuccessful attempt to achieve South Carolina ratification of the Equal Rights Amendment. She also worked to increase public awareness and support for victims of domestic violence. She chose not to run for re-election in 1982 but served in 1983–1984 as co-chair of the steering committee for Ernest Hollings's presidential campaign and as a member of the national Democratic platform accountability and steering committee. In 1984 she ran unsuccessfully for the Second Congressional District seat held by Republican congressman Floyd Spence.

Stevenson moved to the Washington, D.C., area in 1985 and turned her major efforts from politics to art. She established the Winston Gallery in Washington, which specialized in contemporary art. After a long struggle with breast cancer, Stevenson died at her home in Floyd, Virginia, on May 31, 2001. ALICE H. HENDERSON

Bailey, N. Louise, Mary L. Morgan, and Carolyn R. Taylor, eds. *Biographical Directory of the South Carolina Senate, 1776–1985.* 3 vols. Columbia: University of South Carolina Press, 1986.

Stoney, Samuel Gaillard (1891–1968). Nonfiction writer, historian, preservationist. Stoney is considered by many to be the quintessential Charlestonian. Born in Charleston, South Carolina, on August 29, 1891, son of the planter Samuel Stoney, Sr. and Louisa Cheves Smythe, he was descended on his mother's side from the antebellum writer Louisa McCord and was also related to the writer John Bennett and the preservation architect Albert Simons. After graduating from the College of Charleston, Stoney provided military service on the Mexican border followed by a stint as an officer in the 318th Field Artillery, 81st Division in France; in the latter capacity, however, he never saw combat. A degree in architecture from the Georgia Institute of Technology led to work in Atlanta and New York, where his charm and knowledge brought him into contact with artists and scholars. His interest in Gullah enabled him to serve as a dialogue coach for actors in *Porgy* and so piqued the interest of the author Gertrude Mathews Shelby that she convinced Stoney to co-author two books with her: a collection of creation tales told in Gullah, *Black Genesis* (1930) and a novel on the tragedy of miscegenation, *Po' Buckra* (1930).

In 1933, at the MacDowell Colony in New Hampshire, Stoney met and married the New England poet (and later novelist) Frances Frost. They moved to Charleston, and the marriage ended in divorce. Stoney then began a frank love affair with his native city. President of the South Carolina Historical Society, the Preservation Society, Historic Charleston Foundation, the Huguenot Society, and other organizations, Stoney helped document the city's past while fighting to save much of its architecture. His stubborn stands gained him both detractors and devotees. Living simply, he became a familiar sight on Charleston's streets, where he was known as much for his sandals and shirtsleeves as his curiosity, knowledge, and wit. He was a frequent and popular speaker on numerous topics, all colored with his affection for his city. He wrote the text to accompany Bayard Wootten's book of photographs, *Charleston: Azaleas and Old Brick* (1937), and contributed substantially to seminal works on area architecture: *Plantations of the Carolina Low Country* (1938) and *This Is Charleston* (1944), a survey that has been key to the preservation of the city's architectural heritage. Minor works include *The Story of South Carolina's Senior Bank: The Bank of Charleston* and *The Dulles Family in South Carolina* (both published in 1955).

As an author of numerous historical articles, a generous guide to researchers, and a significant contributor to the intellectual life of the city, Stoney built a scholarly foundation for the documentation and study of Charleston, which, in turn, treated him as a favorite son. In May 1968 he was awarded a doctor of letters from the College of Charleston, where he had lectured from 1949 to 1966. He died at his own hand on July 30, 1968. His death, the *News and Courier* noted, "removes a Charleston landmark as real as the architectural treasures he spent his life fighting to preserve." He was buried at St. James Goose Creek Episcopal Church, which he had served as senior (and sole) warden for forty years. In 1991, Stoney was posthumously inducted into the South Carolina Academy of Authors. HARLAN GREENE

"Article Features Stoney and City." Charleston *News and Courier,* April 12, 1964, C11.

Bowles, Billy E. "Stoney's Death Takes Away City Landmark." Charleston *News and Courier,* August 4, 1968, C12.

Greene, Harlan. *Mr. Skylark: John Bennett and the Charleston Renaissance.* Athens: University of Georgia Press, 2001.

Leland, Jack. "Samuel Gaillard Stoney: 1891–1968." *Preservation Progress* 13 (November 1968): 1, 6.

Rigney, Harriet Stoney Popham. "Samuel Gaillard Stoney: 'If I Were a House....'" *Carologue* 8 (autumn 1992): 6–7, 18–19.

Thompson, Dorothy Perry (1944–2002). Poet, scholar, educator. Born Dorothy Perry in Springfield, South Carolina, in 1944, Thompson grew up with five siblings in the Wheeler Hill neighborhood of Columbia, South Carolina, which has figured so prominently in many of her poems, especially those which appear in *Fly with the Puffin.* A child of two working parents, her father as a carpenter and her mother as a shirt presser in a laundry, Thompson described her childhood as "rich with people, talk, things to do" although it was "bare of material things." She also described her early years as "naive, happy, and passionate (about everything: folks, school, books, boys, dancing)."

Thompson was educated in the public schools, graduating from Booker T. Washington High School in 1962. She received her B.A. in English from Allen University in 1968 and a master of arts in the teaching of English from the University of South Carolina in 1974. After receiving her M.A.T., Thompson taught for several years in the public schools of South Carolina, notably Riverside High School in Saluda, Lower Richland High School in Hopkins, and Dreher High School in Columbia. She then returned to graduate school and earned her Ph.D. in English from the University of South Carolina in 1987; she holds the double distinction of being the second African American in USC's history to earn a doctorate in English and the first African American to do a creative writing dissertation at that university (under the direction of James Dickey). Of her landmark position as a minority woman in graduate studies in English at the University of South Carolina, she recalled getting "lots of support from the clerical staff (mostly African American women) in the English department, and from fellow graduate students. Some professors breathed more easily and actually talked to me once they saw I could write my name; others tried their best to ignore me."

As a poet, scholar, and teacher, Dorothy Perry Thompson lent a vibrant voice to scholarship and the arts. Her first book of poems, *Fly with the Puffin* (96 Press, 1995) reveals a distinctly female and distinctively African American sensibility. Thompson's poems confront issues including race and gender, as well as celebrating the strength and the enduring quality of love that enliven family and community. Her subsequent books, *Priest in Aqua Boa* (96 Press, 2001) and *Hurrying the Spirit: Following Zora* (Palanquin Press, 2002) mark the resilience and flexibility of the African American spirit. Thompson's poems have also been published in an impressive array of journals and anthologies including the *African American Review, Catalyst, Carolina Literary Companion, Caesura, Black American Literature Forum*, the *Sucarnochee Review, Spirit and Flame, 45/96*, the *Baltimore Review*, and *Southern Poetry Review*.

Two poems in particular serve to illustrate Thompson's central concerns. The first, "God After Atheism," presents God as a movie maker and the poet as a human being who has picked up the camera for her own creative purposes. In effect, the poem demonstrates the importance of black identity, citing hard, black pieces of obsidian as part of earliest creation, and then explains the necessity for the poet to surrender the camera to its original owner. The poem's title suggests that the speaker is re-establishing a connection with God after a period of denying God's existence. Of this God, the reader must conclude that he is both powerful and mysteriously inconsistent; sometimes he helps the speaker in her work (singing songs, decorating her dress, making her share with her son the wonderful things she sees) and sometimes he punishes her with terrible, threatening dreams—perhaps for being too creative on her own. Thus, when the speaker in the poem promises to give this god the camera "to begin again," she is not only giving herself another chance in life but also giving the movie-maker God a second chance as well. The second poem, "To Danya, My Daughter," is a profound and moving testimony to the power of maternal love and the importance of a spiritual consciousness shared by generations.

Like her poems, Thompson's scholarly work is deeply concerned with the place and presence of African Americans. Published works include an essay, "Daddy Saved in Snatches: The Quilting," which appears in *Father Songs: Testimonies by African American Sons and Daughters*, and a chapter entitled "Africana Womanism in Gloria Naylor's 'Mama Day' and 'Bailey's Café'" in *Gloria Naylor's Early Works*, edited by Margaret Anne Kelley. Asked about writers who most deeply influenced her, Thompson cited Toni Morrison, Gloria Naylor, Gwendolyn Brooks, Djuna Barnes, Ernest Gaines, Alice Walker, Rita Dove, Zora Neale Hurston, and Nikki Giovanni.

At the time of her death, Dorothy Perry Thompson held the rank of professor of English at Winthrop University where she taught courses in American literature, writing, verse composition, and African American studies and where she also coordinated the African American Studies Program. She was a member of Delta Sigma Theta and the South Carolina Academy of Authors (2002). She and her husband Johnnie C. Thompson, also a 1962 graduate of Booker T. Washington High School, raised three children: Johnnie (III), Danya, and Jene. PHEBE DAVIDSON

Dorothy Perry Thompson. Personal Interview. 12 June, 1998.

———. "Daddy Saved in Snatches: The Quilting." *Father Songs, Testimonies by African American Sons and Daughters*. Edited by Gloria Wade-Gayles. Boston: Houghton, Mifflin, 1997.

Timrod, Henry (1828–1867). Poet, essayist. Timrod was born on December 8, 1828, in Charleston, South Carolina, the only son of a bookbinder, William Henry Timrod, and his wife, Thyrza Prince. Hedged by poverty, frail health, and the cataclysm of the Civil War, Timrod led a brief tubercular life that bore the stamp of the romantic tradition that he revered and defended among his neoclassical contemporaries in Charleston's antebellum literary circles.

Timrod attended the prestigious Classical School, where he befriended his lifelong ally and fellow poet Paul Hamilton Hayne. As a young man, Timrod enjoyed solitude, nature, and the contemplation of romantic love and death. William Gilmore Simms found Timrod "morbid," but the ever-loyal Hayne memorialized him as "passionate, impulsive, [and] eagerly ambitious." When scant resources precluded his graduation from the University of Georgia, Timrod returned to Charleston in 1846 to study law with James L. Petigru. However, as one contemporary put it, Timrod "was too wholly a poet" to find the regimen compatible. Until the outbreak of the Civil War, he tutored the children of lowcountry planters while publishing his poetry and essays in *Russell's Magazine* (which he helped to found in 1857 with Hayne), the *Southern Literary Messenger*, and the Charleston newspapers. *Harper's* magazine hailed "the true poetical genius" of Timrod's *Poems* (1860), the only collection published in his lifetime.

Scholars generally concur that slavery and its ideological defense retarded the intellectual evolution of the antebellum South, particularly in the realm of letters. Timrod's 1859 essay "Literature in the South" buttresses this point of view. Southern readers at best, he wrote, were indifferent to southern writers, but more often criticized them "as not sufficiently Southern in spirit." According to Timrod, literature served merely as "epicurean amusement" for the South's "provincial" people. Even among the most learned, said Timrod, the "fossil theory of [classical] criticism" remained de rigueur. A devotee of romanticism, Timrod argued that the embracement of new modes of expression was not inherently subversive. In his other notable essay, an exchange with William J. Grayson titled "What Is Poetry?" (1859), Timrod vehemently rebutted Grayson's defense of verse as simply "form and order." Precisely for its disavowal and articulation of the modern sensibility in southern voices, the literary scholar Richard J. Calhoun has called this exchange "one of the more interesting critical debates in antebellum literary history."

Although Timrod opposed secession, the opening of the Confederate Congress in February 1861 elicited from him the exultant "Ethnogenesis," which prophesied the world made over in the image of a utopian South free "from want and crime." But as the war dragged on, Timrod's poems—"The Cotton Boll" (1861), "Carolina" (1862), "Charleston" (1862), "Christmas" (1862), "The Unknown Dead" (1863), and the postwar "Ode" (1866)—turned from ardor to apprehension and gloom, earning for him the sobriquet "Poet Laureate of the Confederacy." Lauding the "controlled eloquence" of his wartime compositions, Louis D. Rubin wrote, "Nothing in Timrod's pre-secession verse really prepares us for this sudden maturation as a poet. It is as if the advent of secession and the war had jarred him loose from his preoccupation with his own personality, the obsessive self-consciousness of his role as sensitive spokesman for aesthetic Ideality, into an abrupt confrontation with his identity as a member of the civil community." Even so harsh a critic as Ralph Waldo Emerson chose to read Timrod's war poetry to New England audiences after the Civil War, a tribute to his artistry and evocation of the sectional crisis.

Timrod enlisted in the Confederate service several times, but his chronic tuberculosis led to repeated discharges. In the spring of 1862, as a war correspondent for the *Charleston Mercury,* Timrod witnessed the retreat of the Confederate army from Shiloh. Overwhelmed by the horror, he returned home and in January 1864 assumed the editorship of the *South Carolinian,* a daily newspaper published in Columbia. He married his long-betrothed Kate Goodwin, the English sister of his brother-in-law, and on Christmas Eve their son Willie was born. Timrod remained at his desk while Sherman's troops destroyed the capital city, issuing "thumbsheets" until the occupation forced him into hiding. Facing ruin and starvation, Timrod futilely sought employment, depending on the charity of friends and the sale of his meager possessions for survival. The poet's bloodstained manuscripts still attest to his precipitous physical decline after the death of Willie, "our little boy beneath the sod," in October 1865. Henry Timrod died from tubercular hemorrhages on October 7, 1867, and was buried in the cemetery at Trinity Episcopal Cathedral in Columbia. In 1911 the South Carolina General Assembly adopted Timrod's "Carolina" as the state song; he was inducted into the South Carolina Academy of Authors in 1992. ELIZABETH ROBESON

Parks, Edd Winfield, ed. *The Essays of Henry Timrod.* Athens: University of Georgia Press, 1942.

———. *Henry Timrod.* New York: Twayne, 1964.

Parks, Edd Winfield, and Aileen Wells Parks, eds. *The Collected Poems of Henry Timrod.* Athens: University of Georgia Press, 1965.

Rubin, Louis D. *The Edge of the Swamp: A Study in the Literature and Society of the Old South.* Baton Rouge: Louisiana State University Press, 1989.

Tuttle, Jon (b. 1959). Playwright, scholar, educator, administrator. Jon Tuttle was born in Salt Lake City, Utah, in 1959. He moved to New Mexico in the early 1960s and graduated from Manzano High School in Albuquerque in 1977. While working as a sports writer for the *Daily Lobo* and the *Albuquerque Tribune,* Tuttle enrolled at the University of New Mexico but left after one year, moving back to Utah and finishing his B.S. in Mass Communication at the University of Utah in 1982. Tuttle credits David Kranes, a professor of theater at the University of Utah, for sparking his interest in theater. As a student of Kranes, Tuttle wrote his first play *Remembering Us*, which received a staged reading by the Salt Lake Acting Company and which was later produced by the community theater Vortex in Albuquerque, New Mexico.

In 1983 Tuttle moved back to New Mexico and pursued graduate studies at the University of New Mexico. There, he worked with Bob Hartung, a professor of theater and the founder of Summerfest, a month-long theater festival that produced student-written plays. Tuttle's next three plays—*A Rose Nocturne, A Fish Story,* and *Terminal Café*—were performed at Summerfest, and though Tuttle would later express mixed emotions about these early plays, calling them "sweaty and emotionally indulgent melodrama," he also called his work at Summerfest "the single most valuable formative experience I've ever had. [Summerfest] taught me so much about practical theater and rewarded the time I spent writing with actual productions and not simply 'development.'" Tuttle finished his M.A. in 1984 and his Ph.D. in 1989 with a dissertation on the work of playwright Arthur Miller. After working as a lecturer in English and composition at the University of New Mexico from 1988 to 1990, Tuttle moved to South Carolina and joined the English department at Francis Marion University. In 1998 he became playwright-in-residence at Trustus, a theater in Columbia, South Carolina, with which he continues to have a close and productive relationship. From 1999 to 2009, Tuttle also worked as the literary manager for Trustus, reading scripts for possible production.

In 2002 Tuttle married the former Cheryl Roberts, who directs student housing at FMU. Together, he and Cheryl have three children—her daughters Staci and Jill and Tuttle's son by a previous marriage, Joshua. Tuttle's writings include scholarly essays on Arthur Miller, David Mamet, Jean-Paul Sartre, and Truman Capote. In 2011, he edited *David Kranes: Selected Plays* (Level 4 Press), a collection of his former teacher's plays. Tuttle is best known, however, for the existential themes and compelling mix of humor, wit, and tragedy in his own mature work for the stage. *Sonata for Armadillos,* a road-trip story about three "idiots stuck on a Greyhound," was a finalist for the 1990 Heidemann Award. *The Hammerstone,* an academic satire that juxtaposes two college professors with opposing philosophies of education, won the 1994 South Carolina Playwrights' Festival Award and was a finalist at the prestigious Actors' Theatre of Louisville's Humana Festival. *Drift,* a bitter meditation on marital mistrust and infidelity, won the 1998 South Carolina Playwrights' Festival Award and a silver medal in the 2003 *Pinter Review* International Competition. Scenes from *Drift* were published in *Best Scenes 2001, Best Women's Monologues 2001,* and *Best Men's Monologues 2001.* Furthermore, *The Hammerstone, Drift,* and a later play, *Holy Ghost,* were collected by Intellect in *The Trustus Plays* in 2009.

In 2001 the University of South Carolina commissioned Tuttle's play *The White Problem*, a historical tragedy about Richard Greener, the first African American to graduate from Harvard and a leading figure in the post-Reconstruction conflict between W. E. B. Du Bois and Booker T. Washington. Greener was also the first black professor to teach at the University of South Carolina. *The White Problem* premiered at the Piccolo Spoleto Festival in Charleston, South Carolina. Tuttle's second historical play, *Holy Ghost*, revolves around inmate suicides in a South Carolina P.O.W. camp where German prisoners during World War II are monitored by African American and Jewish guards. *Holy Ghost* premiered at Trustus in 2005 and won the Sprenger-Lang/Nathan Miller History Play contest and was a runner-up for National New Play Network's Smith Award and a finalist for the Next Generation Playwriting Contest. *The White Problem* and *Holy Ghost* were later published together in a collection *Two South Carolina Plays* (Hub City, 2006), accompanied by essays written by Michael Mounter and John H. Moore.

Surprised and overwhelmed by the emotions provoked by the 2006 death of a family pet, Tuttle wrote *The Sweet Abyss*, which focuses on a woman grieving for her cat and the impact of that grieving on the woman's daughter. Premiered by Trustus in 2009, *The Sweet Abyss* was published by Next Stage Press in 2011 and reprinted in the 2011 *Regional Best* anthology. Tuttle's most recent play, *The Palace of the Moorish Kings*, is based on a story by American author Evan Shelby Connell about a friend returning to America in 1970, which Tuttle originally read in the mid-1980s. First produced by the Trustus Theater in 2012, *The Palace of the Moorish Kings* is set at a Thanksgiving Day family gathering and depicts the psychic surrender of members of the Greatest Generation now settled into middle class suburban lives. Tuttle calls *The Palace of the Moorish Kings* his "most reasonable, adult, and linear play."

Currently, Tuttle teaches courses in playwriting, theater, and the literature of the Vietnam War as professor of English at Francis Marion University, where in 2005 he was named a Francis Marion University Trustees Research Scholar. In 2011–2012, he coordinated FMU's international program and in 2013 accepted appointment as director of the honors program.

Tuttle has served on the board of governors of the South Carolina Academy of Authors and on the board of directors of the Florence Regional Arts Alliance since 2011. He has received the South Carolina Theatre Association's Founders Award and fellowships from the South Carolina Arts Commission and the South Carolina Academy of Authors. DAVID BRUZINA

Tuttle, Jon. Personal Interview. 14 Sept. 2012.
———. *The Trustus Plays*. Chicago: Intellect-U of Chicago Press, 2009.
———. *Two South Carolina Plays*. Spartanburg, S.C.: Hub City Writers Project, 2009.

Walker, William (1809–1875). Composer, author, teacher. Walker was born on May 6, 1809, near Cross Keys in the Union District of South Carolina, the son of Absalom Walker and Susan Jackson. The family moved to the Cedar Springs section of Spartanburg District when he was seventeen. In 1832 Walker joined the Cedar Springs Baptist Church. About 1835 he married Amy Golightly, a member of the same congregation. The couple moved to the town of Spartanburg in the same year. They were the parents of five sons and five daughters.

In September 1835 Walker published *Southern Harmony,* a shaped-note hymnal using a four-shape (fa-so-la) system. The shaped-note style is a simplified musical notation developed to make it easier for untrained congregations to sing in harmony without instrumental accompaniment. Shapes (triangle=fa, oval=so, rectangle=la, and diamond=mi) were added to the note heads to help singers find pitches within major and minor scales. *Southern Harmony* included some of Walker's own compositions, and it marked the first publication of the tune "New Britain" with the words "Amazing Grace." Some older hymns and psalms in standard usage at the time were included as well as new compositions by other southern composers. The work was immensely popular across the South, going through several editions and selling more than 600,000 copies by 1854. Thenceforth, when he signed his name, Walker added the initials "A.S.H." ("Author of Southern Harmony"), and he was affectionately known as "Singing Billy" Walker.

In 1846 Walker published *Southern and Western Pocket Harmonist.* Twenty years later he brought out a publication in the seven-shape (or do-re-mi) system entitled *Christian Harmony.* It contained many of the same hymns and psalms as his earlier publications but with the addition of several modern tunes "more suitable to church use." A second and enlarged edition was published in 1873 and underwent printings as late as 1979. Other editions of his *Christian Harmony* and reprints of *Southern Harmony* are still available and remain in use. His last publication was *Fruits and Flowers* for use in Sunday schools.

Some groups remain dedicated to continuing the tradition of singing Walker's *Southern Harmony* and the shaped-note style. The "Big Singing," for example, is an annual event, held continually since 1884, on the fourth Sunday in May in Benton, Kentucky. The music group the Black Crowes named their 1992 album *The Southern Harmony and Musical Companion* after Walker's work. In May 2002 Wofford College in Spartanburg hosted a gathering of *Southern Harmony* enthusiasts.

In addition to his musical publications, Walker traveled over the South conducting singing schools. As early as 1849 he was an agent for the *Spartan,* the weekly newspaper in the town of Spartanburg. In June, 1862, he was sent to Richmond to nurse Confederate soldiers. He also maintained a bookstore for a time in Spartanburg. Walker died in Spartanburg on September 24, 1875, and was buried in that city's Magnolia Cemetery. BRENT HOLCOMB

Eskew, Harry L. "*Southern Harmony* and Its Era." *The Hymn* 41 (1990): 28–34.

Landrum, John B. O. *History of Spartanburg County, South Carolina.* 1900. Reprint, Spartanburg, S.C.: Reprint Company, 1977.

Walker, William. *The Southern Harmony and Musical Companion.* Edited by Glenn L. Wilcox. Lexington: University Press of Kentucky, 1987.

Wentworth, Marjory Heath (b. 1958). Poet, educator. Born in Lynn, Massachusetts, on June 3, 1958, Wentworth is the daughter of John Heath and Mary Tully. She received a bachelor's degree from Mount Holyoke College in anthropology and political science in 1980 and an M.A. in literature and creative writing from New York University in 1984. On June 27, 1981, she married the filmmaker Peter Wentworth. They have three sons.

Wentworth went to work as a book and film publicist soon after graduate school and has been involved in publicity and marketing ever since. In 1989 the Wentworth family moved to Sullivan's Island, South Carolina. In 1992 Wentworth began teaching creative writing at an arts center in the Charleston area, and a year later she became an adjunct instructor of English at Trident Technical College. Since then, she has taught creative writing to children and adults in a variety of settings across the state, including the Art Institute of Charleston, the Roper St. Francis Cancer Center "Expressions of Healing" program, and the Poets in the Schools program sponsored by the Lowcountry Initiative for the Library Arts (LILA).

Wentworth conducts creative writing workshops and presents readings of her own work throughout the United States. She has performed with poets Coleman Barks and Lisa Starr and with the Paul Winter Consort. Her poems have been displayed at the National Science Foundation and the Duke University Museum of Art, and she collaborates extensively with visual artists and composers. Her poems have been nominated for the Pushcart Prize five times, and her work has been published in numerous magazines and anthologies. Her work is included in the South Carolina Poetry Archives housed at Furman University.

Her books of poetry include *Noticing Eden* (2003), *Despite Gravity* (2007), and *The Endless Repetition of an Ordinary Miracle* (2012). Her children's story, *Shackles* (2009), is set in Sullivan's Island. She is the coauthor, with artist Mary Edna Fraser, of *What the Water Gives Me* (2002); and she and human rights activist Juan E Mendez are the authors of *Taking a Stand: The Evolution of Human Rights* (2011).

Wentworth read her poem "Rivers of Wind" at the inauguration of Governor Mark Sanford in January 2003. She was named South Carolina's poet laureate later the same year. As poet laureate, she has initiated projects designed to bring the enjoyment and writing of poetry into the lives of South Carolinians. JULIA ARRANTS

Watts, Judy. "Hard Times Have Inspired New Poet Laureate of South Carolina to Become an Advocate for Writing." Charleston *Post and Courier,* August 30, 2003, F1, F3.

White, Benjamin Franklin (1800–1879). Composer, publisher. White was born on September 10, 1800, in the Padgett's Creek section of Union District of South Carolina, the youngest of fourteen children born to Robert White and Mildred Whitehead. He attended school for only a short time but inherited a musical inclination from his father. On December 30, 1825, he married Thurza Golightly, the sister of Amy Golightly, the wife of the shaped-note composer William Walker. The Whites were the parents of fourteen children, nine of whom reached adulthood. The family moved to Harris County, Georgia, about 1842.

White was probably a contributor to Walker's *Southern Harmony,* though he received no credit. While earning his livelihood as a farmer in Georgia, in 1844 he published *The Sacred Harp,* a shaped-note singing book, in conjunction with E. J. King. Shaped-note singing in the South evolved from the eighteenth-century New England singing-school movement. Itinerant music teachers taught the shaped-note system to church congregations. The easy-to-learn system made it possible for congregations to sing in harmony without musical accompaniment and also without the singers having to be trained to read formal sheet music. Shapes (triangle=fa, oval=so, rectangle=la, and diamond=mi) were added to the note heads to help singers find pitches within major and minor scales. The 1850 census lists White's occupation as "music teacher," but by 1860 he identified himself to census takers simply as "Author of Sacred Harp." White used the four-shape (or fa-so-la) system and became one of the most prominent figures in promoting that method. While some others changed to a seven-shape (or do-re-mi) system, White admonished his followers to "ask for the old paths and walk therein." He composed the tunes and harmony to many hymns in his book. *The Sacred Harp* went through many printings and remains in use, with its most recent republication occurring in 1991. Singers across the South have kept the *Sacred Harp* tradition of shaped-note singing alive into the twenty-first century.

In 1852 White began the first newspaper in Harris County, the *Organ,* and served as the county's clerk of the inferior court in 1858. He formed the Southern Musical Convention in Upson County, Georgia, in 1857 and served as its president until 1862. In 1865 he served as mayor of Hamilton, Georgia. He died on December 6, 1879, in Atlanta, Georgia, and was buried in that city's Oakland Cemetery. *The Sacred Harp* tradition remains prominent in upstate South Carolina, western North Carolina, eastern Texas, and parts of Kentucky. BRENT HOLCOMB

Chase, Gilbert. *America's Music.* 3d ed. Urbana: University of Illinois Press, 1992.

Cobb, Buell. *The Sacred Harp: A Tradition and Its Music.* Athens: University of Georgia Press, 1978.

Coleman, Kenneth, and Charles Stephen Gurr, eds. *Dictionary of Georgia Biography.* 2 vols. Athens: University of Georgia Press, 1983.

White, John Blake (1781–1859). Playwright, painter. White was born on September 2, 1781, near Eutaw Springs at Whitehall Plantation, St. John's, Berkeley Parish, to Blake Leay White and Elizabeth Borquin. A pioneer in early American painting and literature, White was a leading figure in both art forms in antebellum South Carolina.

After growing up at Whitehall and reading law in Columbia, in 1800 White sailed for England, where he studied painting under Benjamin West, the American-born official historical painter to King George III. In 1803 White returned to South Carolina and settled in Charleston. Finding little market for the grand historical subjects he wished to execute, he applied to the bar and attempted to make a living painting portraits. In 1806 his first two plays, *Foscari, or the Venetian Exile* and *The Mysteries of the Castle*, were performed at the Charleston Theatre. He was admitted to the bar in 1808, greatly improving his financial and social standing. In 1818 he was elected by the city parishes of St. Philip's and St. Michael's to the General Assembly, where he served one term. He became a director of the South Carolina Academy of Fine Arts the year it was chartered in 1821. Beginning in 1826, he was engaged in running the state's only paper mill, in Lexington District, but he moved back to Charleston in 1832 after a fire destroyed the plant. There he took a position at the U.S. Custom House, where he worked for the next twenty-five years. In 1845 he was made an honorary member of the National Academy of Design. He was married twice, first to Elizabeth (Eliza) Allston on March 28, 1805, and then to Anna Rachel O'Driscoll on October 2, 1819, two years after Eliza's death. His first marriage produced four children, and his second produced eight.

Although White's earliest plays are Gothic romantic tragedies set in Europe, his other dramas are notable for addressing contemporary American concerns. *Modern Honor,* which opened at the Charleston Theatre in 1812, was the first anti-dueling play in American literature and attacked the practice as "sanctioned murder." Unafraid of controversy, White also spoke out against capital punishment and allied himself with opponents of nullification. *The Forgers,* written in 1829 and published in 1837, was one of America's first temperance plays. *The Triumph of Liberty, or Louisiana Preserved* ostensibly celebrated Andrew Jackson's victory at the Battle of New Orleans during the War of 1812. However, the play, published in 1819, also attempted to justify the execution in 1818 of two British citizens convicted of inciting Indians during the Seminole War.

Both of White's parents served in the Revolutionary War, his father at Fort Moultrie and his mother as a spy for Francis Marion. Some of his paintings depict dramatic scenes from the conflict. Four of these, *General Marion Inviting a British Officer to Share His Meal, Sergeants Jasper and Newton Rescuing American Prisoners from the British, Mrs. Motte Directing Generals Marion and Lee to Burn Her Mansion to Dislodge the British,* and *The Defense of Fort Moultrie,* all painted between 1810 and 1815, hang in the U.S. capitol. Among his portraits are those of South Carolina luminaries John C. Calhoun, Charles Cotesworth Pinckney, and Henry Middleton. White died on August 24, 1859, in Charleston and was buried in the family plot at St. Philip's Church. HUGH DAVIS

Moore, Alexander, ed. *Biographical Directory of the South Carolina House of Representatives.* Vol. 5. Columbia: South Carolina Department of Archives and History, 1992.

Partridge, Paul W., Jr. "John Blake White: Southern Romantic Painter and Playwright." Ph.D. diss., University of Pennsylvania, 1951.

Turner, Mary Ellen. "John Blake White: An Introduction." *Journal of Early Southern Decorative Arts* 16 (May 1990): 1–17.

Watson, Charles S. *Antebellum Charleston Dramatists.* Tuscaloosa: University of Alabama Press, 1976.

Woods, Sylvia Pressley (1926–2012). Cookbook author, restaurateur, businesswoman. Woods was born in Brooklyn, New York, on February 2, 1926, the only child of Van and Julia Pressley. Her father died three days later, and Sylvia Pressley and her mother moved to Hemingway, South Carolina, to live with her maternal grandparents on their thirty-five-acre farm. It was here that Woods learned to cook traditional southern and African American food.

Sylvia Pressley married Herbert Woods in Hemingway on January 18, 1944. They started a family, which would eventually grow to include four children, and she owned a beauty parlor. In 1950 the family moved to Harlem, and in 1954 she began waiting tables at Johnson's Restaurant on the corner of Lenox Avenue and 127th Street. Eight years later she bought the eatery with a $20,000 loan from her mother, who mortgaged the family farm to raise the money, and renamed it Sylvia's.

Sylvia's became a popular neighborhood restaurant, but it was not until *New York* magazine's food critic Gael Greene wrote a 1979 article dubbing Woods "the queen of soul food" that the business gained worldwide attention. Her simple southern dishes—many of which were created by Hemingway native Ruth Gully, who ran the restaurant's kitchen from 1975 until her death in 1995—attracted throngs of tourists each year and have spawned a multi-million-dollar empire, Sylvia Woods Enterprises. The company includes the Harlem restaurant, an Atlanta branch, cookbooks, and a successful line of packaged food products sold in stores across the country.

By the early twenty-first century Wood's four children ran the business, and she divided her time between Hemingway and Harlem until her death in July of 2012. At just one of several memorial services, hundreds of mourners packed the church to hear eulogies by former President Bill Clinton and New York mayor Michael Bloomberg. Her 1999 cookbook, *Sylvia's Family Soul Food Cookbook,* is an homage to her childhood in Hemingway, a town that, she wrote, "has more great cooks per square inch than you would find in most cooking schools." BRUCE LANE AND SCOTT WYATT

Woods, Sylvia. *Sylvia's Family Soul Food Cookbook: From Hemingway, South Carolina, to Harlem*. New York: Morrow, 1999.
Woods, Sylvia, and Christopher Styler. *Sylvia's Soul Food: Recipes from Harlem's World-Famous Restaurant*. New York: Morrow, 1992.

Woolsey, Gamel (b. Elizabeth Gamel Woolsey, 1897–1968). Poet, novelist, memoirist. The exact year of Woolsey's birth is not known—estimates vary from 1895 to 1900—but what is certain is that she was born and raised on Breeze Hill Plantation just outside of Aiken, South Carolina. The daughter of Charleston socialite Elizabeth Gammell and New York banker William Walton Woolsey, Gamel Woolsey—in adulthood she adopted as her first name a shortened version of her mother's maiden name—spent what she later recalled as an idyllic childhood on the rural property that her father had purchased and that is still occupied by a branch of the family.

After the death of her husband in 1910, Woolsey's mother packed up her two daughters and returned to Charleston where both girls attended Ashley Hall, an exclusive school for young ladies. As a member of Charleston society, Woolsey savored the often glittering social opportunities available to young women of her circle but also bristled at the restrictive gender roles imposed by the social conventions of that time. Very early, she sought escape through creative pursuits, acting in student dramatic productions and leading the editorial staff of the school literary magazine.

A diagnosis of tuberculosis in 1917—her father had suffered from the same condition and had moved to Aiken because of its reputation as a health resort—cut short the path that her family had set for her, which included an eventual marriage to a young man of her social station, and freed Woolsey to pursue her artistic inclinations. Accordingly, after a recuperative period in a sanitarium, she set out for New York City, found a place in Greenwich Village, and actively pursued a career as a poet.

All the while, men pursued her. First came a marriage to New Zealand journalist Rex Hunter—although they never officially divorced, the couple separated within four years of tying the knot—and then a long transatlantic affair with British writer Llewelyn Powys, who was himself married at the time to American writer Alyse Gregory—the latter fretted over her husband's affection for Woolsey but supported his quest to have a child by the younger woman—and, finally, a forty-year relationship with writer Gerald Brenan. Woolsey's delicate beauty and innate sensitivity aroused in her male admirers a desire to protect her from the larger world.

In England, while slowly extricating herself from the Powys entanglement and slowly awakening to the possibility of a life with Brenan, Woolsey published one book of poems entitled *Middle Earth* in 1931. A year later, in 1932, she confronted the aborted publication of her first novel *One Way of Love*—it was eventually released posthumously in 1987. Fearing legal problems because of the book's rather straightforward depiction of a young woman's determination to find a lover to match her dreams, the publisher Victor Gollancz changed his mind at the last minute. The book, which incorporates largely autobiographical material in a poetic style, focuses on the fate of Mariana, a southern girl who moves to the big city where she is immersed in a bohemian world of writers and artists and where she faces a number of challenges, including an unwanted pregnancy, in her quest to find romantic fulfillment.

Woolsey and Brenan moved to Spain in 1935; and except for a period during World War II when they were forced to return to England, Woolsey lived in Andalusia until her death in 1968. Her first-hand account of the Spanish Civil War, published in England as *Death's Other Kingdom* in 1939 and in America as *Malaga Burning* in 1998, is probably the most important of her works published during her lifetime. It is an eyewitness record of the early years of the war by a foreign resident whose life and the lives of the natives of the coastal city of Malaga are forever changed by the bloody conflict.

Her other book inspired by her adopted country is a collection of popular folk tales that she translated into English; first published in 1944, *Spanish Fairy Stories* was reissued in an expanded edition with illustrations by Anglo-Spanish artist Armengol in 1946.

As with her first novel, however, most of Woolsey's works have seen the light of day after her death. Her poetry was issued in a number of volumes by Kenneth Hopkins and the Warren House Press in the United Kingdom: *Twenty-Eight Sonnets* (1977), *The Last Leaf Falls* (1978), *Middle Earth* (reprint, 1979), *The Seeds of Demeter* (1980), *The Weight of Human Hours* (1980), and *Collected Poems* (1984). The very best of these poems are either nostalgic—"All That the Child Remembers Now" and "On Breeze Hill Plantation" hearken back to her formative years in Aiken— or echo some of the themes of her adult fiction—"For the Flesh" captures the urgency of physical love.

Much of this poetic sensibility is also evident in her long lost novel *Patterns on the Sand,* which she wrote in England in 1947 but withdrew from submission when it suffered rejection by just one publisher. Rediscovered in manuscript form in a library in Texas in 2000, the novel is set in the South Carolina lowcountry during the period that Woolsey herself was reaching early adulthood in Charleston. The book finally found a publisher in 2012 when Sundial Press in the United Kingdom released a hardcover edition, a project spurred in part by the author's posthumous induction into the South Carolina Academy of Authors in 2011. TOM MACK

Mack, Tom. *Circling the Savannah*. Charleston, S.C.: The History Press, 2008.
Ozieblo, Barbara. Introduction. *Patterns on the Sand*. By Gamel Woolsey. Sherborne, U.K.: The Sundial Press, 2012.

Workman, William Douglas, Jr. (1914–1990). Journalist, editor. Workman was born on August 10, 1914, in Greenwood, South Carolina, the son of William D. Workman and Vivian Watkins. Following his 1935 graduation from the Citadel, he was a reporter for the *News and Courier* in Charleston. On June 10, 1939, he married Rhea Thomas of Walterboro. They had two children. Workman entered the U.S. Army in 1941 and was on active duty for five years during World War II.

After military service, Workman returned to the *News and Courier* and was the paper's Columbia-based capital correspondent from 1946 until 1962. By the late 1950s, as a result of his reporting on government, politics, and racial issues throughout the South; his widely syndicated columns; and his frequent appearances as a television commentator, his name recognition in the state was so great that his newspaper byline was simply his initials, "W.D.W." His conservative political attitudes were similarly known, especially with the 1960 publication of his first book, *The Case for the South,* which asserted his own views of the constitutionality and wisdom of maintaining racial segregation in the southern states.

In 1962 leaders of the state's fledgling Republican Party, especially J. Drake Edens, Jr., persuaded Workman to run as a Republican for the U.S. Senate seat held by Democrat Olin D. Johnston. South Carolina Republicans had only rarely nominated candidates for local, much less statewide, office. Johnston, a staunch segregationist, was not directly vulnerable on the race issue. Consequently, Workman painted him as a supporter of President John F. Kennedy and intimated that a vote for Johnston was a vote for the invasion of Mississippi by federal troops. Johnston held on to win the election, but Workman's remarkable forty-four percent of the vote was a clear sign that the Republican Party in South Carolina had become a viable force.

Workman returned to journalistic duties when he joined the editorial department of the Columbia *State* in 1963, and he served as the paper's editor from 1966 to 1972. He remained with the *State* until his retirement in 1979. In 1982 Workman, to the surprise of friends and contrary to the advice of his 1962 campaign manager, Drake Edens, announced his candidacy for the Republican nomination for governor to face the Democratic incumbent Richard W. Riley. Suffering from a mild form of Parkinson's disease, Workman waged a lackluster campaign in which he acknowledged that there were few issues. Riley was overwhelmingly reelected, and Workman failed to win any of the state's forty-six counties.

The 1982 contest marked Workman's final quest for office, and thereafter his progressive illness began to worsen. He died in Greenville on November 23, 1990, and was buried in Greenlawn Memorial Park in Columbia. His obituary in the *State* called Workman "a singular influence in establishing a two-party political system in the state." NEAL D. THIGPEN

Merritt, Russell. "The Senatorial Election of 1962 and the Rise of Two-Party Politics in South Carolina." *South Carolina Historical Magazine* 98 (July 1997): 281–301.

Wickenberg, Charles, Jr. "Journalist, GOP Crusader William Workman Dies." Columbia *State,* November 24, 1990, A1, A7.

Workman, William D., Jr. Papers. Modern Political Collections, South Caroliniana Library, University of South Carolina, Columbia.

www.ingramcontent.com/pod-product-compliance
Lightning Source LLC
Chambersburg PA
CBHW031103020726

47495CB00007B/2020